why

POWERFUL ANSWERS AND
PRACTICAL REASONS FOR LIVING LDS STANDARDS

JOHN HILTON III AND ANTHONY SWEAT

DESERET
BOOK

Salt Lake City, Utah

Design by Ken Wzorek and Barry Hansen

Library of Congress Cataloging-in-Publication Data
    Hilton, John, III.
     Why? : powerful answers and practical reasons for living LDS standards
    / John Hilton III and Anthony Sweat.
        p. cm.
     Includes bibliographical references.
     ISBN 978-1-60641-040-0 (hardbound : alk. paper)
     1. Mormon youth—Religious life. 2. Mormon youth—Conduct of life. 3.
    Parent and teenager—Religious aspects—Church of Jesus Christ of
    Latter-day Saints. 4. Church of Jesus Christ of Latter-day
    Saints—Doctrines. I. Sweat, Anthony. II. Title.
     BX8643.Y6H55 2009
     248.8'3088289332—dc22
                                2008036295

Printed in China
R. R. Donnelley, Shenzhen, China
10   9   8   7   6   5   4   3   2

To all the youth of the Church who desire
to understand "Why?"

"It isn't always easy to give you a 'why' for everything. But we owe it to you of the coming generation to do more than just say, 'Don't!'"

—President Boyd K. Packer

contents

Acknowledgments

We owe many people a debt of gratitude for their assistance in this project. To the amazing people at Deseret Book for their insights and talents that made this book what it is: Sheri Dew, Chris Schoebinger, Lisa Mangum, Derk Koldewyn, Tonya Facemyer, Richard Erickson, and Kayla Hackett. Thanks also to Patrick Muir for his hard work on the ldswhy.com web site and to Brian Clark and Bryan Beach for the wonderful illustrations.

We would also like to thank all those who read draft versions of the book for their valuable feedback and suggestions. To the many teachers who have influenced us in our teaching careers and shared ideas which are used in this book, we say thank you.

Finally, we would like to thank our spouses, Lani Hilton and Cindy Sweat, who are the "why" behind all that we do.

Introduction:
Why Ask "Why"?

Would you throw this beautiful baby out the window?

Of course not! But recently there was a family who did throw their baby out the window.[2]

WHY Quote **#1**

"*Why* is among the first and favorite words pronounced early by children and especially teenagers." —Elder Charles Didier[1]

Why would they do such a thing?

As you can see from the illustration on the left, the building was on fire—by throwing the baby out of the window to someone below, they saved its life.

Just like there was a good reason why this baby was thrown out the window, there are good reasons why God gives us commandments and standards. The problem is, sometimes we don't know why those standards exist.

Most Latter-day Saints know *what* the standards of the Church are. For example, we know what fasting is, what temple marriage is, what it means to be morally clean, what is and is not modest (sometimes down to the square-inch of fabric!). But *why* have those standards been given? More importantly,

WHY Quote **#2**

"All too often in the world, a teacher's relation to a student is one of giving counsel with . . . no explanation of the reasons *why* there are commandments, rules, and standards."—Elder Richard G. Scott[3]

why should we obey those commandments? Answering why usually proves more difficult for people (even parents) because, as Elder Richard G. Scott said, it is something we don't teach and talk about enough.

WHY Quote #3

"Of all the creations of the Almighty there is none more beautiful, none more inspiring than a lovely daughter of God who walks in virtue with an *understanding of why she should do so.*" —President Gordon B. Hinckley[4]

WHY Quote #4

"It concerns me as I see young people in our Church who know all the correct things they should do and do not have a clue as to why. . . . Do we understand why? *If we do not understand the why, then the power available to us through the doctrine of Christ will not be evident in our lives.*"—Elder David A. Bednar[5]

It is good to obey simply because we have been commanded to. Sometimes we need to act on faith because God does not give us a reason why (see Conclusion: Sometimes We Do Not Need to Know *Why*). Yet, as Elder David A. Bednar taught, knowing why we do what we do often makes for even more powerful obedience.

Many Want to Know "Why"— And the Lord Often Tells Them

The word "why" appears 366 times in the scriptures.

WHY Quote #5

"I think we underestimate youth. They're in a searching age—it's the 'why' age. There's a reason for that: the Lord wants them to get their own testimonies. It's leaders' and parents' job to give them the doctrinal 'whys' and to back up standards by teaching about the reasons for them."—Sister Julie B. Beck[6]

Asking why is not limited to youth. Many individuals in the scriptures also wondered "why?" Our first parent Adam asked, "Why is it that men must repent and be baptized in water?" (Moses 6:53). The great Moses wanted to know "Why these things are so?" (Moses 1:30). Even the greatest of us all, our Lord and Savior, asked in his most trying hour, "My God, my God, why hast thou forsaken me?" (Matthew 27:46).

The great news is, the Lord wants us to know why and often will tell us. For example, when Adam didn't know why he was offering sacrifices, an angel explained why Adam was commanded to do it (see Moses 5:7). The Lord also explained why the name of the higher priesthood was changed to Melchizedek (see D&C 107:1–4), why "many are called, but few are chosen" (D&C 121:40), why he spoke in parables (see Matthew 13:10–13), and why his disciples couldn't heal a child (see Matthew 17:19–21). There are powerful truths behind why things are the way they are. The Lord desires us to understand these and many other "whys" and to explain them to others.

WHY Quote #6

"Young people wonder 'why?'—*Why* are we commanded to do some things, and *why* are we commanded not to do other things? . . . Let them know what it's all about, then they will have the '*why*.'"
—Elder Boyd K. Packer[7]

There *Are* Reasons Why We Do What We Do

Perhaps the most common answers people give as to why we should or should not do certain things are "Because it's a commandment" or "Because the prophet said to." While those responses show admirable faith, they may not persuade a friend or family member to understand why something is a true principle they should follow. Answers like "Because God said so" have much of the same effect as a parent saying to a questioning child, "Because I said so."

WHY Quote #7

Because I'm the mommy, that's why.

"I've always been one that wants to know 'why.' . . . On the wall of our kitchen is a picture of a hen talking to her chicks with the caption, 'Because I'm the mommy, that's why.' . . . However, we have been given good, logical, and spiritual reasons to the vast majority of things we are asked or commanded to do."—Elder Glenn L. Pace[8]

The good news is that when it comes to the gospel, there are many good reasons why we have the standards that we have. Elder Richard L. Evans said, "There is real reason for every commandment."[9] In fact, Joseph Smith taught that every commandment we are given is designed to make us happy.[10] There are reasons why those commandments make us happy, and asking why will help us learn those reasons.

More Likely to Obey

A powerful reason why we should desire to know the principles behind the practice is because when we understand the logical reasons behind what we are being asked to do, *we are more likely to obey*. Some people are disobedient—not out of rebellion, but out of ignorance and uncertainty. They simply don't understand the principle behind the practice.

YUMMY... WANNA COOKIE?

If a mother tells her children, "Don't eat those cookies on the table" without explaining why, some kids will still swipe a cookie when Mom isn't looking. But if Mom says, "Don't eat those cookies on the table because they are doggie biscuits," there would be no problem.

> **WHY** Quote #8
>
> "It isn't always easy to give you a 'why' for everything. But we owe it to you of the coming generation to do more than just say, 'Don't!'"— Elder Boyd K. Packer[11]

Learning why the Lord gives us certain commandments helps us see his wisdom and the purpose behind his commandments. Understanding why makes us more likely to obey—and to obey more sincerely. Perhaps this is why Elder Boyd K. Packer said we need to do more than just tell the youth "Don't."

We hope that as you read the following chapters, you will come to learn why God has given us the commandments we have today. And as a result, that you will have a greater desire to obey, inviting more spiritual power into your life.

1 ^{ch} Why Should I Keep the Commandments?

Pretend for a moment that you had to walk through a minefield with hidden explosives buried all around you. Luckily, you have a map that can show you all the potential bombs. There are explicit instructions on the map, telling you exactly which paths lead to destruction and which paths lead to safety. Would you follow the map or ignore it and say, "I don't need anyone telling me what to do. I hate all these restrictions and rules. Just let me walk where I want to walk! I can figure it out for myself!"?

WOULD YOU RATHER CROSS A MINEFIELD LIKE THIS?

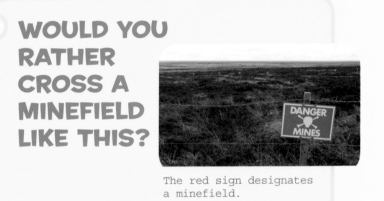

The red sign designates a minefield.

OR LIKE THIS?

Each stick marks an unexploded land mine.

The commandments of God are similar to that minefield map. God knows which steps in life will hurt and even kill us spiritually, and which steps will lead us along a path of safety and happiness. When he tells us, "Don't lie" or "Serve your neighbor," he is saying, "Don't step there—it will lead to tragedy" and "Do step here, it's a better path." Ignoring God and his divine commandments is like ignoring the map and walking blindly through a minefield. Let's take a look at why that is true.

Commandments and Happiness

Although people who break commandments may seem to be momentarily happy, eventually their disobedience causes them to become miserable. One reason why we should keep the commandments is that "wickedness never was happiness" (Alma 41:10). Since this is a book

about why we should keep the commandments, we could almost end the discussion right here. Most everyone wants to be happy. Not many people wake up and say, "I hope I can be miserable today." The problem is that sometimes people seek happiness from the wrong sources. Some people think that money, fame, popularity, or physical beauty will make them happy. Sadly, some even believe sin will bring happiness.

YOU CAN'T REALLY BUY HAPPINESS

A study on happiness printed in the *Washington Post* said:

"A wealth of data in recent decades has shown that once personal [savings] exceeds about $12,000 a year, more money produces virtually no increase in life satisfaction. From 1958 to 1987, for example, income in Japan grew fivefold, but researchers could find no corresponding increase in happiness."[1]

In reality, none of those things will ever make anyone truly happy. Possessions get lost, beauty fades, money is spent, and after high school nobody really cares who the head cheerleader or captain of the football team was. Similarly, sin only produces sorrow, guilt, and regret.

FALLING STARS

Although they have talent, money, fame, and beauty, many celebrities live lives that are out of control and seem to be the opposite of happiness. We should keep our focus on the true source of light—the Son of God—and not on celebrity stars that can fade or fall.

So what *does* make people truly happy? Joseph Smith taught the key to happiness when he said that God "never has—He never will—institute an ordinance or give a commandment to His people that is not *calculated* in its nature to promote that *happiness* which He has designed, and which will not end in the greatest amount of good and glory to those who become the recipients of his law and ordinances."[2]

Gospel Math

1. Commandments + Obedience = Happiness
2. Commandments − Obedience = Misery

It really is that simple—obedience brings happiness. No calculus required to figure this one out.

IF YOU'RE HAPPY AND YOU KNOW IT . . . DON'T DO METH

The following pictures show a drug addict and the toll that meth took on her in just a ten-year period. It is obvious that doing drugs does *not* produce happiness.

Start

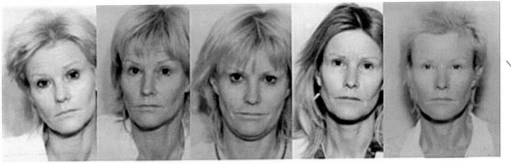

10 Years of Meth Use

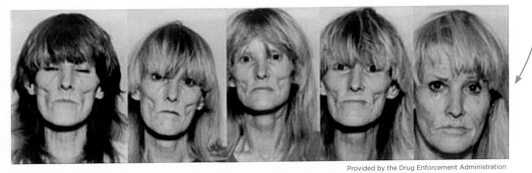

Provided by the Drug Enforcement Administration

End

Please notice that the Prophet Joseph used words like "happiness," "good," and "glory" when he spoke about obedience, and not words like "fun," "entertaining," and "exciting." Sometimes people think that just because something is fun or exciting that it will produce happiness. Some sins appear fun or enjoyable, but that doesn't mean they bring long-lasting joy.

It is impossible to find true happiness in sin, as deceivingly appealing and fun as it may appear, because being in the "bonds of iniquity" is "contrary to the nature of happiness" (Alma 41:11). As you read the different commandments outlined in this book, you can put them to the test by living them and discovering this truth for yourself: The more we obey God's laws, the more happiness, peace, and joy we will have in our lives.

Guidance, Direction, and Protection

A second reason to keep the commandments is that they give us needed guidance. The Lord taught, "I give unto you a new commandment. . . . Or, in other words, I give unto you *directions*" (D&C 82:8–9; emphasis added). The commandments show us the right way and are for our benefit and protection. Returning to the minefield analogy, we can either ignore our all-knowing and wise Heavenly Father and get hurt in the process, or we can be obedient and free from unnecessary pain.

WARNING: DON'T HEAD-BUTT THE ANIMALS

John Says:

Once when I went to the zoo with my children, we came to a station where we could feed the giraffes.

Although a sign was posted warning us that the giraffes could be dangerous, I thought it would be fun to take a picture with a giraffe.

As I stood posing next to one, the giraffe pulled his head away from me, and then with surprising speed, he moved his neck in a circular motion, whacking me on the head. It hurt! If you think giraffes are wimps, you're wrong. In the final picture, I kept my distance from the giraffe.

The sign mentioned above warning zoo guests to be cautious of the giraffes was meant to give helpful guidance and keep visitors safe. It's the same with the commandments—they are there to direct us to stay safe from those things which will inevitably bring pain and sorrow.

EVERY WARNING HAS A REASON . . .

TOUCHING WIRES CAUSES INSTANT DEATH ☠ $200 FINE ☠

IF DOOR DOES NOT OPEN DO NOT ENTER

CAUTION THIS SIGN HAS SHARP EDGES

Please Be Safe.

Do not stand, sit, climb, or lean on zoo fences.
If you fall, animals could eat you and that might make them sick.
Thank you.

Obedience and Freedom

A third reason why keeping the commandments is so important is because of the following truth: Obedience leads to freedom, and disobedience leads to slavery. When we obey God's commandments, we can avoid many of those limiting, addictive, and controlling practices and behaviors that can take away our freedom. Elder Bruce C. Hafen taught:

"Curiously, the invitation to submit to God's will initially looks like a restriction on our freedom, yet ends by bringing us the full-blown liberty of eternal life. Laws and rules may seem to limit rather than free us; but it is only because of the law of gravity that we can walk. Only by adhering to the laws of physics can we compose beautiful music and send up spaceships. Obedience is liberating, not confining.

"By contrast, Satan's invitation to disobey God's laws initially looks like an expansion of our freedom; yet, if we follow Satan, we will end up in bondage to him."[3]

According

to the U.S. Department of Justice, as of June 30, 2007, there were more than 2,299,116 prisoners in the United States. The leading causes of imprisonment were violent offenses (52%)—such as murder, rape, sexual assault, and robbery. Property offenses—such as burglary, fraud, and vandalism—accounted for 21%. And drug offenses were another 20%. Can you think of any crime that does not break some sort of commandment? Talk about sin taking away our freedom . . . literally![4]

Keeping commandments helps us remain in control of ourselves, our desires, our passions, and the direction of our lives. As the Savior taught, "The truth shall make you free" (John 8:32).

COMMANDMENTS AND KITE STRING

Here is an interesting thought: Does the string on a kite hold it down, or keep it up, so it can fly? How is that similar to having commandments? What happens to a kite when someone cuts the string? What happens when someone breaks the commandments? Think about it . . . there are a lot of similarities.

That Which We Persist in Doing . . .

A fourth reason why keeping the commandments is so important is that the more we obey, the easier it is to continue obeying. This is because each time we obey, we are blessed with an increased amount of the Spirit of the Lord, which strengthens us to withstand temptation. As you read these next verses keep in mind that the word "light" in the scriptures can be a synonym for the Spirit of Jesus Christ (see D&C 84:45).

"He that keepeth his commandments receiveth truth and light, until he is glorified in truth and knoweth all things" (D&C 93:28).

We can invite the Light of Christ into our life by living the commandments. Notice what happens when we receive light:

"He that receiveth light, and continueth in God, receiveth more light; and that light groweth brighter and brighter until the perfect day" (D&C 50:24).

In other words, when we gain light and continue to do what is right, we will receive more light—and that light continues to grow brighter. One of the great things about receiving light is that it makes us less likely to want to do bad because "light and truth forsake that evil one" (D&C 93:37). Truly, the more we obey, the easier it is to be obedient, and to be more like our Savior.

DO TRY THIS AT HOME!

Pull out an old board game that you don't know how to play, and try to play it *without reading the rules or instructions*. Or, if you do know the rules, play the game with someone who doesn't know them. See how long it takes before they start to ask questions about how the game should be played. Compare this to the commandments of God. How hard would life be if we were left on our own without God giving us guidance, rules, and commandments so that we can know how to play the "game" of life successfully?

SPIRITUAL ACCLIMATIZATION

Have you ever noticed yourself breathing hard at higher altitudes? It's because your body isn't acclimatized, or used to the thin amount of oxygen in the air. But, if we stay at the new altitude, we will get used to it. For example, if a person hikes to 10,000 feet and spends several days at that altitude, their body acclimatizes. If the person then climbs to 12,000 feet, their body will acclimatize again in another 1 to 3 days.[5] Keeping the commandments is similar. Living a "higher" way of life, although it may be hard at first, becomes easier the more time we spend doing it.

When we obey now, we increase our capacity to obey in the future by receiving an increased amount of the Spirit—like an upward spiral of light.

HOW DO YOU VIEW THE COMMANDMENTS?

One indicator of our spirituality is how we view the commandments. President Ezra Taft Benson taught, "When obedience ceases to be an *irritant* and becomes our *quest*, in that moment God will endow us with power."[6] The way we view obedience affects our power to be obedient.

Commandments can be seen as an *irritant*, like blurred vision, or . . .

Commandments can be seen as a focused *quest* . . . either way, our view affects our ability to follow them clearly.

Ye Shall Prosper in the Land

Another reason why we should be obedient is explained repeatedly in the scriptures. Put simply, each time we obey the commandments we will be blessed. Lehi taught his sons the Lord's words: "Inasmuch as ye shall keep my commandments ye shall prosper in the land" (2 Nephi 1:20). This promise is repeated numerous times throughout the scriptures. We are blessed with happiness, peace, freedom, and the Spirit of God. Even in the inevitable times of trial, God will "expand [our] vision, and strengthen [us]. He will give [us] the help [we] need to meet [our] trials and challenges"[7] if we are faithful.

These blessings will not only be rewarded in the next life, but in our life *now*. King Benjamin taught that when we obey, God will "immediately" bless us (Mosiah 2:24).

Why Should I Keep the Commandments?

1. **When we obey, we experience true happiness. On the negative side, "wickedness never was happiness" (Alma 41:10).**
2. **The commandments give us needed guidance and direction that help us avoid unnecessary pain and sorrow.**
3. **Obedience leads to freedom, and disobedience leads to slavery.**
4. **The more we obey, the more of the Spirit of the Lord (light) we receive in our lives making it easier for us to obey in the future.**
5. **Each time we keep the commandments, we are blessed.**

NOW that we have reviewed some of the *principles*, let's answer some of the questions regarding the *practices* connected to why we should keep the commandments:

Why are there so many commandments and rules?

As the first three principles in the chapter emphasize, God's commandments primarily exist to produce happiness for his children and to help them avoid unnecessary pain. There are many ways we can produce sorrow through our actions. Therefore, our loving Heavenly

Father commands us to avoid those practices that produce unhappiness (adultery, dishonesty, anger, etc.), and he also commands us to do those things that produce happiness and will help us become like him (forgive, love, serve, be humble, etc.). There are a lot of commandments, but that also means there are a lot of blessings.

Why do some people who break the commandments appear happy?

The key word in that question is *appear*. While those who break commandments may have momentary pleasure through disobedience, eventually disobedience leads to sorrow, suffering, or slavery. Remember the analogy of the kite string from earlier in the chapter—when the kite breaks away from the string, it might appear "free," perhaps even suddenly darting up higher in the sky, but it won't take long before it spins out of control and crashes to the ground. Remember, there is an eventual consequence to all disobedience, some consequences just take longer than others to become apparent.

Why are some commandments more important than others—or are they?

The Savior said that the most important commandments were to love God and to love our neighbor (see Matthew 22:36–40). There are obviously some commandments that hurt God or hurt our fellow man more than others. According to Alma 39:5, the three worst sins that can be committed are denying the Holy Ghost, murder where innocent blood is shed, and sexual immorality.

2ch Why Should I Listen to and Follow the Prophet?

Imagine a beautiful river scene like this one.

Wouldn't you love to be canoeing along this river, enjoying the view? But what if we expand our view of this scene?

Suddenly the river trip takes on a whole new meaning. This object lesson, adapted from a talk by Elder Neil L. Andersen, shows one reason why it is so important for us to follow the prophets—because they see things we cannot.

Do You See What I See?

Just like an expanded view of the river changes our perspective, prophets can give us an expanded view of the world, which helps us avoid equally dangerous pitfalls. One of the gifts given to prophets is this gift of vision; thus, prophets are called seers, or *see*-ers. The Book of Mormon says that "A seer can know of things which are past, and also of things which are to come, and by them shall all things be revealed, or, rather, shall secret things be made manifest, and hidden things shall come to light, and things which are not known shall be made known by them, and also things shall be made known by them which otherwise could not be known" (Mosiah 8:17).

Consider all the ways people try to "see" the future.

Only one comes with a guarantee. (See D&C 1:37–38 for the promise.)

Through revelation, prophets are able to see things before they happen. The scriptures repeatedly demonstrate how those who listened to seers were blessed. Whether it was Joseph in Egypt seeing the seven-year famine, or Noah building his ark before the flood, or Lehi and his family leaving Jerusalem before the city was destroyed, blessings came to those who obeyed what they could not see themselves.

Prophecies Fulfilled

We have many modern examples of how seers have seen and told of events before they unfolded. For example, Joseph Smith prophesied of the Civil War thirty years before it happened—he even named where the rebellion would begin (see D&C 87). Years before his martyrdom and the Saints moved west to Utah, Joseph saw in a vision that some members of the Church would "live to go and assist in making settlements and build cities and see the Saints become a mighty people in the midst of the Rocky Mountains."[1]

Joseph Smith

saw that the Latter-day Saints would become a "mighty people" in the Rocky Mountains years before they went west. Lucky guess? We think not.

Joseph also saw the worldwide growth of the Church. Speaking at a time when all the priesthood holders in the world could fit in a log cabin, he prophesied, "This Church will fill North and South America—it will fill the world."[2] Today, we are literally seeing this prophecy fulfilled.

LDS CHURCH GROWTH WORLDWIDE

"This Church will fill North and South America—it will fill the world." —Joseph Smith

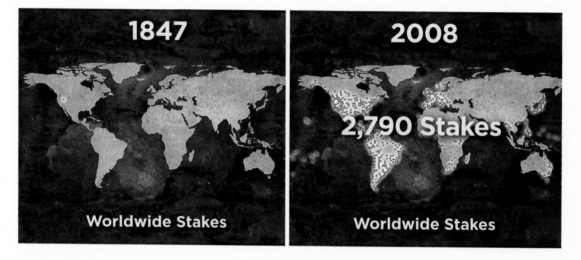

1847 — Worldwide Stakes

2008 — 2,790 Stakes — Worldwide Stakes

The gift of seership is alive and well today. In general conference, we sustain each member of the First Presidency and Quorum of the Twelve as a prophet, *seer,* and revelator. "The Family: A Proclamation to the World," given in 1995, provides a recent example of their prophetic power to see.

The first sentence of the Proclamation reads: "We, the First Presidency and the Council of the Twelve Apostles of The Church of Jesus Christ of Latter-day Saints, solemnly proclaim that marriage between a man and a woman is ordained of God."[3] At the time this Proclamation was made there was little public debate that marriage should be defined as being "between a man and a woman," and at that time no government on earth permitted same-sex marriage.

However, within six years of the Proclamation, the Netherlands became the first country to legalize same-sex marriage, followed by Belgium, Spain, Canada, and South Africa.[4]

Parts of the United States have also legalized same-sex marriage. Modern-day seers saw this increased global pressure to redefine marriage and called "upon responsible citizens and officers of government everywhere to promote those measures designed to maintain and strengthen the family as the fundamental unit of society."[5]

DO TRY THIS AT HOME!

We're not prophets, but we've made a prediction. We need your help to see if it's correct. Pick a number between one and ten in your head. Multiply that number by nine. Then add the two digits of your answer together (for example, if you got 42, 4+2=6). Now subtract five from that number (for example, 6-5=1). Have your new number? Now, think of the alphabetical equivalent to the number (1=A, 2=B, 3=C, etc.). Now, think of a country that starts with your letter (Albania, Bosnia, Croatia, etc.). Take the last letter in the country's name and think of an animal whose name starts with that letter. (It must be a one-word animal—"black widow," for example, would not count.) Finally, take the last letter of the animal's name and think of a color that starts with that letter. (If you had "bear," the color could be "red.") So you should have a color, an animal, and a country. We think we've predicted what you picked. Turn to page 20 and see if we were correct!

Dodging Destruction and Being Protected from Plagues

Another reason why we should follow the prophet is because those who heed the prophet's counsel have been promised safety and protection from many of the foretold calamities and problems of the last days. Some people are afraid of the Second Coming because of the widespread destruction and misery that has been foretold will accompany it. In the words of Elder Bruce R. McConkie, "There will be earthquakes and floods and famines. The waves of the sea shall heave themselves beyond their bounds, the clouds shall withhold their rain, and the crops of the earth shall wither and die.

"There will be plagues and pestilence and disease and death. An overflowing scourge shall cover the earth and a desolating sickness shall sweep the land. Flies shall take hold of the inhabitants of the earth, and maggots shall come in upon them. (See D&C 29:14–20.) 'Their flesh shall fall from off their bones, and their eyes from their sockets' (D&C 29:19).

"Bands of Gadianton robbers will infest every nation, immorality and murder and crime will increase, and it will seem as though every man's hand is against his brother."[6]

That sounds scary! But one theme repeated in the scriptures and in the words of the prophets is that the people who follow God's prophet will be safe from many of the problems that await the wicked and rebellious (see 1 Nephi 22:16–17). There was terrible devastation and death in the Americas following Christ's crucifixion, but as Mormon teaches us, "It was the *more righteous* part of the people who were saved, and it was *they who received the prophets* and stoned them not; and it was they who had not shed the blood of the saints, who were spared" (3 Nephi 10:12; emphasis added). Although *all* the righteous will not be spared *all* of the destructions that will come, it is certain that following the prophet will maximize our protection.

Elder McConkie also promised, "We do not say that all of the Saints will be spared and saved from the coming day of desolation. But we do say there is no promise of safety and no promise of security except for those who love the Lord and who are seeking to do all that he commands."[7]

Much of the protection that will come to the Saints in the last days will be "Noah-like," meaning that as we follow prophetic counsel, we will be prepared in order to make it through potential trials and problems (such as the counsel to store food and stay out of debt). Some of the protection will also be "Moses and Pharaoh-like," in that obedience will help us avoid many modern-day plagues (such as sexually transmitted diseases).

Given the prophesied calamities that will happen before the Second Coming, the divine safety, preparation, and peace promised to the righteous is another powerful reason why we should follow the counsel of God's living prophets in the latter days.

Never Led Astray

On May 11, 1996, eight people died trying to summit Mount Everest, making it one of the deadliest days in the mountain's history. One factor that led to this disaster was that the guides permitted their climbers to try to summit the mountain after the 2:00 PM turn-around time that had been designated. Being that close to the success of summiting the world's tallest peak caused some of the guides to put pleasing their clients ahead of their expedition's safety.[8]

Who's guiding you?

A KEY THAT WILL NEVER RUST

Joseph Smith said, "'I will give you a key that will never rust—if you will stay with the majority of the Twelve Apostles . . . you will never be led astray.' The history of the Church has proven this to be true."[9]

DO TRY THIS AT HOME!

Go to http://lds.org and re-read the prophet's most recent counsel from general conference. You may also want to download some conference talks and listen to them. What insights do you gain from the living prophet?

Fortunately, we have been promised that the latter-day prophets will never bend to the pressures of society and lead the people of God astray. Prophets and apostles will *always* lead the Church and its members in a straight course. President Wilford Woodruff promised, "The Lord will never permit me or any other man who stands as President of this Church to lead you astray. It is not in the program. It is not in the mind of God. If I were to attempt that the Lord would remove me out of my place, and so He will any other man who attempts to lead the children of men astray from the oracles of God and from their duty."[10]

If we follow the prophet, we will never be led astray as we strive to find our way back into the presence of our Heavenly Father.

TELL ME ONE MORE TIME!

Why Should I Listen to and Follow the Prophet?

1. **Prophets can see coming events more clearly and direct us accordingly—they are see-ers!**
2. **Those who follow the prophet have been promised safety from and preparation for many of the calamities of the last days.**
3. **When we follow the prophet, we will never be led astray.**

NOW that we have reviewed some of the *principles*, let's answer some of the questions regarding the *practices* connected to following the prophet:

Why is it so important to listen to general conference?

General conference is the time when the Lord's prophets publicly declare God's will for the worldwide Church. President Harold B. Lee said, "If you want to know what the Lord would have the Saints know and to have his guidance and direction for the next six months, get a copy of the proceedings of this conference, and you will have the latest word of the Lord as far as the Saints are concerned."[11] It is also a time when we can publicly raise our hands to sustain the living prophets and leaders of the Church and express our faith that they are truly prophets, seers, and revelators.

Why do modern prophets sometimes teach things that are different from what past prophets taught?

In times past, as new circumstances have arisen, the Lord, through his prophets, has directed inspired changes to meet the new challenges and opportunities of the day. Since this is a "true and living church" (D&C 1:30), change is a sign of continuing revelation, and we should expect more changes in the future. Although programs, practices, and policies of the Church might change because of new revelation, the eternal truths that those practices are based on—the doctrines of the gospel—don't change.

Why should I listen to prophets who are so much older than I am? They don't know what it's like to be a teenager today.

You might be surprised how much Church leaders *do* know about what it's like to be a youth in today's world. Consider this: God the Father, the Savior, and the Holy Ghost—the Godhead—know more about being a teenager today than you do because they have the knowledge and experience of ALL the world's teenagers combined, and you just have yourself! If we believe that prophets truly do receive revelation and that they are truly seers, then there is no doubt that they know exactly what spiritual issues are facing teenagers today.

THERE ARE NO ORANGE KANGAROOS IN DENMARK!

Let's see, you picked the number 4, the letter D, Denmark as the country, kangaroo as the animal, and orange as the color. We were right, weren't we?

Again, we are *not* prophets. This is a simple math trick, and real prophets don't use tricks. How blessed we are to live in a time when seers walk the land.

3 ch Why Does It Matter Who My Friends Are?

Which of these photos do you think is an arctic fox? Actually, they both are! During the winter, the arctic fox's coat is white to blend in with the surrounding snow. But when the seasons change, so does the fox. With the coming of summer and its attendant browns and yellows, the fox's coat changes to match its environment.

Are we different? Depending on who we surround ourselves with, we may tend to change just like the arctic fox does. In order to understand why it matters so much who our friends are, we must accept this universal truth: Our friends affect who we are.

The Influence of Friends

For the Strength of Youth says, "Choose your friends carefully. They will greatly influence how you think and act, and even help determine the person you will become."[1]

The prophets say friends *will* influence how we think and act, not "friends *might* influence," or "*perhaps* friends will influence how we think and act." Rather, friends *will* influence us.

Friends influence us in different ways. Some influences are obvious, like friends who directly try to pressure us to do things we wouldn't normally do. But friends also can influence us subtly. Just being with a person increases the likelihood that we will become more like that person. For example, have you ever caught yourself unconsciously using the same slang phrases that your friends use?

MERRY GRINCHMAS!

John Says:

A few years ago, my wife and I went to Universal Studios in Orlando, Florida. It was December, and we were able to see a holiday show called "Grinchmas" (like Christmas—get it?). As part of the show, you could stand in a line to meet the Grinch instead of Santa.

The Grinch looked unbelievably real, and he was unbelievably mean. When it was time for a child to take a picture with the Grinch, the child began to cry. "Fine," said the Grinch. "I don't like you either."

When two giggling teenage girls came to take their picture with him, he burped in their faces! Later, I saw one of the attendants come in and ask the Grinch to go outside to get his picture taken with somebody who could not come in. The Grinch stormed outside to find a person in a wheelchair. Do you think he showed compassion? Nope! He looked at her and said, "Well, what makes you so special?"

I thought the Grinch was so funny that I watched him for an hour. Later that day, I found myself talking like the Grinch—and my wife didn't like it! Just hanging around the Grinch for a short period of time had affected how I acted.

Have you ever started liking a certain music group, or TV show, or style of clothing because a friend introduced it to you? If you don't think that friends influence each other, pay attention the next time you are with a group of teenagers. Odds are they will dress the same way, have similar hairstyles, have common interests, and talk the same way.

WHAT DO YOUR FRIENDS BRING OUT IN YOU?

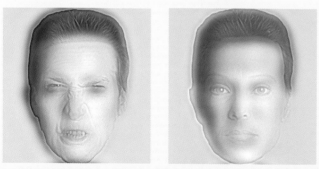

Looking at these two faces close-up, the left face appears to be an angry man, and the right face appears to be a woman with a neutral emotion. Have somebody hold the book and step back from it (perhaps several feet). Squint, blink, or let your eyes become unfocused, and watch the faces change expression—even genders! The angry man should change into the face of the woman, and the neutral woman should change into an angry man.[2] Our friends have the same ability to bring out different sides in us, positive or negative.

Simply being around people has an influence on how we think and act. The proverb says, "Make no friendship with an angry man; and with a furious man thou shalt not go: *Lest thou learn his ways, and get a snare to thy soul*" (Proverbs 22:24–25; emphasis added).

One young woman wrote, "When I was a teenager I never would admit it, but now I can see that my friends had a negative influence on me more than I thought. I thought I was strong and that my 'wild' friends wouldn't affect me. I was strong and stood up against their teasings and temptings, but in my efforts to 'save' them I can see that over time I started to compromise my standards and accept things that weren't right.

Hanging out with bad friends will affect you even if you think it won't."[3]

To illustrate the power of peer pressure, the television show *Candid Camera* did an experiment with people entering an elevator. When the elevator doors opened, an unsuspecting person saw that everyone inside the elevator (all actors) were facing the back wall of the elevator. What did each person do as they got on the elevator? In succession, they all turned around and faced backward as well.

Why would grown adults stand backwards in an elevator? It is simply because they were influenced by what they saw and heard around them. If we are influenced by complete strangers, what happens to us when

DO TRY THIS AT HOME!

Now . . . Which Way Do I Face?

Check out the video of the *Candid Camera* elevator experiment at http://ldswhy .com

we are with our friends? This is the first reason why it is so important that we choose friends carefully: They will influence us and help determine the kind of person we become.

Positive Peer Pressure

Now let's look on the bright side of things. Peer pressure isn't always used for *bad;* in fact, it can often be used for *good.* Friends can be an incredibly positive influence in your life. If you are down and discouraged, or tempted and wavering, good friends can encourage you to do the right thing.

As if That Weren't Enough . . .

Researchers have found that the number one reason LDS youth do bad things is pressure from their friends.[4]

CAUTION: PEER PRESSURE

A powerful example of this appears in the Old Testament. David (the same one who killed Goliath) was going through a difficult time. He was alone in the woods and feeling extremely discouraged. Notice what his friend Jonathan did: "And Jonathan Saul's son arose, and went to David into the wood, *and strengthened his hand in God*" (1 Samuel 23:16; emphasis added). True friends will "strengthen [your] hand in God" and influence you for good in difficult times.

Speaking of the strengthening effect that good friends can have, President Thomas S. Monson cited an interesting Church study: "In a survey made in selected wards and stakes of the Church, we learned a most significant fact: those persons whose friends married in the temple usually married in the temple, while those persons whose friends did not marry in the temple usually did not marry in the temple. The influence of one's friends appeared to be a highly dominant factor—even more so than parental urging, classroom instruction, or proximity to a temple."[5]

"As you walk the road of life, be careful of your friends. They can make you or break you. Be generous in helping the unfortunate and those in distress. But bind to you friends of your own kind, friends who will encourage you, stand with you, live as you desire to live; who will enjoy the same kind of entertainment; and who will resist the evil that you determine to resist."—President Gordon B. Hinckley[6]

A TRUE BFF

Would a *real* friend ever tell on you, or scold you, or set you straight? They should! Does a *real* friend let you do whatever you want? They shouldn't! Sometimes we think our BFFs (best friend forever!) are good friends because they "like me for me" and don't care how we act. A true friend *does* care how you act. *For the Strength of Youth* says we should "strengthen and encourage each other in living high standards. A true friend will encourage you to be your best self."[7]

Influence Your Friends for Good

This study leads to a second reason why our choice of friends matters so much: We can help lift up those around us. The Savior taught, "Ye are the light of the world. A city that is set on an hill cannot be hid" (Matthew 5:14). As we are a light to others, we have the potential to have an eternal influence on them.

Many people are lonely—and we can lift them up. *For the Strength of Youth* says, "Make a special effort to reach out to new converts and to those who are less active. Help them feel welcome among your group of friends. You can strengthen them by sharing your testimony and by setting a good example."[8] To our friends of other faiths, we can invite them "to [our] Church meetings and activities, where they can learn about the gospel,"[9] and continue to be their friend even if they aren't interested in the Church.

"More than half the members of the Church today chose to be baptized after the age of eight."—Elder Henry B. Eyring[10]

The Doctrine and Covenants tells us that we should "succor the weak, lift up the hands which hang down, and strengthen the feeble knees" (D&C 81:5). Strengthening others and setting a positive example is another reason why it is so important who we choose as our friends.

TELL ME ONE MORE TIME!

Why Does It Matter Who My Friends Are?

1. **Friends influence how we think and act—for good or bad—and help determine the kind of person we become.**
2. **You can be a positive influence in the lives of others who need strengthening.**

NOW that we have reviewed some of the *principles*, let's answer some of the questions regarding the *practices* connected to friendship:

Why is it OK to still be friends with people if they aren't LDS?

For the Strength of Youth tells us to "choose friends who share your values so you can strengthen and encourage each other in living high standards."[11] Millions of people of other faiths have high standards. The question is not whether they are LDS, but whether they help you live your LDS standards. Also, as the second principle in the chapter emphasizes, by sincerely befriending those who are not LDS, we may find ways to share the gospel with them.

Why can a friend still be bad if they aren't pressuring me to break the commandments?

We need to pay attention to how we *feel* when we are with certain friends. Do they physically or verbally harm us? Does their influence make us feel bad about ourselves, or encourage us to adopt a negative or bad attitude when we are around them? *For the Strength of Youth* teaches that "a true friend will encourage you to be your best self."[12] Even if they don't encourage us to do wrong, some friends may indirectly *discourage* you from being your best self.

Why is it wrong for me to "cover" for my friends and not tell on them? Isn't that what good friends do?

A good friend should be a positive influence and strengthen their friends in living the gospel. When we cover for our friend's mistakes or wickedness, we act like Kishkumen who "was upheld by his band, who had entered into a covenant that *no one should know his wickedness*" (Helaman 2:3; emphasis added). A true friend will have the courage to stand up to friends who are doing things wrong, set a positive example for them, and try to persuade them to be righteous.

4 Why Should I Keep the Word of Wisdom?

We could make this a very short chapter just by showing you a few pictures.

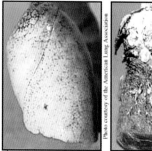

Photo courtesy of the American Lung Association

Photo courtesy of the American Lung Association

└ healthy lung tissue ┘ └ diseased lung tissue ┘

The lung tissue on the left is healthy. The tissue on the right has been damaged by cigarette smoke.[1] Which do you want inside your body?

This picture was taken at the scene of an automobile accident involving a drunk driver.

The three leading causes of death for fifteen- to twenty-four-year-olds are automobile crashes, homicides, and suicides. Alcohol is a leading factor in all three. The question "Why should I keep the Word of Wisdom?" has some pretty obvious answers.

Health Benefits of the Word of Wisdom

First, the health benefits. Although there was little medical evidence in 1833 when the Word of Wisdom was first received, today nobody doubts that it contains good health advice and that living the Word of Wisdom will help us live longer.

The Word of Wisdom says that, "inasmuch as any man drinketh wine or strong drink among you, behold it is not good" (D&C 89:5).

"It is not good" is an understatement! Did you know that a 2006 report of all the U.S. alcohol-related deaths listed 41% as automobile fatalities (25% of which were teenage deaths), 31% as homicides, and 20% from boating accidents.[2]

That definitely doesn't sound good!

As you already know, there is a clear correlation between smoking and cancer: The more you smoke, the likelier you are to get lung cancer.

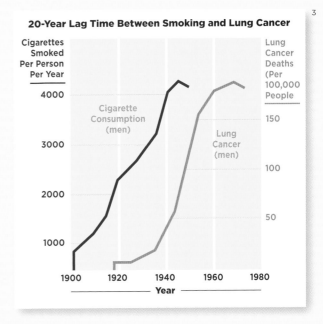

20-Year Lag Time Between Smoking and Lung Cancer [3]

Negative health effects of breaking the Word of Wisdom include nausea, increased stress, loss of muscle control, birth defects, shortness of breath, yellowing of the skin, damaging the liver, and much more.

Numerous studies over the years have shown that those who obey the principles found in the Word of Wisdom enjoy healthier lives and an increased life expectancy. If we live the Word of Wisdom, we are promised that "the destroying angel shall pass by [us]" (D&C 89:21), and we will live longer and healthier lives than if we don't live the Word of Wisdom.

Not only will obeying the Word of Wisdom help us live longer, it will also help us live a life of higher quality and health. A fourteen-year selective study conducted by UCLA epidemiologist James E. Enstrom tracked the health of 10,000 moderately active LDS people in California. Of these non-smoking, monogamous, non-drinkers, Enstrom concluded "that LDS Church members who follow religious mandates barring smoking and drinking have one of the lowest death rates from cancer and cardiovascular diseases—about half that of the general population. . . . Moreover, the healthiest LDS Church members enjoy a life expectancy eight to eleven years longer than that of the general white population in the United States."[4]

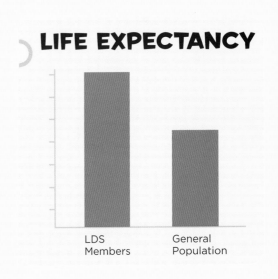

LIFE EXPECTANCY

There are some funny anti-smoking ads out there. If you want to hear a good message (and get a good laugh), you can link to these ads at http://ldswhy.com.

Intellectual Benefits of the Word of Wisdom

Keeping the Word of Wisdom is not only good for our body, it's good for our brain. Perhaps this is part of what the Lord meant when he promised that those who lived this law would "find wisdom and great treasures of knowledge, even hidden treasures" (D&C 89:19).

President Heber J. Grant taught, "No man who breaks the Word of Wisdom can gain the same amount of knowledge and intelligence in this world as the man who obeys that law. I don't care who he is or where he comes from, his mind will not be as clear, and he cannot advance as far and as rapidly and retain his power as much as he would if he obeyed the Word of Wisdom."[5]

As a second witness, Brigham Young said that if we follow the Word of Wisdom it "will increase [our] intelligence."[6]

In addition to these prophetic words, medical evidence clearly shows that living the Word of Wisdom will make us smarter.

WHICH BRAIN DO YOU WANT?

Drinking alcohol affects our brain. The brain on the left belongs to a healthy, fifteen-year-old non-drinker, the one on the right belongs to a fifteen-year-old heavy drinker. The pink and red spots represent brain activity. Whose brain is working better?

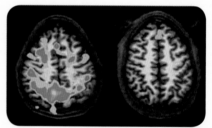

This picture demonstrates what alcohol does to the brain. The image on the left is a scan from a healthy non-drinker. The one on the right is from a heavy drinker. The holes that appear in the image on the right indicate areas of reduced brain activity.[7] Do you want holes in your brain?

Images used by permission of Daniel G. Amen, M.D. and The Amen Clinics - www.amenclinics.com

There is even a correlation between drinking alcohol and academic success. A study reported that at both two-year and four-year colleges the heaviest drinkers receive the lowest grades.[8]

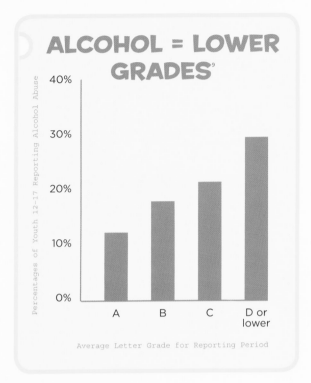

ALCOHOL = LOWER GRADES[9]

Percentages of Youth 12–17 Reporting Alcohol Abuse

40%

30%

20%

10%

0%

A   B   C   D or lower

Average Letter Grade for Reporting Period

Our Heavenly Father desires that we "do many things of [our] own free will" and that we be "agents unto [ourselves]" (D&C 58:27–28). On the other hand, Satan wants to take away our freedom, limit our ability to choose for ourselves, and bind us (see Moses 7:26). One of the ways the adversary does this is through harmful and addictive substances such as drugs, alcohol, nicotine, and caffeine—substances prohibited in the Word of Wisdom. When we keep the Word of Wisdom, we remain in control of our actions and our own free will.

Those who violate the Word of Wisdom run the risk of losing part of their freedom and agency by becoming enslaved to these controlling influences. Also, when we are under the influence of these substances, it becomes increasingly difficult to think clearly and make good decisions. We tend to act more impulsively and emotionally, without realizing the consequences of our behavior. It becomes nearly impossible for us to watch our thoughts, words, and deeds (see Mosiah 4:30) because we are not in complete control of ourselves.

Addiction Isn't Freedom . . .

The following statements were all made by an addict describing how trapped he felt because of his addictions:

"Addiction is missing my mother's birthday because I was high."

"Addiction is the tingling on both sides of my tongue, near the back, when I haven't had a cigarette in 2 hours."

"Addiction is cutting a date short so I can go home and get high."

"Addiction is leaving the party thinking I'm sober enough to drive, backing up the car, and realizing that I'm not."

"Addiction is a box in the back of my closet where I hide my cigarettes."

"Addiction is realizing that I can never introduce my girlfriend to my friends at work, because they know I smoke and she doesn't."

"Addiction is a persistent cough."

"Addiction is never having quiet, much less peace."[10]

Spiritual Benefits of the Word of Wisdom

The spiritual blessings of the Word of Wisdom are perhaps the most important reason why we should obey this divine command. President Boyd K. Packer taught, "The Word of Wisdom was given so that you may keep the delicate, sensitive, spiritual part of your nature on proper alert. . . . And I promise . . . you shall be warned of dangers and shall be guided through the whisperings of the Holy Spirit."[11]

These spiritual blessings are certainly part of the "great treasures of knowledge" promised in Doctrine and Covenants 89.

One of the ways police officers determine whether somebody is under the influence of alcohol is to see how well they follow verbal instructions. Think about it, if somebody who has been drinking struggles to follow verbal instructions, how will they be able to respond to the soft, spiritual promptings of the Holy Ghost?

The Spirit does not shout at us. Coffee, alcohol, tobacco, and other harmful substances create a barrier of insensitivity that prevents us from receiving the revelation we need.

The Lord has promised, "And all saints who remember to keep and do these sayings, walking in obedience to the commandments, shall receive health in their navel and marrow to their bones; And shall find wisdom and great treasures of knowledge, even hidden treasures; And shall run and not be weary, and shall walk and not faint. And I, the Lord, give unto them a promise, that the destroying angel shall pass by them, as the children of Israel, and not slay them" (D&C 89:18–21).

Living the Word of Wisdom will bless you physically, intellectually, and spiritually. There should be no doubt as to why this commandment is so important.

Prophetic Spiritual Promises and the Word of Wisdom

"The Lord . . . gave us the Word of Wisdom . . . that our faith might be strengthened, that our testimony . . . might be increased."
—President George Albert Smith[12]

"I would like it known that if we as a people never used a particle of tea or coffee or of tobacco or of liquor . . . we would grow spiritually; we would have a more direct line of communication with God, our Heavenly Father."
—President Heber J. Grant[13]

"[The] Word of Wisdom . . . was given . . . for the benefit, the help, and the prosperity of the Latter-day Saints, that they might purify and prepare themselves to go nearer into the presence of the Lord."
—President Joseph F. Smith[14]

TELL ME ONE MORE TiME!

Why Should I Keep the Word of Wisdom?

1. **Living the Word of Wisdom will bring better physical health.**
2. **You will be smarter if you keep the Word of Wisdom.**
3. **You will remain in control of your actions and avoid the addictions that are connected to violating the Word of Wisdom.**
4. **You will be more receptive to promptings from the Holy Ghost and will receive other spiritual blessings.**

NOW that we have reviewed some of the *principles*, let's answer some of the questions regarding the *practices* connected to the Word of Wisdom:

Why shouldn't I "try" alcohol just to see what it tastes like?

One reason we shouldn't ever touch alcohol (or anything addictive) is that we don't know how our bodies will respond to it. Even one drink could create an addictive appetite for something that can kill our minds and bodies and take away our freedom. Furthermore, even if we take only one drink of alcohol, we immediately lose our ability to be led by the Spirit. There have been many people who have ruined their lives due to *one* night of drinking and the poor decisions they made on that one occasion.[15]

Why shouldn't I take something into my body if science says it's good for me?

Even *if* substances prohibited by the Word of Wisdom were *good* for our bodies, the Word of Wisdom is about more than just physical health. It is also about remaining in control of our actions and decisions and being in tune with the delicate promptings of the Holy Ghost (reasons #3 and #4). For those reasons alone, we should avoid taking anything into our body that

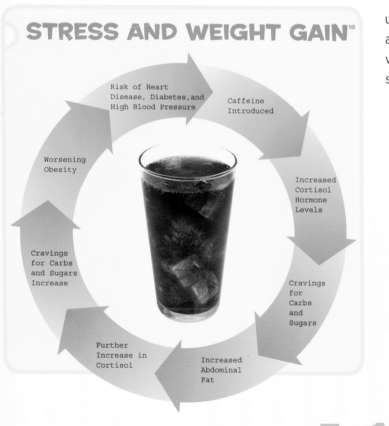

could dull our senses, take away our agency, or lead to addiction. The Lord, who created our bodies, knows what is best for them. When he specifically states that things forbidden in the Word of Wisdom are "not for the body" (D&C 89:8), we should trust him.

Why should I avoid drinking highly caffeinated soft drinks or "energy" drinks?

Although the Church has no official position on drinking caffeinated beverages, "The leaders of the Church have advised . . . against use of any drink containing harmful habit-forming drugs."[16]

In recent years, medical research has been done on the dangers of highly caffeinated energy drinks and the results are surprising. Dr. Thomas J. Boud lists some of the side effects of caffeine-related medical conditions, which include jitteriness, agitation, insomnia, difficulty concentrating, rapid heart rate, elevated blood pressure, gastrointestinal disorders, osteoporosis, acid reflux, weight gain, and decreased blood flow. High levels of caffeine can even lead to depression and death.[17]

President Thomas S. Monson has urged us to "keep our bodies—our temples—fit and clean, free from harmful substances which destroy our physical, mental, and spiritual well-being."[19]

STRESS AND WEIGHT GAIN[18]

Caffeine Introduced

Increased Cortisol Hormone Levels

Cravings for Carbs and Sugars

Increased Abdominal Fat

Further Increase in Cortisol

Cravings for Carbs and Sugars Increase

Worsening Obesity

Risk of Heart Disease, Diabetes, and High Blood Pressure

A JOLT TO THE SYSTEM

In 2006,

- 500 new brands of energy drinks were introduced

- 7.6 million young people reported having used an energy drink

- The energy drink industry reached the $3 billion-a-year mark[20]

5 ^{ch} Why Shouldn't I Pierce or Tattoo My Body?

Words of the Prophet

Something that makes Latter-day Saints peculiar is the counsel we have been given by Church leaders to not pierce or tattoo our bodies. Many people view tattoos and multiple piercings as not only acceptable, but fashionable; therefore, this standard makes us stand out from those around us. Notice the clear counsel given by President Gordon B. Hinckley:

"You Mormons are peculiar."

"A tattoo is graffiti on the temple of the body.

"Likewise the piercing of the body for multiple rings in the ears, in the nose, even in the tongue. Can they possibly think that is beautiful? It is a passing fancy, but its effects can be permanent. Some have gone to such extremes that the ring had to be removed by surgery. The First Presidency and the Quorum of the Twelve have declared that we discourage tattoos and also 'the piercing of the body for other than medical purposes.' We do not, however, take any position 'on the minimal piercing of the ears by women for one pair of earrings'—one pair."[1]

YOU WOULDN'T DO THIS TO A TEMPLE . . .

SO WHY WOULD YOU DO THIS TO YOUR TEMPLE?

FAST FACT
There is a significant correlation between tattoos and piercings and such risk-taking behaviors as smoking cigarettes, doing drugs, drinking alcohol, and sexual activity.[2]

Some people might think, "Tattoos and piercing are no big deal." But do you remember the story of Naaman? He was a leper and was told by the prophet Elisha that bathing in the Jordan River would cure his disease. Naaman didn't want to follow Elisha's counsel because it seemed so small and insignificant. But one of his servants said to him, "My father, if the prophet had bid thee do some great thing, wouldest thou not have done it? how much rather then, when he saith to thee, Wash, and be clean?" (2 Kings 5:13).

In other words, "You would obey the prophet if he told you to do something really important, so why not obey when he tells you to do something small and simple?"

Why do prophets speak about such seemingly small things as tattoos and piercings? President Harold B. Lee taught, "Do not underestimate the important symbolic and actual effect of appearance. Persons who are well groomed and modestly dressed invite the companionship of the Spirit of our Father in Heaven and are able to exercise a wholesome influence upon those around them."[4]

Private Property

One of the first reasons why we don't believe it is right to pierce and tattoo our bodies has to do with the fact that we don't own our bodies. They are not our personal property. The apostle Paul taught the Corinthians this important doctrine: "Know ye not that ye are the temple of God, and that the Spirit of God dwelleth in you? If any man defile the temple of God, him shall God destroy; for the temple of God is holy, which temple ye are" (1 Corinthians 3:16–17).

If we were to say to Paul, "It's my body, I can get a tattoo or pierce it up if I want," we think he would say: "What? know ye not that your body is the temple of the Holy Ghost which is in you, which ye have of God, and ye are not your own? *For ye are bought with a price:* therefore glorify God in your body, and in your spirit, *which are God's*" (1 Corinthians 6:19–20; emphasis added).

Notice that first word: "What?" Paul would be totally shocked to hear somebody say, "It's my body. I can do what I want with it." Paul's response is, "What are you talking about? Your body has been purchased with the blood of Jesus Christ—it isn't *your* body at all."

A COMMANDMENT AS OLD AS THE OLD TESTAMENT

"Ye shall not make any cuttings in your flesh for the dead, nor print any marks upon you: I am the Lord."—Leviticus 19:28

If a friend loaned you a car, would you return it with a bunch of holes in it and painted all over with little symbols and personal pictures?

Because our bodies actually belong to the Savior, we should follow the counsel of the one who owns it and not defile our bodies with tattoos or multiple piercings.

Making the Right Impression on Others

Another powerful reason why we shouldn't tattoo or pierce our bodies is that it negatively affects how we feel and how other people view us. *For the Strength of Youth* says, "Your dress and grooming send messages about you to others and influence the way you and others act."[5]

Before It Was Borrowed . . .

"Yeah, you can borrow my car. Just take good care of it because it cost a lot."

After It Was Returned . . .

"Dude, check out what I did to your ride! I hope you like it! Think I can borrow it again?"

Elder David A. Bednar shared a story about a recently returned missionary who began dating a young woman. As time passed, the returned missionary wanted to get more serious in their relationship, even thinking about marriage. About this same time, President Hinckley counseled the women of the Church to have only one pair of earrings. The young man waited for several weeks, but the young woman did not remove her extra earrings. He decided to stop dating her.

After relating this story, Elder Bednar said, "You may believe the young man was too judgmental or that basing an eternally important decision, even in part, upon such a supposedly minor issue is silly or fanatical. . . . I simply invite you to consider . . . [that] the issue was not earrings!"[6]

What was the issue? It was that the young man wanted to date somebody

DO TRY THIS AT HOME!

If you are a young man, set a goal for yourself that you will never get a tattoo and never have any piercings. If you have any piercings, remove them. If you are a young woman, set a goal for yourself that you will never get a tattoo and never have more than one pair of modest earrings. If you have more than one piercing, remove them.

who was obedient, not rebellious. He wanted to date someone who followed the prophet, not the trends and fads of the world.

After hearing this story one young woman wrote: "The story . . . about the young man who would not date a young woman because she refused to heed the prophet's counsel and remove her second set of earrings really impacted me. I likewise had refused to take out my three earrings. I decided that I did not want to be like [that] young woman. . . . After the talk, I took out my earrings. I also was more cautious about the skirts I wore, making sure I would not show any skin. But something more important happened as a result of . . . following [this] counsel. *I became more susceptible to the Spirit.*"[7]

The Trendy Tattoo

"According to the most recent Harris Poll, conducted in the summer of 2003, approximately 15% of Americans (or about 40 million people) have at least one tattoo. The increased popularity of the tattoo is apparent if you compare those findings to the 1936 *Life* magazine estimate that 10 million Americans, or approximately 6% of the population, had a tattoo."[8]

Whether we want to admit it or not, tattooing and piercing are trends that send messages to others that we are caught up in following the fashions of the world. The prophet Isaiah prophesied of worldly people in the last days by writing of "their tinkling ornaments" and "the rings, and nose jewels" (Isaiah 3:18, 21). Isaiah said "their countenance doth witness against them; and [declares] their sin as Sodom" (Isaiah 3:9). Sending the right message to others is another reason why we shouldn't pierce and tattoo our bodies.

SO DID I GET THE JOB?

"Conspicuous tattoos and other boy modification can make gainful employment difficult in many fields."[9]

OUCH!

"The most common method of tattooing in modern times is the electric tattoo machine, which inserts ink into the skin via a group of needles that are soldered onto a bar, which is attached to an oscillating unit. The unit rapidly and repeatedly drives the needles in and out of the skin, usually *80 to 150 times a second.*"[10]

TELL ME ONE MORE TiME!

Why Shouldn't I Pierce or Tattoo My Body?

1. **Our bodies belong to the Savior, not to us. Therefore, we can't do "whatever we want" with them without his permission.**
2. **Tattoos and body piercings negatively affect the way we act and the way others see us.**
3. **Tattoos and body piercings reflect an increased concern with following worldly trends and images at the expense of following prophetic counsel.**

NOW that we have reviewed some of the *principles*, let's answer some of the questions regarding the *practices* connected to tattoos and piercings:

Why is having two pairs of earrings such a big deal? Or is it?

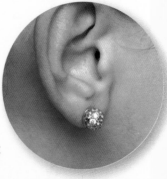

Compared to the "big" commandments such as living the law of chastity or the Word of Wisdom, multiple piercings may seem relatively minor. But if we are willing to be obedient on smaller issues, we will be faithful on the large ones as well. As principle #3 reminds us, multiple piercings send a message that we are becoming increasingly caught up in the trends, fads, and standards of the world. As we adopt the world's appearance, it doesn't take long before we adopt the world's behavior, too.

Why is it wrong to get a religious tattoo, such as a scripture reference or "CTR"?

Principle #1 teaches us that our bodies belong to the Savior, not to ourselves. Those who get religious tattoos probably have the best of intentions—but we have still been told not to do it. The Savior has already given us the way to remember him: partake of the sacrament each week, pray daily in his name, and keep his commandments. Those covenants and commandments will do more to help us honor his name and remember his life and teachings than any religious tattoo ever could.

Cont.

Why shouldn't I get a tattoo or piercing if it is acceptable in my culture?

Elder Dallin H. Oaks taught that as members of the Church we should adopt the "gospel culture" as our way of life, "giving up all of our practices—personal, family, ethnic, and national—that are contrary to the commandments of God. . . . We say to all, give up your traditions and cultural practices that are contrary to the commandments of God and the culture of His gospel, and join with His people in building the kingdom of God."[11] Part of having "no other gods before me" (Exodus 20:3) includes the god of our culture when it conflicts with the gospel of Jesus Christ.

6 ch Why Should I Dress Modestly?

What we wear and how we cover our bodies has been a gospel principle ever since Adam and Eve were found naked in the Garden of Eden and God made "coats of skins, and clothed them" (Genesis 3:21). Why has God always been so concerned about how his children clothe themselves? Perhaps a fishing story can help explain the answer.

FISHING FOR PIRANHAS
Anthony Says:

While in the Amazon jungle, I had the opportunity to go fishing for piranhas with some friends and a native guide. I'll never forget the moment I was handed my fishing gear for the trip as we set out in the little boat across the muddy waters of the Amazon River.

Nobody in the group was given conventional fishing poles with reels or lures to catch these mean piranhas. Instead, we were given a thick, three-foot-long stick, with roughly six feet of fishing line tied around it, and a large, finger-sized hook dangling off the end, Robinson Crusoe style.

For bait, the guide pulled out a slab of raw meat. He slapped it down on the bottom of the boat and told us to cut off a chunk, fasten it to our hooks, and simply drop the line over the side of the boat. The guide must have sensed our skepticism of the simplicity of the process. He explained that the piranhas would *come to us*, attracted by the raw meat. There was no need to cast out a line and go after them.

I dropped my hook over the side of the boat, and within seconds, there was a ripple in the water and a bite on the line. With a quick tug of the line, I pulled a piranha into the boat. Although the fish was small, the razor-sharp teeth and menacing look of the fish's mouth were enough to keep me at a distance. So, like a true man, I let the guide remove the hook from the fish's mouth.

I attached a new piece of raw meat, dropped it into the water, and caught piranha after piranha. It was amazing to see the power of attraction the raw meat had to bring in these frightening fish.

The Principle of Attraction

So what do piranhas, hooks, and raw meat have to do with hemlines, midriffs, and modesty? What does casting out bait have to do with putting on clothing? A statement from the *For the Strength of Youth* pamphlet provides the connection. It teaches, "The way you dress is a reflection of what you are on the inside. *Your dress and grooming send messages about you to others.*"[1]

The parable of the piranha serves to illustrate this very important point: Whatever you cast out is what you catch. It's true for fishing, and it's true for our dress standards.

Just as the meat sent a message to the piranha, our dress and appearance send messages as well, attracting and repelling different kinds of people in the world. If you don't want to be surrounded by piranhas, don't toss meat into the Amazon. Similarly, if we wanted to catch a nice trout out of a mountain lake, we wouldn't use raw meat. The trout simply wouldn't be attracted to or interested in it.

This principle of attraction is one of the primary reasons why prophets of God have always counseled us to dress modestly. Prophets understand that everything we wear and how we cover or reveal our bodies sends messages to others. If a young woman is constantly revealing her skin, who will she attract? She will attract "piranha" boys who are primarily interested in her flesh. On the other hand, if a young woman casts out righteousness, intelligence, spirituality, humor, and confidence (the "power bait"☺) that is exactly who she will attract: young men who appreciate righteousness, intelligence, spirituality, humor, and confidence.

The Lord taught, "For intelligence cleaveth unto intelligence; wisdom receiveth wisdom; truth embraceth truth; virtue loveth virtue; light cleaveth unto light" (D&C 88:40).

Remember this principle of attraction: What we choose to wear directly affects the level of character of those who we attract.

President Thomas S. Monson linked low *dress* standards with low *moral* standards by categorizing them together as the "Twin Demons of Immodesty and Immorality."[2]

Immorality   **Immodesty**

Does Your Dress Attract?

What Kind of Attention

Modesty and Men

Being modest has just as much to do with boys as it does with girls. We tend to define modesty only by tight shirts or short skirts (therefore exempting all but the boys who wear Scottish kilts), but modesty is much more than that.

The actual definition of modesty uses such words as "unassuming," "humble," and "decency,"[3] which all apply to a young man's appearance and demeanor just as much as a young woman's. Elder Robert D. Hales said that "modesty is at the core of our character" and that it "reflects who we are and what we want to be."[4] For young men, the issue with modesty usually is dressing too sloppily, too casually, too worldly, or in such a way that draws a lot of attention to themselves (such as extreme hairstyles). Dressing in this way not only violates the "humble" definition of modesty, but it also sends the message that we are a sloppy, casual, worldly, and selfish person (since how we dress is at the core of our character). For this reason, *For the Strength of Youth* tells young men to "always be neat and clean and avoid being sloppy or inappropriately casual in dress, grooming, and manners."[5]

It is especially important that a young man dress neat, clean, and unassuming when administering the sacrament. Elder Dallin H. Oaks told young men to live by the "principle of non-distraction" during the sacrament. This principle suggests that young men "should not do anything that would distract any member from his or her worship and renewal of covenants."[6] Elder Jeffrey R. Holland added that, wherever possible, a white shirt should be worn by those young men who handle the sacrament.[7]

Dressing in a sloppy, casual, worldly, or distracting way causes a young man to be just as immodest as a young woman dressed in tight or revealing clothing.

The Stumbling Block of Pornography

Few Latter-day Saint women would support pornography, let alone become an active participant in that evil industry. Yet when women dress immodestly, they become a source of living pornography that can act as an immoral temptation to those around them. Elder Dallin H. Oaks said, "Young women, please understand that if you dress immodestly, you are magnifying this problem by *becoming pornography* to some of the men who see you."[8]

This truth does not justify men in their actions nor place the blame solely upon immodest women. (The Lord expects both men and women to use their agency to control their eyes and thoughts.) But we must

IN THE BLINK OF AN EYE . . .

"It only takes three-tenths of a second for an image to enter the eye and start a chain reaction in the body."[9]

Control your *eyes* and you can control your *thoughts*!

understand that when women dress in a revealing and immodest way, they become part of the problem of pornography.

One young woman said, "It's not my fault if boys can't control their eyes!" While boys should control their eyes, why would a faithful sister want to create a problem for her brother? The apostle Paul spoke to some of the saints who were following the trends of idol worship in his day, warning them to "take heed lest by any means this liberty of yours become a stumblingblock to them that are weak" (1 Corinthians 8:9). In other words, don't do anything that would cause others to falter.

No one should knowingly want to be a source of temptation to another—especially not in matters of modesty.

Physical Obsession and Spirituality

A third reason why we should dress modestly relates to the effect that revealing our bodies has on our self-esteem and spirituality. If we constantly make our physical body a source of attention and public display, then that is where our focus will be. As the Savior taught, "For where your treasure is, there will your heart be also" (Matthew 6:21).

When we become overly self-conscious about how we look and are perceived—our dress size, our waistline, our tan, our biceps, our nails, our hair, and everything else in between—then other people's opinions about our bodies begin to affect our self-confidence and self-worth. What *other* people think becomes more important than what *we* think. That can rob us of peace and happiness—and it shouldn't be that way. Elder Jeffrey R. Holland explained: "I plead with you young women to please be more accepting of yourselves, including your body shape and style, with a little less longing to look like someone else. . . . As one adviser to teenage girls said: 'You can't live your life worrying that the world is staring at you. When you let people's opinions make you self-conscious you give away your power.' . . .

"The [world's] pitch is, 'If your looks are good enough, your life will be glamorous and you will be happy and popular.' That kind of pressure is immense in the teenage years, to say nothing of later womanhood. In too many cases too much is being done to the human body to meet just such a fictional (to say nothing of superficial) standard. . . .

"[This] fixation on the physical . . . is more than social insanity; it is spiritually destructive, and it accounts for much of the unhappiness women, including young women, face in the modern world."[10]

CHECK OUT THE SCRIPTURAL PATTERN!

Look up these scriptures to see how the Book of Mormon teaches about the way clothing is linked to sins such as pride and selfishness.

- Jacob 2:13
- 4 Nephi 1:24–26
- Mormon 8:37

DO TRY THIS AT HOME!

The Dove company released an incredible video that illustrates how makeup and computer software create unrealistic physical standards that truly are fictional. See for yourself by watching the clips at http://ldswhy.com

Clothed with Righteousness

With modesty able to influence our spiritual lives so dramatically, it should be obvious why the prophets of God have consistently stressed the importance to dress in such a way that we, "can show the Lord that [we] know how precious [our] body is."[11] Notice how the scriptures speak of being "clothed with purity, yea, even with the robe of righteousness (2 Nephi 9:14), being "clothed with salvation" (D&C 109:80), and "with power and authority" (D&C 138:30), "and above all things, clothe yourselves with the bond of charity" (D&C 88:125). This type of clothing is sure to attract peace and joy to all who see it.

TELL ME ONE MORE TiME!

Why Should I Dress Modestly?

1. **How we dress affects who we attract, whether positively or negatively. (Don't go fishing for piranhas!)**
2. **Dressing in a sloppy or worldly fashion sends the message that our character is sloppy and worldly.**
3. **Those who choose to dress immodestly become "living pornography" and a source of temptation to those around them.**
4. **Wearing revealing clothing causes us to become more self-conscious about our physical appearance. This can lead us to obsess over our appearance and become increasingly self-centered, which negatively affects our pride, our charity toward others, our self-worth, our happiness, and our spirituality.**

NOW that we have reviewed some of the *principles*, let's answer some of the questions regarding the *practices* connected to dressing modestly:

Why can't I wear a strapless prom dress one night of the year?

For the Strength of Youth answers this question clearly, "Never lower your dress standards for any occasion. Doing so sends the message that you are using your body to get attention and approval and that modesty is important only when it is convenient."[12] Lowering our dress standards one night of the year is similar to lowering our language standards one game of the year, or our moral standards one date of the year, or our Word of Wisdom standards one party of the year. The true tests of our conversion and commitment are those moments when it is difficult to live our standards. Holding fast to our standards of modesty, especially on prom night, is a great way to show your Heavenly Father that you are willing to do what is right when things are difficult, not just when they are easy.

Why shouldn't I let skin show between my shirt and my pants?

This has become a trend recently, and some don't see why it is a big deal. Principle #4 applies because if we are showing off our mid-section, we become self-conscious about how that mid-section looks. If we don't have rock-hard abs or zero cellulite around our belly, then we can begin to obsess about our physical appearance. Also, revealing our mid-section with low-cut pants and short shirts is a trend connected to worldly sexuality (along with showing the back of the underwear, belly piercings, and tattoos), so principle #1, the law of attraction, applies here as well. Furthermore, showing this skin can become a stumbling block to the young men who are trying to avoid looking.

Why is it a big deal if boys "sag" their pants or have long hair?

The principle of attraction applies to both girls and boys. A boy who dresses sloppily, "sags" his pants, and has long, unkempt hair sends a message to others just as much as a girl who dresses in a revealing way. If a boy dresses like he uses drugs (even if he doesn't), then he will attract others who use drugs. If a boy dresses like he is in a gang, then people will treat him like a gangster. Remember, the way we dress affects how we act and behave. If we dress sloppily and according to the trends of the world, then it doesn't take long before our behavior becomes sloppy and we adopt the standards of the world.

Why Should I Be Sexually Pure?

Lisa was in an awkward situation. She was on a double date and didn't really know any of the people she was with. The four of them had been having a picnic at a park. It was nice, but now the sun was going down and the other couple had gone off on a walk together—she was alone with her date. She could tell that her date had some intimate expectations, so she decided she better explain her standards.

She had scarcely begun when he said, "Lisa, I know you're Mormon and that you don't believe in pre-marital sex. But I don't get it— why does your Church care about it so much? What's the big deal?"

Tips to Staying Sexually Pure: PROPHETIC PRINCIPLE #1

Avoid being alone with someone you are attracted to.

For the Strength of Youth advises that "when you begin dating, go in groups or on double dates."[1]

"When you're on a date, plan to be in groups and avoid being alone."—Elder David E. Sorensen[2]

Don't be afraid to be like Joseph in Egypt and run away from a compromising situation (see Genesis 39:9-12)!

Many teenagers find themselves in a situation where they have to explain to others— or perhaps they wonder to themselves—why morality is such a big deal. Before we talk about why we should stay sexually pure, think about this question: "Why would somebody *not* stay sexually pure?"

There may be lots of reasons— peer pressure, to feel accepted, to solidify a relationship, to try to show someone you "love" them, crazy hormones, and so on. President Ezra Taft Benson gave this reason when he said, "Most people fall into sexual sin in a misguided

Tips to Staying Sexually Pure: PROPHETIC PRINCIPLE #2

Don't date before you are 16.

"Dating before [age 16] can lead to immorality, limit the number of other young people you meet, and deprive you of experiences that will help you choose an eternal partner."[3]

Tips to Staying Sexually Pure: #3
PROPHETIC PRINCIPLE

Only date those with high moral standards.

"Date only those who have high standards and in whose company you can maintain your standards."[4]

If even your dad knows that other people call your date "the harlot Isabel," you probably shouldn't go out with her (see Alma 39:3).

attempt to fulfill basic human needs. We all have a need to feel loved and worthwhile. We all seek to have joy and happiness in our lives. Knowing this, Satan often lures people into immorality by playing on their basic needs. He promises pleasure, happiness, and fulfillment.

"But this is, of course, a deception."[5]

Take a minute to think about your own or other people's experiences. Do you know of instances in which somebody violated the law of chastity so that person would feel love? Did it work?

The truth is that it doesn't. This is one reason why it is so important to stay sexually pure—so that we can experience the respectful love that we deeply desire. When we violate the law of chastity, feelings of guilt, sorrow, regret, shame, and bitterness usually result instead of the love we seek.

President Gordon B. Hinckley compared breaking the law of chastity with the implosion of a building. To see an implosion and hear President Hinckley's comparison visit http://ldswhy.com.

Immorality and Hate

In the Old Testament there was a guy named Amnon who was infatuated with a woman named Tamar. The scriptures say he was so "sick for [her]" that he couldn't do anything else but think about her. Unfortunately, this obsession with Tamar led Amnon to want to be immoral with her, and he "[raped] her, and lay with her" (2 Samuel 13:14).

What do you think the result of this immorality was? Do you think that Amnon fell in love with her after stealing her virtue? He did not. Second Samuel 13:15 says, "Then Amnon hated her exceedingly; so that the hatred wherewith he hated her was greater than the love wherewith he had loved her." For Amnon, immorality led to hate, not love.

Why can something that is an "expression of love between husband and wife"[6] result in guilt and hate between those who aren't married? If "physical intimacy between husband and wife is beautiful and sacred"[7] then why is it not so between boyfriend and girlfriend? It hinges on the timing, or the *order* of when the physical intimacy takes place. There is a time and a season for everything, and God has commanded that marriage must come before physical intimacy. If we do this in the wrong order, something sweet can become bitter.

DO TRY THIS AT HOME!

Think the order isn't important? Try this experiment. Pour a tall glass of orange juice and drink half of it. Tasty, isn't it? Now, brush your teeth and rinse with mouthwash. Nice and fresh! Now, drink the other half of your orange juice. How does it taste? Isn't it interesting that if we do this in the wrong order, something sweet can become bitter? Physical intimacy is no different.

not be misled by Satan's lies. There is no lasting happiness in immorality. There is no joy to be found in breaking the law of chastity. Just the opposite is true. There may be momentary pleasure. For a time it may seem like everything is wonderful. But quickly the relationship will sour. Guilt and shame set in. We become fearful that our sins will be discovered. We must sneak and hide, lie and cheat.

Tips to Staying Sexually Pure: PROPHETIC PRINCIPLE #4

Know "the line" and stay far from it.

For the Strength of Youth says we should not participate in passionate kissing or anything that arouses powerful emotions.[8]

Just like if we were driving next to a cliff, the further we stay away from "the line," the safer we will be.

Physical intimacy is similar to orange juice and mouthwash. If physical intimacy comes *after* the marriage covenant, it is beautiful and sacred. If physical intimacy comes *before* marriage, it leads to a whole list of ugly results. Read what President Benson taught: "Do

Tips to Staying Sexually Pure: PROPHETIC PRINCIPLE #5

Don't steady date before a young man's mission.

"Avoid going on frequent dates with the same person."[9]

"When you are young, do not get involved in steady dating. When you reach an age where you think of marriage, then is the time to become so involved. But you boys who are in high school don't need this, and neither do the girls."—President Gordon B. Hinckley[10]

Tips to Staying Sexually Pure: PROPHETIC PRINCIPLE #6

Avoid pornography like a foul disease.

If someone released a jar of mosquitoes that carried malaria or West Nile Virus in a room, what would you do? Do the same when your computer, TV, or a movie releases pornography.

"Do not attend, view, or participate in entertainment that is vulgar, immoral, violent, or pornographic in any way.

"Pornography . . . can lead you to sexual transgression."[12]

Love begins to die. Bitterness, jealousy, anger, and even hate begin to grow. All of these are the natural results of sin and transgression."[11]

One reason why we should stay sexually pure is that immorality leads to negative and bitter feelings, not love. Let's look at some other reasons why it is so important to live the law of chastity.

Making a Mockery of the Atonement

Another reason why we should avoid breaking the law of chastity is that when we do, we mock the Savior's Atonement. Elder Jeffrey R. Holland explained this concept. "In exploiting the body of another—which means exploiting his or her soul—one desecrates the Atonement of Christ, which saved that soul and which makes possible the gift of eternal life. And when one mocks the Son of Righteousness, one steps into a realm of heat hotter and holier than the noonday sun. You cannot do so and not be burned."[13]

That sounds pretty serious! Keep reading:

"'Flee fornication,' Paul cries, and flee 'anything like unto it,' the Doctrine and Covenants adds. Why? Well, for one reason because of the incalculable suffering in both body and spirit endured by the Savior so that we could flee. We owe Him something for that. Indeed, we owe Him everything for that. 'Ye are not your own,' Paul says. 'Ye [have been] bought with a price: therefore glorify God in your body, and in your spirit, which are God's.'"[15]

LOSS OF THE SPIRIT

Another major reason why we should stay sexually pure relates to the Holy Ghost. The Lord warned that "if any shall commit adultery in their hearts, they shall not have the Spirit" (D&C 63:16). If we are sexually immoral, we will lose the guidance of the Holy Ghost.

Elder Richard G. Scott said, "Recognize that an individual who is violating commandments of the Lord will find it very difficult to discern a prompting of the Spirit from the powerful emotions that can be stimulated through transgression. I am confident that is one of the reasons that some marriages fail. Two individuals who have allowed themselves to violate the laws of chastity during courtship cannot expect to clearly perceive the answer to their prayer regarding marriage."[14]

The time of dating and courtship is one time when we desperately need the Holy Ghost. Staying sexually pure will help you qualify for that divine companionship.

According to Elder Holland, our bodies are gifts that should not be tarnished by immoral activities. We must stay morally clean because our bodies are sacred. First Corinthians 3:16–17 teaches, "Know ye not that ye are the temple of God, and that the Spirit of God dwelleth in you? If any man defile the temple of God, him shall God destroy; for the temple of God is holy, which temple ye are."

Tips to Staying Sexually Pure: PROPHETIC PRINCIPLE #7

Dress modestly.

"Your dress and grooming send messages about you to others."[16] When we display our body immodestly, we send a message to others that our body isn't important to us.

The Savior purchased our bodies with his blood in the Garden of Gethsemane; we owe it to him to keep them clean. If we desecrate our bodies through immorality, we desecrate the atonement of Christ that saved that body.

Hurting the Soul of the One We "Love"

Another reason why it's so important to stay morally clean is that when we are immoral, we harm the very soul of the person we are immoral with and supposedly love.

Joseph Smith taught a key doctrine about the relationship between our physical bodies and our spirits when the Lord revealed through him, "the spirit and the body are the soul of man" (D&C 88:15). In other words, our bodies and our spirits are *connected.* When we harm or abuse our physical body, we harm or abuse our spirit. Likewise, when we harm the body of another person through immorality, we not only harm our spirit, but *theirs* as well. Elder Jeffrey R. Holland warned, "We declare that one who uses the God-given body of another without divine sanction abuses the very soul of that individual."[17]

Sometimes people are physically intimate outside of marriage and rationalize it by saying that they love each other. If we truly love someone, would we ever do anything to intentionally harm them? Would we ever want to harm their *very soul?* Would we want to be the cause of someone not being able to enjoy the gift of the

Tips to Staying Sexually Pure: PROPHETIC PRINCIPLE

Have a curfew and keep it. #8

Being out late at night when we are tired and unsupervised can lead to immorality. As President Hinckley said, "Nothing really good happens after 11 o'clock at night."[18]

"When you [get enough sleep] you . . . gain the blessings of a healthy body, an alert mind, and the guidance of the Holy Ghost."[19]

Tips to Staying Sexually Pure: #9
PROPHETIC PRINCIPLE

Keep the Word of Wisdom.

Speaking of the Word of Wisdom, the modern prophets warn, "Being under the influence of alcohol weakens your judgment and self-control and could lead you to break the law of chastity."[20]

Holy Ghost, attend the temple, or partake of the sacrament? Do we want to be a contributing party of causing someone to lose self-respect, to feel shame and guilt? That is *not* how we show someone we love them!

Please remember, when we violate the law of chastity, we violate not only our body and soul, but the body and soul of someone we claim to love.

Some Temporal Reasons Too

We've focused on some of the doctrinal reasons why it is so important to stay morally clean. Common sense also provides several other reasons. For example, when you live the law of chastity, you avoid contracting sexually transmitted

Tips to Staying Sexually Pure: #10
PROPHETIC PRINCIPLE

Pray daily.

President Gordon B. Hinckley said that youth should "kneel alone in prayer before they leave home on a date that they may remain in control of themselves."[21]

CHILDREN OUT OF WEDLOCK

- Of all births out of wedlock, only 16% of those parents were married five years after the birth.[23]
- "80 percent of teenage mothers end up in poverty and must rely on welfare."[24]

Only 16% Still Married Five Years Later

80% of Teenage Mothers in Poverty

diseases. The *New York Times* reported that in the United States alone about 19 million new cases of sexually transmitted diseases are reported each year and that 1 in 4 sexually active teenage girls in the U.S. have a sexually transmitted disease.[22]

Furthermore, by staying morally clean, you avoid the heartache and hardships that come from pregnancy outside of marriage, including dropping out of school, losing friends, missing out on the wholesome fun and freedom of youth, and taking on the financial worry and time commitment of bearing, supporting, and raising a child. The Proclamation on the Family says that "Children are entitled to birth within the bonds of matrimony, and to be reared by a father and a mother who honor marital vows with complete fidelity."[25] As you live the law of chastity, you give your future children this right.

At the beginning of this chapter, we wrote about how immorality leads to all sorts of negative emotions, not love. The good news is that the opposite is also true: Staying sexually pure leads to increased love. President Ezra Taft Benson taught, "When we . . . keep ourselves morally clean, we will experience the blessings of increased love and peace, greater trust and respect for our marital partners, deeper commitment to each other, and therefore a deep and significant sense of joy and happiness."[26]

Why Should I Be Sexually Pure?

1. **Immorality leads to bitterness, jealousy, anger, and even hate—not love.**
2. **Breaking the law of chastity makes a mockery of the Atonement.**
3. **Sexual transgression harms the soul of the person we claim to love.**
4. **Staying morally clean helps us avoid pre-marital pregnancy or sexually transmitted diseases.**

NOW that we have reviewed some of the *principles*, let's answer some of the questions regarding the *practices* connected to being sexually pure:

Why is it going too far to passionately kiss someone?

In the *For the Strength of Youth* pamphlet, the prophets have clearly defined "the line" of chastity by saying, "Do not participate in passionate kissing."[27] The pamphlet also says, "Before marriage, do not do anything to arouse the powerful emotions that must be expressed only in marriage."[28] In other words, *anything* that sexually arouses someone should be avoided before marriage. *Anything.* By the very definition of the word, passionate kissing is supposed to elicit "passion," or arousal, and should therefore be avoided. Also, when you are involved in passionate kissing before marriage, you and your partner are usually alone and in a place or situation where you might be more easily tempted to break the law of chastity. It can become difficult to control your emotions, and you can easily end up doing something more serious that will only bring sorrow and regret.

Why are NCMOs bad?

"NCMOs" (or "non-committal make outs") are when two people have short-term connection (a weekend or a one-night romance) just for the sake of being able to kiss or make-out with someone with no further expectations of a long-term relationship. A NCMO flies in the face of almost all the principles of chastity that have been emphasized in this chapter. They are selfish in nature and show a lack of respect for the sanctity of the body and of God's children. They also pervert "kissing" into a cheap act of self-pleasure; kissing should be an expression of love, not lust.

Why is it wrong to be physically intimate with someone if I love them?

For the Strength of Youth teaches that, "Physical intimacy between husband and wife is beautiful and sacred. It is ordained of God for the creation of children and for the expression of love between husband and wife."[29] One of the purposes of physical intimacy is to bring children into the world and to have a family. When we are physically intimate before marriage, we are not ready to bring children into a family (principle #4 in the chapter) because "children are entitled to birth within the bonds of matrimony, and to be reared by a father and a mother."[30] The other purpose of physical intimacy is to express love between husband and wife. If we become physically intimate outside of marriage, "moral schizophrenia" can result.[31]

8 ch Why Shouldn't I Date Until I'm 16?

In researching some of the reasons why we shouldn't date until we are 16 years old, we came across an interesting blog post. An inquiring person asked why Mormons can't date until they are 16. A frustrated teenager responded, "There aren't any real reasons why! They just want to control us!"

Hmmm . . . Makes us wonder if that comment was made by a bitter 15½ year old somewhere.

Do you really think that Church leaders sit around asking, "What can we do to really bug the youth?"

"I know—how about no dating until 16?"

"Great idea, let's put that in the pamphlet!"

Of course they don't! God has a purpose in all he does and all he reveals, even for things like when we should begin dating.

NOT JUST MORMONS

In a study of almost 300 parents of teens nationwide, "eighty-seven percent of parents of teens said teens should be at least 16 before they begin steady, one-on-one dating."[1]

Morally Clean and Sixteen

Perhaps the most powerful reason why we should wait until we are 16 to date has to do with keeping the law of chastity. Prophets have repeatedly warned—and statistics have shown—that the earlier we begin to date, the more likely we are to break the law of chastity. *For the Strength of Youth* says, "Do not date until you are at least 16 years old. Dating before then can lead to immorality."[2]

Researchers studied the connection between when a youth began dating and if they remained sexually pure through high school. Take a look at the results:

Age when students began dating and the percentage who became sexually involved before marriage.[3]

Age	Percentage
12	90%
15	60%
16	20%
17	12%

The younger a person is when he or she begins to date, the more likely he or she is to become sexually active. The most dramatic decrease in the likelihood of becoming sexually active in high school was for those students who chose to wait until they were 16 years old to start dating.

Logically, the sooner we begin to date, the quicker we will move into serious relationships before we are ready to handle them. Anytime we enter into serious relationships in our early teens, we increase the moral temptation and therefore the chances of breaking the law of chastity. President Spencer W. Kimball said: "Dating in the earlier teen-age years leads to early steady dating with its multiplicity of dangers and problems, and frequently early and disappointing marriage."[5]

Sweet Sixteen . . . Sorry Fifteen

"While about 70 percent of [LDS youth] who did not date until they were 16 had avoided immoral behavior, more than 80 percent of those who reported dating before age 16 had become sexually involved enough to require a bishop's help for repentance."—Bruce Monson[4]

In other words, you are almost *three times* more likely to commit serious sexual sin if you begin dating before age 16.

THE "MULTIPLICITY" OF DATING DANGERS

Dating in early adolescence is connected with such at-risk behaviors as poor school performance, drug use, delinquency, having poor social skills that last through the later teenage years, depression, and sexual activity.[6]

Growing Pains

The "bitter blogger" from the beginning of the chapter was right about one thing, though. One of the reasons why we should wait to date *is* about control. Not parental or Church control—but *self*-control. Just listen to most 12- to 15-year-old boys speak, and we'll quickly get a good auditory reason why we should wait to date a little bit. Boy's voices fluctuate from low to high and from high to low during these years, sometimes squeaking like a mouse and other times sounding like a tuba. If a young teenage boy finds it difficult to control his voice, how much more difficult is it to control his physical emotions?

Simply stated, we are not yet physically or emotionally stable while we are in our early teens to begin dating. Our bodies are going through massive changes. It is wise to postpone dating until we have begun to figure ourselves out. We simply don't need to get involved romantically before we form our own personal identity. Part of dating is to get to know other people, which is hard to do if we don't even know ourselves.

LET'S USE OUR BRAIN . . . WELL, THE PARTS WE CAN

Research shows that brain development goes through a second wave of change around age 12 and isn't complete until our late teens.[7]

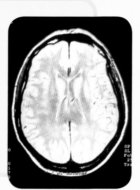

DUDE, I THINK YOU GREW OVERNIGHT!

The average teenager grows between 3 to 5 inches per year during their early teens.

Paul's counsel about milk and meat is appropriate here. He taught, "I have fed you with milk, and not with meat: for hitherto ye were not able to bear it, neither yet now are ye able" (1 Corinthians 3:2).

In other words, you don't feed a baby a sizzlin' steak until they are older and ready for it.

There will come a time for the "steak" of dating, but we make a serious "mi-stake" if we start too soon.

YOU WANT TO RIDE ON BACK?

A practical reason why we should wait until we are 16 to date is that we can't drive yet. It is very hard to look cool pulling up on your tandem bike to pick up your date.

"I'll pick ya up at seven . . . you're on back!"

But I'm 15.99999 Years Old . . . Does it Really Matter?

Maybe you say that you are *almost* 16, that you are mature for your age, that you don't have any "romantic" interest in anyone, but you just want to have "fun" on a date. Can you be the exception to the rule?

You may not change a lot between the day before you turn 16 and the day after, but remember this principle: Waiting to date until you are 16 helps you develop a pattern of obedience that will bless you for the rest of your life. Sticking to this standard will help you stick to other standards when you are tempted to excuse yourself as the exception. It's not about digits . . . it's about discipleship! We extend the promise of the First Presidency to you that, "as you keep these standards [such as not dating until 16] . . . , you will feel good about yourself and will be a positive influence in the lives of others."[8] You will never regret living this standard of waiting to date until you are 16.

ARE WE JUST "HANGING OUT" . . . OR IS IT A "DATE"?

FYI: A "date" is officially defined in the dictionary as "a social engagement between two persons that often has a *romantic* character." But even staying home alone with a member of the opposite sex should be avoided. Studies have shown that the most common time of day when teens break the law of chastity is not late at night on Friday, but after school on weekdays at home![9]

DO TRY THIS AT HOME!

Work on developing your friendships during your teenage years. Learning how to be a good friend will help you more to have a successful marriage in the future than learning how to be in a romantic relationship will.

TELL ME ONE MORE TIME!

Why Shouldn't I Date Until I'm 16?

1. **The prophets have warned and statistics show that the earlier we begin to date, the more likely we are to break the law of chastity.**
2. **We are not sufficiently physically or emotionally ready to date while we are in our early teens.**
3. **Not being able to stick to a numerical standard (dating at age 16) threatens our ability to stick to other spiritual standards. It's not about digits . . . it's about discipleship!**

NOW that we have reviewed some of the *principles*, let's answer some of the questions regarding the *practices* connected to not dating before we are 16:

Why is 16 the magical age? Is it all that different than 15?

If you look at the studies, then the answer is, yes, 16 appears to be a magical age and very different than 15. (Somebody is 300% more likely to break the law of chastity if they begin dating at age 15 instead of age 16).[10] Principles #1 and #3 both apply here. If we can stick to our dating standards and wait until we are 16, then we will develop a pattern of obedience that will help us more easily stick to other important relationship standards, such as group dating, keeping the law of chastity, and not steady dating.

Why isn't it a good idea to hang out at the house of someone of the opposite gender who I really "like"?

Remember, the dictionary definition of a "date": "a social engagement between two persons that often has a *romantic* character." It doesn't matter where you go out to—the park, meeting at a movie theatre, attending a school game, or even "hanging out" at someone's house—it is still a romantic engagement. More importantly, being at the house of someone you really like is a seedbed of temptation, probably more so than a public setting. In a study of more than 2,000 teenagers who had had pre-marital sex, 91% reported doing so in a home setting.[11]

Why is it still considered a date if a group of my friends goes to the park to meet a group of the opposite gender whom some of us like?

Once again, it is our intent that matters. The Lord said he "knowest thy thoughts and the intents of thy heart" (D&C 6:16). If we are trying to disguise a "date," or a social engagement of romantic interest, by grouping it together with a large conglomerate of friends who are all meeting together, it is still a date. We shouldn't look for loopholes or try to deceive our parents in this way, because when it comes right down to it, the Lord knows exactly what we are doing.

Why Shouldn't I Steady Date in High School?

Chapter 9

Did you read that title clearly? It says, "Why shouldn't I steady date *in high school.*" Let's not make the assumption that we should never steady date, or we would have a major problem in the Church in our quest for exaltation. (Can anyone say, "eternal singles ward"?) The question is not *if* we steady date, but *when.* The Lord does want us to become involved in serious relationships that will lead us to the temple—but "in *his* time" (Ecclesiastes 3:11; emphasis added). The Lord has made it clear through his prophets that steady dating in high school is not the right time.

Timing Is Everything

IS TIMING IMPORTANT? YOU BE THE JUDGE

- Try getting to the airport five minutes after your plane left.
- Try asking somebody on a date by calling at 5:30 AM.
- Try showing up to a party a half-hour early.
- Try eating cookies that are three minutes under-baked.

President Spencer W. Kimball taught, "There is definitely a time for . . . the date, and even for the steady date that will culminate in the romance which will take young people to the holy temple for eternal marriage. *But it is the timing that is so vital. It is wrong to do even the right things at the wrong time in the wrong place under the wrong circumstances.*"[1]

The Familiarity Factor

A major reason why we should avoid forming serious relationships in high school is that *steady dating* leads to *steady temptation.*

Steady Dating and Steady Temptation

In a study of LDS teens conducted by Bruce Monson, he found that "of the 308 11th graders surveyed, 95 reported having a current boyfriend or girlfriend. Of those 95, only six had never been involved in making out (or kissing for a long time)."[2] (Remember that *For the Strength of Youth* says "Do not participate in passionate kissing."[3]) Furthermore, *more than half* of those who had steady-dated had even more seriously transgressed the law of chastity.

Of **308** eleventh-graders . . .

95 had a boyfriend or girlfriend

Of those 95, only **6** had never been involved in making out

The physical familiarity that comes from spending so much time with one person to whom you are attracted can lead to moral temptations and moral trouble. President Gordon B. Hinckley said: "Steady dating at an early age leads so often to tragedy. . . . Have a wonderful time, *but stay away from familiarity.* Keep your hands to yourself. It may not be easy, but it is possible."[4]

When we begin to feel familiar with those we date, there is a tendency to continue pushing the line of familiarity further and further. Soon holding hands isn't as fun, and a quick kiss gets old; it doesn't take long before passionate kissing (making out) becomes the norm—and deeper sin ensues. President Spencer W. Kimball taught: "A vicious, destructive, social pattern of early steady dating must be changed. . . . *The change of this one pattern of social activities of our youth would immediately eliminate a majority of the sins of our young folks.*"[5]

IF YOU THINK YOU CAN HANDLE THE TEMPTATION . . . THINK AGAIN

"Dr. Phil . . . aired a program in which he staged an experiment to demonstrate the [temptation and] danger of guns in the home. Amid a group of playing little girls and boys, a teacher placed two fake guns inside a dollhouse. *The teacher warned the kids not to play with the guns,* and then left the room. The boys promptly began playing with the guns. Dr. Phil came in, *warned the boys again,* and after eliciting a promise not to play with the guns, which he put on a table, he left the room. Again, the boys promptly began playing with the guns."[6]

One moral of the experiment is that it is better to avoid the temptation than to resist the sin. When it comes to steady dating in high school, it is better to just not start.

BUT WE'RE GOOD KIDS!

Some may think, "But we're not like that. We are both active and have high standards!" President Spencer W. Kimball taught, "The devil knows how to destroy our young girls and boys. He may not be able to tempt a person to murder or to commit adultery immediately, but he knows that if he can get a boy and a girl to sit in the car late enough after the dance, or to park long enough in the dark at the end of the lane, *the best boy and the best girl will finally succumb and fall.* He knows that all have a limit to their resistance."[7]

The Emotional Rollercoaster

Another reason why we should not steady date in high school is that we are not emotionally ready to handle serious relationships in our teens. Evidence of emotional instability in the teen years is supported by the fact that problems such as anorexia, bulimia, suicide, and self-hurting (cutting), are higher among teens than for any other group of people. Research says teenagers are the least stable with their self-identity and are the most susceptible to peer influence than any other age group.[8]

With so many social pressures, anxieties, and worries during our teenage years, we don't need the added emotional drama, stress, temptation, and worry that comes along with a serious boyfriend or girlfriend.

Early Steady Dating: An Emotional Roller Coaster

RELATIONSHIP STRESS

- "53% of teens who are involved with a boyfriend or a girlfriend say their relationship causes them stress."[9]

- "61% of teens who had been in a relationship stated they had a boyfriend/girlfriend who made them 'feel bad or embarrassed' about themselves."[10]

- "25% of [teens] in a 'serious' relationship were 'hit, slapped, or pushed.'"[11]

Most romantic relationships among 12- to 18-year-olds are short-lived. One college student said, "I got a girlfriend in junior high. That was one of the worst choices I have ever made. Because of that relationship I had my heart broken and stomped on when I was way too young to handle it. It wasn't just the girl's fault either, I know I hurt her too. We would have both been so much better off if we had just waited."

WHAT EMOTION DO YOU SEE IN THIS FACE?

"In a recent study mapping differences between the brains of adults and teens, [researcher Deborah Yurgelun-Todd] put teenage and adult volunteers through an MRI and monitored how their brains responded to a series of pictures. Volunteers were asked to discern the emotion in a series of faces like this one. The results were surprising. All the adults identified the emotion as fear, but many of the teenagers saw something different, such as shock or anger. When she examined their brain scans, Todd found that the teenagers were using a different part of the brain when reading the images."[12] In addition, researchers found that some parts of the brain do not even function in the teenage years. These studies show that teenagers process information in a manner substantially different than adults—which may be a factor in why teenage relationships often lead to heartbreak.[13]

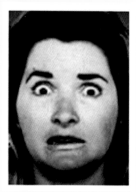

We have our entire lives to be involved in a serious relationship, so let's not rush into it during our developing teenage years. It is better to do so when we are emotionally ready to handle it.

Fish in the Sea

He's a little too puffed up for me.

For the Strength of Youth gives another reason why we should avoid steady dating in our teens. Steady dating can "limit the number of other young people [we] meet."[14] One of the purposes for dating during our teen years is to develop friendships and learn what kinds of people we enjoy being with. This takes a *variety* of dating experiences.

"Dating and especially steady dating in the early teens is most hazardous. It distorts the whole picture of life. It deprives you of worthwhile and rich experiences; *it limits friendships;* it reduces the acquaintances which can be so valuable in selecting a partner for time and eternity." —President Spencer W. Kimball[15]

We will be much better off by following President Gordon B. Hinckley's advice: "It is better, my friends, to date a variety of companions until you are ready to marry."[16]

Girlfriends and Missions

Some may think that it's okay for young men to steady date after high school but before their missions. But President Ezra Taft Benson taught: "*Avoid steady dating with a young man prior to the time of his mission call.* If your relationship with him is more casual, then he can make that decision to serve more easily and also can concentrate his full energies on his missionary work instead of the girlfriend back home."[17]

An Actual Dear John?

Dear John (Jim),

Yes, this is a "Dear John" letter (email). Sorry to have it start off like that, but you always said I was blunt, well I guess you're right.

I'm engaged to be married at the end of this month! I'm soooo excited! The same day I got the internet like you suggested (so that I could email you) I also saw a commercial on TV about [an LDS dating site]. Well, I signed up for that too and they matched me up with Desidorio, from Spain!

I thought it was interesting that I got matched up with someone living in the same country as your mission! We've been communicating ever since and we've fallen in love and will be getting married! We've never met in person, but we don't need to. We prayed over the phone and we felt the Spirit soooooo strong I think it would be wrong NOT to get married!

So, if anything, I wanted to THANK YOU for suggesting that I get the internet. If it wasn't for you listening to the Spirit to tell me that, then I would have never met Desidorio! You truly are a great friend!

You will always have a place in my heart!

Com Amor,

Valerie

P.S.—Desidorio and I want to vacation with you and your family before you leave Spain! Is that okay? Aren't you excited?[18]

Simply put, having a girlfriend back home distracts the missionary. Instead of being able to dedicate 100% of his focus on the Lord's work, part of his energy is focused on his girl back home. Remember the principle: We want to delay forming serious relationships *until the time we are ready to be married.* Young men are not ready to be married when they are called and set apart as a full-time missionary.

Being obedient to the Lord's commandments—including not steady dating in high school—will help you be happier. Depending on your personal circumstances, avoiding a serious relationship in your teens may be the toughest standard for you to live. But, for all the reasons listed in this chapter and many more, we promise you it will be worth it.

DO TRY THIS AT HOME!

Attracted to One Another

Take two magnets that are strongly attracted to each other and place one on the table. Holding the other in your hand, bring it down as slowly as possible until you are as close as you can get to the other magnet without causing them to come together. What happened? Liken the results to pushing "the line" with physical familiarity and staying morally clean.

TELL ME ONE MORE TIME!

Why Shouldn't I Steady Date in High School?

1. When we steady date we become increasingly familiar with our boyfriend/girlfriend. Steady dating leads to steady temptation to break the law of chastity.

2. **We are not emotionally ready to handle serious, romantic relationships in our teens.**
3. **Steady dating in high school limits the number of other young people we meet.**
4. **Steady dating distracts missionaries from being able to serve the Lord with *all* their "heart, might, mind and strength" (D&C 4:2).**

NOW that we have reviewed some of the *principles*, let's answer some of the questions regarding the *practices* connected to not steady dating in high school:

Why date other people if I only like one person?

High school is not the time to be looking for a spouse but a time for building friendships. If you truly do only like one person, then dating other people until you are both at a marriageable age (translation: after the young man's mission) will only confirm that he or she is the one for you. After all, it's hard to know what your favorite ice cream is if you have tried only vanilla and chocolate. More importantly, we should date a variety of people in order to limit the emotional bond that is created when two people who care for each other spend a lot of time together. Remember, when we form an emotional bond with someone, we naturally want to express those feelings physically, which could result in breaking the law of chastity.

Why is it wrong to steady date someone in high school if we both have high standards?

Principle #1 applies best here. No matter how high your standards are, steady dating leads to steady temptation. Emotions and desires connected to physical intimacy are among the strongest human emotions we have. There is simply no good reason to subject two good LDS youth to increased moral temptation when you don't need it. It would be much better to keep the relationship at a safe distance, date other people, and then pursue a steady relationship when you reach an age when you are ready to be married.

Why is it OK to steady date after my mission, but not before?

One mistake that young men often make is thinking that it is OK to have a serious girlfriend between the end of high school and the beginning of their mission. As principle #4 in this chapter teaches, many times this only serves to distract the potential missionary from serving with all his heart. Prophets have repeatedly stated that steady dating is in preparation for marriage . . . not mission letters and care packages! A young man should not steady date before his mission because he is not ready to be married until he returns home. And when should a young woman begin steady dating? When she is ready to be married and *he* is home from his mission. ☺

10^{ch} Why Should I Get Married in the Temple?

In order to understand why we should be married in the temple, we must first have an accurate understanding about why we were sent to earth. What is the purpose of the plan of salvation? Many people answer that question by saying something along the lines of, "To live with God again." While enjoying our Heavenly Father's presence will be one of the benefits of a celestial life, it is not the primary reason we were sent to earth. After all, if the point is simply to live with God, then why did we ever leave the pre-mortal life? We could have just stayed in our Father's presence eternally!

YOU'RE IN THE MTC: A QUIZ

John Says:

On one of my first days in the Missionary Training Center, my teacher said, "I want to see what you know about the plan of salvation. Who can come and draw it on the board?"

Sadly, nobody in the room (including myself) felt confident enough to do it. Once the teacher outlined it, I felt silly because I realized I could have done it. Let's see if you can do better. Number the following points of the plan of salvation in the right order.

#_____ War in Heaven   #_____ Birth

#_____ Resurrection   #_____ Death

#_____ Mortal Life   #_____ Spirit World (paradise/prison)

#_____ Final Judgment   #_____ Council in Heaven

#_____ Eternal Kingdoms   #_____ Pass through Veil
        (Celestial/Terrestrial/Telestial)

Answers: 1. Council in Heaven; 2. War in Heaven; 3. Pass through Veil; 4. Birth; 5. Mortal Life; 6. Death; 7. Spirit World; 8. Resurrection; 9. Final Judgment; 10. Eternal Kingdoms

Obviously, the plan of salvation has a deep purpose. President Gordon B. Hinckley taught, "The whole design of the gospel is to lead us onward and upward to greater achievement, even, eventually, to godhood."[1] President Lorenzo Snow immortalized this grand concept of becoming like God in his famous phrase: "As God now is, man may be!"[2] Understanding this doctrine provides the primary reason why we must be married in the temple for time and all eternity.

Becoming Like God

When we see that the purpose of the plan is not simply to *live* with God but to *become* like God, then we must ask, "What is God like?" We know that "the Father has a body of flesh and bones as tangible as man's" (D&C 130:22). He is all-knowing and all-powerful, kind, loving, forgiving, and possesses all the attributes of perfection (see Matthew 5:48). But we must not overlook one of the most fundamental truths about our Heavenly Father: We are not the children of just the Father, but we are each of us "a beloved spirit son or daughter of heavenly *parents*."[3]

The great poet of the Restoration, Eliza R. Snow, penned this doctrinal truth in the hymn "O My Father":

In the heav'ns are parents single?

No, the thought makes reason stare!

Truth is reason; truth eternal

Tells me I've a mother there.

When I leave this frail existence,

When I lay this mortal by,

Father, Mother, may I meet you

In your royal courts on high?[4]

God wants us to fulfill the entire purpose of the plan of salvation—including becoming like him—and has given us guidance on how to achieve that goal.

"In the celestial glory there are three heavens or degrees; and in order to obtain the highest, a man must enter into this order of the priesthood [meaning the new and everlasting covenant of marriage]; and if he does not, he cannot obtain it. He may enter into the other, but that is the end of his kingdom; he cannot have an increase." (D&C 131:1–4)

The phrase, "he cannot have an increase" means that we cannot be like God if we don't have an eternal marriage, one sealed in a temple for time and all eternity. On the other hand, if we do marry in the temple, the Lord has promised us: "Then shall they be gods, because they have no end; therefore shall they be from everlasting to everlasting, because they continue; then shall they be above all, because all things are subject unto them. Then shall they be gods, because they have all power, and the angels are subject unto them. Verily, verily, I say unto you, except ye abide my law ye cannot attain to this glory" (D&C 132:20–21).

Just as a tiny oak seed has the potential to become a great tree, as children of Heavenly Parents, we have the potential to become like them. Our potential will only be fulfilled if we are sealed to a spouse for time and all eternity by the power of the priesthood in the house of God. That great doctrine is a principal reason why we must be married in the holy temple.

"It Is Not Good That the Man Should Be Alone"

Although being single (unmarried) may seem appealing to some people during their late teens and early twenties, most people want to marry and have children. As the Lord said, "It is not good that the man should be alone" (Genesis 2:18). But we should be married in the right place—the temple—and by the right authority—the priesthood.

A COMPELLING CASE FOR MARRIAGE

The book *The Case for Marriage* demonstrates that married people are healthier, wealthier, and happier than single individuals. Some of the statistics cited in the book are as follows:

- "Compared to married people, the non-married . . . have higher rates of [premature death] than the married: about 50% higher among women and 250% higher among men."[5]

- "40 percent of the married said they are very happy with their life in general, compared to just under a quarter of those who were single or who were cohabitating."[6]

- "Husbands earn at least 10 percent more than single men do and perhaps as high as 40 percent more."[7]

To those who choose to marry outside of the temple, the Lord gave a reality check about the permanence of their mortal vows in D&C 132:15–17: "Therefore, if a man marry him a wife in the world, and he marry her not by me nor by my word, and he covenant with her so long as he is in the world and she with him, their covenant and marriage are not of force when they are dead, and when they are out of the world; therefore, they are not bound by any law when they are out of the world."

In other words, if we are not married in the temple, our marriage ends when we die! So what happens next? "Therefore, when they are out of the world they neither marry nor are given in marriage; but are appointed angels in heaven, which angels are ministering servants, to minister for those who are worthy of a far more, and an exceeding, and an eternal weight of glory.

"For these angels did not abide my law; therefore, they cannot be enlarged, but remain separately and singly, without exaltation, in their saved condition, to all eternity; and from henceforth are not gods, but are angels of God forever and ever."

Did you catch that? The Lord warned that we will live "separately and singly . . . to all eternity." And, please keep in mind that not only will we live separately and singly for eternity, but there is no heavenly quick-fix, Las Vegas-style drive-thru wedding chapel to change the eternal marriage we didn't choose in mortality.

If I Don't Have an *Opportunity* for an Eternal Marriage, Am I Doomed?

Those who do not have the *opportunity* to be married in the temple in this life will not forfeit eternal blessings. Elder Dallin H. Oaks taught, "Singleness, childlessness, death, and divorce frustrate ideals and postpone the fulfillment of promised blessings. . . . But these frustrations are only temporary. The Lord has promised that in the eternities no blessing will be denied his sons and daughters who keep the commandments . . . and desire what is right."[8]

We cannot simply dream of loving someone "forever" and think it will just come to pass. Only the priesthood of God can bind, or seal, on earth *and in heaven* (see Matthew 16:19). This sealing power has been restored, but it is only to be had in the holy temple of God. Picturing ourselves as a single angel for eternity, apart from those we love, should provide a powerful visual to anyone as to why we need eternal marriage.

The Celestial Three-Legged Race

Have you ever participated in a three-legged race? You know, you tie your left leg to the right leg of someone else, and then you race toward a finish line. The best way to win a race like that is to make sure you are in step with your partner the whole way. When one partner moves their legs faster, or the other drags their feet a little, they quit working together, get out of step, and lose their momentum.

While it is a fun game to play at the yearly family reunion, it is not so fun if we are trying to build an eternal family relationship with a spouse we are not in step with religiously. The apostle Paul put it this way, "Be ye not unequally yoked together with unbelievers: for what fellowship hath righteousness with unrighteousness? and what communion hath light with darkness?" (2 Corinthians 6:14).

If you fall in love with somebody who is not a member of the Church, you will not be able to be married in the temple. You might think it is more important that you are "in love" than "in the same religion," and that you will work out the religious differences as the relationship goes along. Although it is possible, it is also very difficult. What will you do if you want to pay tithing and your non-member spouse doesn't? Or when you want your children to go to church on Sunday, but your spouse wants to go boating? What will you do when your spouse doesn't see a problem with rated "R" movies, having coffee or alcohol in the house, or using foul language? These differences in religious standards and beliefs will certainly affect your own spirituality and the spiritual development of your children.

President Joseph F. Smith said, "Do not marry those out of the Church, as such unions almost invariably lead to unhappiness and quarrels and often finally to separation. Besides, they are not pleasing in the sight of heaven. The believer and unbeliever should not be yoked together, for sooner or later, in time or in eternity, they must be divided again."[9] Choosing to marry someone worthy to take you to the temple will help you avoid many challenges you would otherwise face with the three-legged celestial race.

Roll the Dice!

Find a six-sided die, and let's play a game. If you roll a 1, 2, 3, 4, or 5, you owe us $1,000. However, if you roll a 6, we will pay you $1,000. Wanna play? Probably not! The odds are stacked against you.

In the same way, if you marry outside the Church, it is unlikely that your spouse will ever get baptized and that you will be sealed together in the temple. President Spencer W. Kimball said: "Of course, most such people who marry out of the Church and temple do not weigh the matter sufficiently. . . . Only about *one out of seven* would be converted and baptized into the Church. This is a great loss. . . .

"We love those few who join the Church after marriage. We praise them and honor them, but the odds are against this happening. . . . The total program of the Lord for the family cannot be enjoyed fully if the people are unequally yoked in marriage.

"We call upon all youth to make such a serious, strong resolution to have a temple marriage that their determination will provide for them the rich promises of eternal marriage with its accompanying joys and happiness. This would please the Lord."[10]

DO TRY THIS AT HOME!

Our exaltation hinges upon our having a celestial marriage. President Spencer W. Kimball said, "Any of you would go around the world for the sealing ordinance if you knew its importance, if you realized how great it is. No distance, no shortage of funds, no situation would ever keep you from being married in the holy temple of the Lord."[11]

YOU DON'T HAVE TO GO AROUND THE WORLD

It took 150 years to build the first 19 LDS temples (1830–1980). But there has been an increased effort to bring the temples to the people of the world. Since 1980, the Church has dedicated more than 100 temples with more under construction every year.[12]

TELL ME ONE MORE TiME!

Why Should I Get Married in the Temple?

1. **The purpose of life is to become like God and have eternal progression. Temple marriage is essential to achieving that goal.**
2. **Those who reject a temple marriage will live life separately and singly as angels to God for eternity.**
3. **Marrying outside the temple and the Church can cause us to be "unequally yoked" with someone who does not share our beliefs or standards.**

NOW that we have reviewed some of the *principles*, let's answer some of the questions regarding the *practices* connected to temple marriage:

Why is it wrong to marry someone outside the Church and temple if I am in love with that person?

In short, if we marry someone of another faith outside the temple, as excellent of a person as he or she might be, we cannot enter into the highest degree of the celestial kingdom and become like God (see D&C 131). This frustrates the very purpose of life.

Cont.

Why shouldn't I marry someone and then hope he or she will later convert to the Church?

Although this does happen for some couples, the odds are stacked highly against it. For every one marriage where the spouse does actually convert to the Church and become temple worthy, there are six others who don't. (See President Kimball's statement on page 68.) That's 85% of spouses who never convert. When dealing with eternal matters, such as temple marriage and exaltation, it is much better to find a potential spouse who already has the qualities we want (such as being a faithful member of the Church), instead of hoping they will change and turn into what we want *after* we are married.

Why is the Lord opposed to homosexual marriage?

Principle #1 is at the heart of why the Lord is opposed to homosexual marriage. Elder Jeffrey R. Holland said, "God . . . wants us to have all of the blessings of eternal life. He wants us to become like Him. To help us do that, He has given us a plan. This plan is based on eternal truths and is not altered according to the social trends of the day. At the heart of this plan is the begetting of children. . . . We are to follow [God's plan] in marrying and providing physical bodies for Heavenly Father's spirit children. Obviously, a same-gender relationship is inconsistent with this plan."[13]

11ch Why Should I Want to Have Children When I'm Married?

If you were asked which person or group of people is the most influential in the world, how would you answer? Would you say the President of the United States? What about billionaires like Bill Gates or Warren Buffett? Perhaps we could even wax sentimental and say "teachers" or "friends" are the most influential people in the world. While all those people are influential, those answers are not accurate. Elder Neal A. Maxwell said: "When the real history of mankind is fully disclosed, will it feature the echoes of gunfire or the shaping sound of lullabies? The great armistices made by military men or the peacemaking of women in homes and in neighborhoods? Will what happened in cradles and kitchens prove to be more controlling than what happened in congresses? When the surf of the centuries has made the great pyramids so much sand, the everlasting family will still be standing, because it is a celestial institution, formed outside telestial time."[2]

MOST INFLUENTIAL OF ALL TIME?

Since 1927, *Time* magazine has chosen a man, woman, or idea that "for better or worse, has most influenced events in the preceding year."[1] Many U.S. Presidents have been awarded the honor. Infamous rulers have won (Adolf Hitler won in 1938). And even an object won the award (the computer in 1982). *Time* has awarded groups of people like "U.S. Scientists" (1960), "The Middle Americans" (1969), "American Women" (1975), "The Peacemakers" (1993), and "You" (2006), but not once in the 80 years of recognition has *Time* awarded the distinction to the people who truly influence everyday events in our world most . . . "parents." As Elder Neal A. Maxwell said, "Greatness is not measured by coverage in column inches."[3]

The Most Influential People of the Most Fundamental Unit

Mothers and fathers are the most influential people on the earth because they shape the most fundamental unit of society: the family. President Ezra Taft Benson said, "A nation is no stronger than the sum total of its families."[4] This is the first reason why being a parent is so important. As parents, we literally have the chance to change our communities and nations for good through the rearing of a righteous family. Speaking of the influence of a righteous mother, President Spencer W. Kimball said: "To be a righteous woman is a glorious thing in any age. To be a righteous woman during the winding up scenes on this earth, before the second coming of our Savior, is an especially noble calling. The righteous woman's strength and influence today can be tenfold what it might be in more tranquil times. She has been placed here to help, to enrich, to protect, and to guard the home—which is society's basic and most noble institution. Other institutions in society may falter and even fail, but the righteous woman can help to save the home, which may be the last and only sanctuary some mortals know in the midst of storm and strife."[5]

The columnist E.T. Sullivan poetically put the influence of mothers on nations this way: "When God wants a great work done in the world or a great wrong righted, he . . . has a helpless baby born, perhaps in a simple home and of some obscure mother. And then God puts the idea into the mother's heart, and she puts it into the baby's mind. And then God waits. The greatest forces in the world are not the earthquakes and the thunderbolts. The greatest forces in the world are babies."[6]

Brigham Young taught that "mothers are the moving instruments in the hands of Providence to guide the destinies of nations."[7] Think of it! The destinies of the nation may depend less on what happens in the White House and more on what happens in *your* house.

A MOTHER'S LOVE

"Many experiments have been made and studies carried out which prove beyond doubt that a child who enjoys mother's love and care progresses in every way much more rapidly than one who is left in institutions or with others where mother's love is not available or expressed.

"Fathers, too, must assume their proper role and responsibility. Children need both parents."
—President N. Eldon Tanner[8]

THINK FATHERS AREN'T IMPORTANT?

Sixty percent of America's rapists, seventy-two percent of its adolescent murderers, and eighty-five percent of youths in prison came from fatherless homes.[9] In other words, children with fathers are much more likely to avoid serious criminal activity. That doesn't mean that without a dad you are doomed (thirty percent of young children live in homes without fathers)—but it does help illustrate the importance of having a father in the home.

In our society, being a parent is not always popular. Some say that having children has a negative effect on society because the world is overcrowded. Young women are told that being a mother is too hard, it's not worth it, and that it will limit their opportunities and potential influence on society. Young men are told to focus on their career, to earn lots of money before thinking about being a father because kids will only tie them down, and that "raising" children isn't their responsibility.

COULD WE ALL FIT IN TEXAS?

To all those who cry the world is overcrowded, economist Dr. Walter E. Williams at George Mason University figured that we could put the entire U.S. population in Texas and that each family of four would live comfortably on 2.9 acres of land.[10]

The Lord has testified that "the earth is full, and there is enough and to spare; yea, I prepared all things" (D&C 104:17).

Why are these messages to avoid parenthood so prevalent in the world, and who is the source of such thoughts? Elder M. Russell Ballard said: "When you stop and think about it from a diabolically tactical point of view, fighting the family makes sense. When Satan wants to disrupt the work of the Lord, he doesn't poison the world's peanut butter supply, thus bringing the Church's missionary system to its collective knees. He doesn't send a plague of laryngitis to afflict the Mormon Tabernacle Choir. He doesn't legislate against green Jell-O or casseroles. When Satan truly wants to disrupt the work of the Lord, he . . . attacks God's plan for His children. . . . Satan knows that the surest and most effective way to disrupt the Lord's work is to diminish the effectiveness of the family and the sanctity of the home."[11]

Heavenly Father and Heavenly Mother

A second reason why the Lord and his Church place so much emphasis on parenthood is because it is a vital part of our learning to become like God. Since the purpose of life is to learn to become like God, what better preparation could we have to eventually become a father or mother in *heaven* than to properly become a father or mother on *earth?* This plan for parenthood was set in motion from the beginning. Notice that Adam called Eve the "mother of all living" (Genesis 3:20) before she ever gave birth. Motherhood is part of every woman, whether or not they are able to have children. Similarly, fatherhood is a divine calling for all males. The Lord wants us to enter into marriage and then accept parenthood in order to help us progress and grow.

Motherhood is so Christlike in nature that the book of Moses compares it to the atonement of Jesus Christ (see Moses 6:59).

The Proclamation on the Family teaches, "The first commandment that God gave to Adam and Eve pertained to their potential for parenthood as husband and wife. We declare that God's commandment for His children to multiply and replenish the earth remains in force."[12]

Elder Russell M. Nelson, quoting the First Presidency said, "Motherhood is near to divinity. It is the highest, holiest service to be assumed by mankind. It places her who honors its holy calling and service next to the angels."[13]

Stand Up for Motherhood

"A few weeks ago . . . I met with a group of about 20 Laurels whom I had never met. I asked them what their goals were. The first few mentioned educational goals like getting a PhD in biology; some said they would like to go on a mission—all worthy goals. Finally one girl timidly expressed the desire to be a mother and have children. Then a few more girls talked about other goals. After one more girl mentioned mother-hood, the rest of them hopped on board. But it was quite courageous for those first two girls to admit they wanted to be mothers. And this was in a very safe setting.

"Besides the fact that admitting this may set the girl up for ridicule, it may also set her up for failure. She may feel that this is a goal that she doesn't have the control to achieve, which may make her feel vulnerable in stating it. It is also a goal that requires great unselfishness; it may require setting aside other more glamorous goals. I am sensitive to the many issues facing our young women, but I still feel that I must teach eternal principles."—Susan W. Tanner, former Young Women general president.[14]

Children and Joy

A third reason why being a mom or dad is so important is that in the eternal scheme of things, parenthood has the potential to bring the greatest joy. Lehi taught concerning Adam and Eve that if "they would have had no children" they would have had "no joy" (2 Nephi 2:23).

THE WISDOM OF CHILDREN

The following are how some little kids "finished" well-known proverbs. A first-grade teacher gave them the first part of the proverb, and the kids finished it . . .

"Better to be safe than . . . punch a 5th grader."

"Don't bite the hand that . . . looks dirty."

"You can't teach an old dog . . . math."

"Where there is smoke, there's . . . pollution."

"A penny saved is . . . not much."

"Children should be seen and not . . . spanked or grounded."

"Laugh and the whole world laughs with you, cry and . . . you have to blow your nose."[16]

Here are a few reasons why being a parent brings joy:[15]

Children help us be a kid again. Having children allows you to continue to do the fun things of youth. Even as an adult, you get to go the park, fly kites, go trick-or-treating (yeah . . . let Dad check that candy to make sure it's "safe"), go swimming, build forts and tree houses, and play with the latest toys. You can repeat all the great experiences from your childhood only this time with your kids! It rocks!

Children encourage us to laugh more. Kids are just downright funny, especially little kids. They say funny things, do silly things, and have a tendency to giggle and belly laugh hysterically. As a parent, you can't help but laugh with them sometimes.

Children surround us with love. There is nothing like one of your children saying, "Mom and Dad, I love you," or getting big hugs when you walk through the door from work. Think of how will you feel when your teenager says something like, "Mom, I want to be just like you when I'm older," or when you overhear, "My Dad can fix anything." Children simply increase the number of people around you that you love, and that love you.

Learn some skills to prepare you for being a mom or dad. Read a book to a younger child or sibling, take them to the park, get them dressed in the morning, or prepare their lunch. If you are feeling really brave, help change a diaper. ☺

Children help us to be less selfish. As any parent would attest, taking care of children and their needs fills up almost any available free time we might have. Although this might seem contradictory to the definition of "joy," caring for others actually increases our joy. The scriptures teach us that the more we forget ourselves in the service of others, the more true happiness we will feel in our lives (see Matthew 10:39).

Children will give us the greatest sense of accomplishment in our lives. Watching your grown children succeed in life brings a greater feeling of accomplishment than almost anything else. How will you feel when your child is in the school play, graduates from college, serves a mission, gets married in the temple, contributes positively to the world, and begins his or her own family? President Gordon B. Hinckley taught, "In terms of your happiness, in terms of the matters that make you proud or sad, nothing—I repeat, nothing—will have so profound an effect on you as the way your children turn out."[17]

Think about it—when you are seventy years old will you really care how many awards you won at work? Probably not. What *will* you be proudest of when you are old and aging? Your children and your grandchildren.

When you consider that families are forever, it becomes clear that the most important work we can do, and the one that will bring us the most joy, is rearing children in a loving family and building a strong and happy family centered on the teachings of Jesus Christ.

TELL ME ONE MORE TIME!

Why Should I Want to Have Children When I'm Married?

1. **Mothers and fathers are the most influential people on the earth because they shape the most fundamental unit of society: the family.**
2. **Parenthood is part of our divine heritage and will help us learn to become like God.**
3. **Parenthood has the potential to bring the greatest amount of joy in our life.**

NOW that we have reviewed some of the *principles*, let's answer some of the questions regarding the *practices* connected to having children:

Why should I want to bring innocent children into such a wicked world?

President Boyd K. Packer answered this question when he said, "When you young people who now look forward to marriage and a family life look around and see the dangers [in the world], there is only one place on this earth where the family can be fully protected, and that's within the ordinances and the doctrines of the gospel of Jesus Christ. Live the gospel, and you're going to be all right."[18] Remember, the Lord has "prepared all things" (D&C 104:17), and we must have faith in his ability to make a way for us to fulfill the command to multiply and replenish the earth. Also, what better way to change the problems of the world than to bring children into a righteous family and raise them faithfully in the gospel so they can be a positive influence on society and help correct the problems of the earth?

Cont.

Why is it more influential to have children than a high-powered career?

Principle #1 in this chapter is clear: Nothing has the potential to change the world for good than faithful people raising faithful families, as the family is the fundamental unit of society. The individual and personalized attention that a parent can offer a child is the kind of long-lasting influence that can change the world.

Why do members of the Church tend to have bigger families than other people?

Although the Church does not dictate a certain number of children to have, we believe "that God's commandment for His children to multiply and replenish the earth remains in force."[19] As principle #3 states, we find joy in the family and in raising children. As Brigham Young stated, there

are "multitudes of pure and holy spirits waiting to take tabernacles [bodies], now what is our duty?—To prepare tabernacles for them; to take a course that will not tend to drive those spirits into the families of the wicked, where they will be trained in wickedness, debauchery, and every species of crime."[20] Following these doctrines, and not societal trends, lead some Latter-day Saints to have families that are larger than the national average.

12^{ch} Why Can't I Watch Whatever I Want?

In August of 2001, President Henry B. Eyring gave a remarkable prophecy. He said that LDS youth cannot just "go with the flow" anymore and expect to remain righteous. He then prophesied of what is to come in the future: "The flow has become a flood and soon will be a torrent. It will become a torrent of *sounds* and *sights* and *sensations* that invite temptation and offend the Spirit of God."[1]

HOW FAST IS A "TORRENT"?

A "torrent" is defined as a large amount of fast-moving or falling water. The photos to the right show the shore of Banda Ache, Indonesia, before and after the tsunami of 2004. Tsunami waves can travel up to 600 miles an hour off-shore. Measurements show the waves that hit Banda Ache were more than 100 feet high in some points and traveled 1.24 miles inland.[2]

BEFORE

AFTER

Just a few short months after President Eyring prophesied of the torrent of sounds, sights, and sensations about to hit our youth, the first iPod was introduced to the general public. Two years later, the first video iPod came out. The youth of today are the first generation to be able to carry thousands of songs, images, and videos in the palm of their hand, twenty-four hours a day, seven days a week.

In the Palm of Your Hand

"With up to 160GB of storage, iPod classic lets you carry everything in your collection—up to 40,000 songs or up to 200 hours of video—*everywhere you go.*"[3]

Not only have iPods blossomed, but since 2001, so have cultural phenomenons like **You-Tube**, **Google Images**, **MySpace**, **Facebook**, **Wikipedia**, **Nintendo Wii**, **Sony PSP**, **satellite radio**, **high-definition TV**, and **home theater systems**. Truly a torrent of sounds, sights, and sensations has washed over this current generation like never before in the history of the world. If ever there was a need to understand why it matters so much what we watch, it is now.

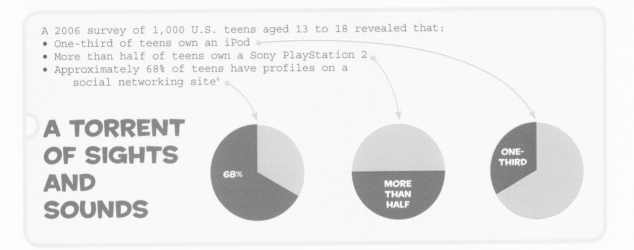

A 2006 survey of 1,000 U.S. teens aged 13 to 18 revealed that:
- One-third of teens own an iPod
- More than half of teens own a Sony PlayStation 2
- Approximately 68% of teens have profiles on a social networking site[4]

A TORRENT OF SIGHTS AND SOUNDS

68%

MORE THAN HALF

ONE-THIRD

Monkey See, Monkey Do

There is an old saying, "Monkey see, monkey do." That is not only true for primates, but also for people as well. *For the Strength of Youth* says, "Whatever you read . . . or look at has an effect on you."[5]

WHATEVER YOU SEE . . .

- By age 18, the average U.S. teen will have seen 16,000 simulated murders and 200,000 acts of violence.
- 64% of all TV shows surveyed in 2001–2002 included sexual content or references.
- Of those shows surveyed, there was an average of 4.4 sexually-related scenes per hour.[6]

Willingness to Have Pre-marital Sex Based on Number of R-Rated Movies Viewed During a Two-Year Period[7]	
Number of "R" Movies Watched	% Willing
0–4	20%
5–15	51%
16–29	65%
30–49	73%
50+	93%

One reason why it is so important to filter what we watch is because what we *see* triggers what we *think*, what we think influences what we *desire*, what we desire affects our *actions*, our combined actions determine our *character*, and our character determines our *eternal destiny*.

Our Eyes and Our Eternity

see=> think=> desire=> actions=> character=> eternity

What We Watch Influences How We Act

The sad downfall of King David is a startling example of how what people view changes their actions. Though David was a great man, he lost everything due to a moment of weakness that began by looking at something he should not have seen.

While on the king's roof, David beheld Bathsheba "washing herself; and the woman was very beautiful to look upon" (2 Samuel 11:2). Instead of looking away and controlling what his eyes beheld, he lusted after her and "sent and inquired after the woman. . . . And she came in unto him, and he lay with her" (2 Samuel 11:3–4). What he saw from the roof created lustful and immoral desires, and those desires led to the sin of adultery, then to the tragic murder of Bathsheba's husband (see 2 Samuel 11:5–17), and eventually the loss of David's exaltation (see D&C 132:39). All because he did not control what he watched!

YO, ROCKY–MONKEY SEE, MONKEY DO

Anthony Says:

When I was a kid, the first *Rocky* movies were popular. My brother and I, with our friends, would watch Rocky train and get in shape for his upcoming fight and then take on his challenger. As Rocky would work out, we would try to do the same things. If he did push-ups and sit-ups, so did we. If he went out for a run, we would run around the family room. When the time for the fight came, one of us would be designated as Rocky and someone else as his opponent, and we would re-enact each scene, fake punch by fake punch. Without even realizing it, the movie influenced how we acted and behaved, down to the last right hook.

We are influenced not only by images we see, but also by the words we read. One scholar ran an experiment where people were divided into two groups. One group read sentences that contained aggressive words, "bold," "rude," "bother," "disturb," "intrude," and "infringe."

The other group was given sentences with the words "respect," "considerate," "appreciate," "patiently," "yield," "polite," and "courteous."

After reading the sentences, the individuals were told to return to an office for their next assignment. But the researcher made sure he was already engaged in a conversation with a co-researcher when the individual arrived. The question was, "Would the people who had read the aggressive sentences be more likely to interrupt the conversation?"

The group who had read the aggressive words interrupted after about five minutes, on average. The group who had read the words that promoted politeness *never interrupted at all!* (The researchers ended the waiting after ten minutes, though who knows how long they would have stood there!)[8]

Proverbs states, "For as [a man] thinketh in his heart, so is he" (23:7). What we see is a primary stimulus for what we think and how we act. This truth is one major reason why it is so important we only watch and view media that helps us to have "virtue garnish [our] thoughts unceasingly" (D&C 121:45).

The Skew of the View

Without our realizing it, media skews or alters our perspective of reality. Video games allow us to shoot, hit, and kill people without any blood or feeling. TV shows depict immoral lifestyles as "normal" and rarely mention the consequences. Beauty magazines and pornographic pictures display women who are so fabricated—nipped, tucked, airbrushed, and digitally manipulated—as to make the average girl wonder why she is the only one with pimples and a bit of cellulite. It is ironic that in our "reality TV" generation, most of what we see in the media is so fake that it couldn't be further from reality. If we are not careful with the media we use, we can start perceiving these false images as reality.

Does the media we watch give us mixed signals?

) DIGITAL DECEPTION

Is She for Real?

To see a digitally altered before and after shot, visit http://ldswhy.com

More than 1,000 studies attest to a causal connection between media violence and aggressive behavior in some children. Studies show that the more "real-life" the violence portrayed, the greater the likelihood that such behavior will be "learned."[9]

Addictive and Restrictive

Media such as pornography is addictive, but other types of visual media—video games, television shows, and internet blogs and chats, for example—can also be addictive. Social networking sites such as MySpace and Facebook have such an all-consuming nature that some of their users have deemed them "cybercrack." Users can't wait to update their personal profiles and read the posts on their personal sites. Their eyes and ears crave it, just like an addict craves another hit or high. As a matter of fact, research has shown that playing some video games raises the amount of dopamine in the brain to a level equivalent to a hit of speed.[10]

THE LAYSAN ALBATROSS

The Laysan albatross is a beautiful, but vulnerable species. The bird frequently mistakes trash for food, and birds have been found with bellies full of trash, including cigarette lighters, toothbrushes, syringes, toys, and clothespins. Because the albatross cannot digest the trash, the garbage stays in the bird's stomach until the stomach becomes so full of trash that it can no longer take in good food or nutrition. In some areas where the bird lives, forty percent of albatross chicks die from dehydration and starvation because of the trash filling their bellies.

Mmm, delicious!

Are we like the Laysan albatross? If we fill our minds with media that is destructive—or even simply a waste of time—we may miss out on the vital nutrients our spirits really need.

One of our tests here in mortality is to have our spirit gain control over our physical bodies, including our eyes and ears. Just like drugs can addict the body, media can enslave our minds. Elder Russell M. Nelson taught, "Addiction to *any substance* enslaves not only the physical body but *the spirit* as well."[11]

As we face the onslaught of sights, sounds, and sensations, we need to be selective about what we watch in order to avoid drowning spiritually in this modern-day river of filth (see 1 Nephi 12:16). What we watch matters.

DO
TRY THIS
AT
HOME!

Are you in control of what you watch? Find out by taking the "no-media" test. Do not watch any visual media for a week—no TV, no computer, no movies, no video iPod. Instead, read books, do some service projects, spend time with your family, or any of the thousand other things that people did for the last 6,000 years before the visual media began to dominate our culture. Can you do it?

TELL ME ONE MORE TiME!

Why Can't I Watch Whatever I Want?

1. **Everything we see affects what we think, and therefore what we desire and how we act.**
2. **Visual media can dangerously skew our perspective of reality.**
3. **Certain forms of visual media are addictive and can take control of our life.**

NOW that we have reviewed some of the *principles*, let's answer some of the questions regarding the *practices* connected to the media we watch:

Why can't I watch a movie if it only has one or two "bad" parts?

Our minds have an amazing ability to record and remember images, and once we have seen something, it is hard to *un*-see it. Elder Dallin H. Oaks said, "The brain won't vomit back filth. Once recorded, it will always remain subject to recall, flashing its perverted images across your mind and drawing you away from the wholesome things in life."[12] When you think of the hundreds or thousands of movies that some people watch during their lives, one or two bad parts in a movie can equal hundreds or thousands of improper images that are recorded in

our minds for recall. The prophet Alma teaches that by small and simple things, great things come about (Alma 37:6). The reverse is also true—by a few small *bad* scenes running through our heads, really *negative* things can be the result.

Why is it wrong to watch a movie that glorifies violence or immorality if it is historically accurate?

Just because it is historical doesn't mean it is good. Seeing glorified violence—whether the violence is historically accurate or not—can dull our spiritual senses and affect our actions. The Church has produced some excellent historical films that, of necessity, contain images of war or bloodshed. But they do it in such a way that the images are not graphic or gruesome and the movies do not glorify the violence taking place. *For the Strength of Youth* says, "Do not attend, view, or participate in entertainment that is vulgar, immoral, violent, or pornographic in any way. Do not participate in entertainment that in any way presents immorality or violent behavior as acceptable."[13] Historical accuracy does not trump spiritual appropriateness, no matter what story is being told.

Why shouldn't I play video games where I fight and kill people if I know it's just pretend?

Even if it is pretend, the images are still seen by our eyes and recorded in our minds. As principle #1 in this chapter teaches, everything we see affects our behavior. Even if the violence is computer-generated, it is still violence and will ultimately affect how we think and act. *For the Strength of Youth* teaches that "Whatever you . . . look at has an effect on you,"[14] even if it is fake. Earlier in this chapter, we talked about people *reading* aggressive words and having it affect their actions. And remember the Laysan albatross? If you are spending your time playing video games, you may be filling your time with "empty" activities when in reality you could be putting your time to much better use.

Why Shouldn't I View Pornography?

If you were in a room with mosquitoes that were carrying the West Nile Virus, would you stick out your bare arm to see if they landed on you? What if you were at a remote hospital and you were about to receive a shot with what might be an HIV-infected needle, would you let yourself be injected? What if somebody poured you a glass of water from a well containing high levels of arsenic, would you drink up? In all three of these examples, you probably said, "Of course not." But what if you were on the computer and a pornographic image came across your screen . . . would you look at it?

Which one of the following is more deadly?

West Nile

HIV needle

Arsenic water

Internet pornography

Only one can cost you your soul.

THE EVIL INDUSTRY OF PORNOGRAPHY

Every second:

28,258 Internet users are viewing pornography

Every second:

372 Internet users are typing "adult" search terms into search engines

Every 39 minutes:

a new pornographic video is being created in the United States[2]

President Hinckley warned of pornography's destructive influence by saying, "Pornography . . . is poison. Do not watch it or read it. It will destroy you if you do. It will take from you your self-respect. It will rob you of a sense of the beauties of life. It will tear you down and pull you into a slough of evil thoughts and possibly of evil actions. Stay away from it. Shun it as you would a foul disease, for it is just as deadly."[1] Pornography is perhaps even more dangerous than a foul disease because it can destroy not only our mortal body, but our eternal soul. Understanding why pornography is so spiritually destructive will help us avoid being tainted by its evil influence.

Pornography Can Lead to Immorality

Perhaps the most obvious reason why we shouldn't view pornography is that its images create immoral and lustful desires that can "lead you to sexual transgression."[3] This is because "whatever you . . . look at has an effect on you."[4] Although this visual process was discussed in chapter 12, it is worth repeating, as the same principle teaches why pornography can lead to immorality: What we *see* triggers what we *think*, what we think influences what we *desire*, what we desire affects our *actions*, our combined actions determine our *character*, and our character determines our *eternal destiny.*

If we view immoral images, then those images can create immoral thoughts and desires, which ultimately can lead to immoral behavior. The prophet Jacob made this connection when he said, "I can tell you concerning your *thoughts*, how that ye are *beginning* to labor in sin" (Jacob 2:5; emphasis added). For those who want to stay morally clean, avoiding pornography is a critical part of keeping our thoughts pure and our sexual desires restrained so they don't lead us to immoral actions.

XLII
VISUAL IMAGES & THE SUPER BOWL

The cost of a 30-second commercial spot during the 2008 Super Bowl was 2.7 million dollars. That's $90,000 a second! Why would advertisers be willing to pay so much? Because they know if they can position their product in front of people's eyes for even as short a time as 30 seconds, it will create a desire for their product. Visual images create desires; marketers know this, and so does the adversary.

CATALOGUES, CLOTHING STORE ADS, AND SWIMSUIT EDITIONS

Just to be clear, many things are not XXX but are still pornography. *True to the Faith* defines pornography as "any material depicting or describing the human body or sexual conduct in a way that arouses sexual feelings."[5] That means some images in underwear ads, books, or sports and car magazines should be avoided. Anthony's mother understood this. He relates, "When I was a teenager, my grandparents gave me a subscription to the magazine *Sports Illustrated*. Unknown to them (but not to my mom), was that once a year the 'swimsuit issue' would also come. My mom would go the mailbox each year and intercept that issue and throw it away so it wouldn't tempt my teenage brother and me. Go, Mom!"

We need to get rid of "*any* material" that could arouse temptation, not just the XXX material.

Pornography Is Addictive

Which do you think is more addictive, cocaine or pornography? Elder Dallin H. Oaks provided the answer when he said: "Pornography is . . . addictive. It impairs decision-making capacities and it 'hooks' its users, drawing them back obsessively for more and more. A man who had been addicted to pornography and to hard drugs wrote me this comparison: 'In my eyes cocaine doesn't hold a candle to this. I have done both. . . . Quitting even the hardest drugs was nothing compared to [trying to quit pornography].'"[6]

"Many rationalizations have been put forth to justify immodest fashion and pornography. . . .

"[But] whatever the rationalizations, you will often find that the real motivation underlying immodesty is someone's desire to profit from titillation, someone's lust for money. The body is a temple of God, and pornography and revealing clothes are evidence that moneychangers are again desecrating the temple."
—Elder D. Todd Christofferson[7]

Consider the following two facts:

"Every second $3,075.64 is being spent on pornography."[8]

"The pornography industry is larger than the revenues of the top technology companies combined: Microsoft, Google, Amazon, eBay, Yahoo!, Apple, Netflix, and EarthLink."[9]

Some people begin to look at pornography out of curiosity, or just to see it once. But its addictive nature makes this a very foolish and dangerous choice. Pornography "leads people to experiment and to seek more powerful stimulations."[10] Because of its addictive and tantalizing nature, pornography can be extremely difficult to get out of our minds. Take a look at the picture below. What do you see?

Can you see the Dalmatian? Look closely. See it? Now the real trick: Once you have seen the Dalmatian, can you look at the picture and *not* see the Dalmatian? Probably not. Once you have seen an image it is extremely difficult *not* to see it again. It's the same with pornography. When we have seen it, it can be *very* hard to get it out of our minds. Elder Dallin H. Oaks said, "The brain won't vomit back filth. Once recorded, it will always remain subject to recall, flashing its perverted images across your mind and drawing you away from the wholesome things in life."[11] The prophets warn, "Pornography in all its forms is especially dangerous and addictive. What may begin as a curious indulgence can become a destructive habit that takes control of your life."[12] We must shun pornography to remain in control of our lives and to avoid this powerful addiction.

Pornography Fire Drill

DO TRY THIS AT HOME!

We practice fire drills at school at least twice a year, and yet the odds of being caught in a building fire are 1 in 111,445.[13] But thanks to those fire drills, we know exactly what to do in a fire . . . just in case we are part of that unfortunate 0.000008973% of people who are caught in a burning building.

According to a recent study of Internet use among 10- to 17-year-olds, "forty-two percent of youth Internet users had been exposed to online pornography in the past year."[14] If we practice what to do to escape from a burning building (which, odds are, we will never need to do), how much more should we practice, rehearse, talk about, and know what to do if we come across pornography, because odds are, we will! *For the Strength of Youth* says, "If you encounter pornography, turn away from it immediately."[15]

Discuss with your parents what to do when you encounter pornography. If you have not already done so, install filters on your computer that will help block pornographic web sites. Decide as a family what you will do to better prepare yourself to avoid this danger that is more deadly than fire.

Pornography Degrades Others

Pornography is degrading to all those who participate—men, women and children. In countries where pornography is prevalent, rape and other violent crimes are higher. President Thomas S. Monson reported, "One study points out that pornography may have a direct relationship to sex crimes. In the study, 87 percent of convicted molesters of girls and 77 percent of convicted molesters of boys admit to the use of pornography, most often in commission of their crimes."[16] In perhaps the most graphic and infamous example of the link between pornography and sex crimes, serial rapist and murderer Ted Bundy blamed his addiction to pornography for his atrocious crimes against women.[18]

PORNOGRAPHY AND WOMEN

Although statistically speaking, more men than women view pornography, 1 out of every 3 visitors to an adult web site is a female, and 17% of women in America admit to having a pornography addiction.[17] Young men *and* young women must learn to avoid pornography.

When we view pornography, we begin to view other people as lustful objects rather than as sons and daughters of God. Instead of seeing and being divinely attracted to a person's intelligence, humor, talents, virtue, spirituality, and abilities, pornography users begin to be only selfishly attracted to a person's body. This degrading view of other people partially fulfills President Gordon B. Hinckley's warning that pornography will "rob you of a sense of the beauties of life."[19]

"By the Mouth of All the Holy Prophets"

Did you know that between 1986 and 2008 about 140 talks in general conference have spoken out against pornography in one way or another? That is almost four talks per general conference for the past 20 years!

Pornography Negatively Affects Marriage

Another powerful reason why we need to avoid pornography is that studies have shown that pornography negatively affects marriage. Those who view pornography often find the following:

- A decreased trust in their spouse.
- An increased risk of cheating on their spouse.
- An increased risk of divorce.
- A decreased desire to marry in the future.[20]

If pornography sounds like a recipe for marital disaster, it is.

One reason why pornography is so destructive to a marriage is that it creates unrealistic ideas about what an average person is supposed to look like and how they are supposed to behave. It also creates distorted expectations

In 2001, a survey of lawyers indicated that 56% of divorces involved one of the partners having an obsessive interest in pornographic web sites.[21]

about physical intimacy and its purpose. A study of 12,000 pornography users found that "one of the most common psychological problems [related to pornography] is a deviant attitude towards intimate relationships such as perceptions of sexual dominance, submissiveness, sex role stereotyping or viewing persons as sexual objects."[22]

Pornography also affects marriage because pornography users are usually hiding their activities from their spouse. They tend to sneak around and deceive their spouses to keep their perverted habit a secret. They tell lies to cover their tracks and often avoid their family and spouse in order to feed their pornography addiction alone. Some pornography users have a very low level of self-worth due to their actions, and many don't feel worthy of marriage or of their spouse. All of these factors can "affect your ability to have a normal relationship with your future [or current] spouse."[23]

One individual was married with children. Unfortunately his use of pornography led him to commit serious crimes, and he wound up in prison. He said, "I can speak both from experience and from talking to my fellow inmates in my unit, which is a sex offender unit, and about 90–95 percent of us viewed pornography on a fairly regular basis. . . . I will be without my wife [and] children [when I am] released [six years from now]."[24]

As a Latter-day Saint youth, you should aspire to have a strong marriage in the future. Viewing pornography will not help you achieve that goal. President Thomas S. Monson said, "Avoid any semblance of pornography. It will desensitize the spirit and erode the conscience. We are told in the Doctrine and Covenants, 'That which doth not edify is not of God, and is darkness.' Such is pornography."[25]

OTHER REASONS WHY WE SHOULD AVOID PORNOGRAPHY . . .

In 1831, the Lord said, "He that looketh on a woman to lust after her . . . shall not have the Spirit, but shall deny the faith and shall fear" (D&C 63:16). Pornography causes us to lose the Holy Ghost, lose our faith, and lose our confidence before God.

TELL ME ONE MORE TIME!

Why Shouldn't I View Pornography?

1. **Pornography creates immoral and lustful desires that can lead to sexual transgression.**
2. **Pornography is addictive (perhaps more so than drugs) and can take control of our life.**
3. **Pornography degrades the sons and daughters of God and changes how we view other people.**
4. **Pornography negatively affects marriage and can affect our ability to have a normal relationship with our spouse.**

Cont.

NOW that we have reviewed some of the *principles*, let's answer some of the questions regarding the *practices* connected to pornography:

Why are romance novels sometimes considered pornography?

Any media—viewed or read—that arouses sexual desires is pornographic. *For the Strength of Youth* points out that "offensive [pornographic] material is often found in . . . books."[26] Although this may be termed "soft" pornography, it is still dangerous. President Monson said, "Some persons struggle to differentiate between what they term 'soft-core' and 'hard-core' pornography. Actually, one leads to another."[27]

Why is pornography a big deal if it doesn't hurt anybody?

The premise of this question is faulty—pornography hurts *everyone* involved with it. All the principles in this chapter show that pornography does not just affect the participant, but it also affects those around them. It leads to immorality, destroys marriages, and contributes to sex crimes, all of which have a negative affect on society. Pornography is not an "isolated" sin; it's a social one.

Why should I see my bishop if I need to repent for pornography use?

True to the Faith explains, "Because of the addictive nature of pornography and the harm it can cause to body and spirit, servants of God have repeatedly warned us to shun it. If you are caught in the trap of pornography, stop immediately and seek help. Through repentance, you can receive forgiveness and find hope in the gospel. Go to your bishop or branch president for counsel on how to overcome your problem."[28] Don't rationalize that you can overcome the sin by yourself without anyone knowing. Many times that is simply the adversary's way of keeping you caught in the sin. Speaking to your parents and bishop will provide the support system, tools, and direction needed to overcome the sin.

DO TRY THIS AT HOME!

If you have viewed pornography and have not yet talked with your bishop, put this book down and call him. Right now.

Why Does the Music I Listen to Matter?

How many times have you heard music today? Think about it. Did you wake up to music from your alarm clock? Was the radio on during your drive to work or school this morning? Did you hear it in the hallways before class? Did you hear it *in* class at some point? (Was your iPod playing when you should have been *listening* in class? ☺) Is the ringtone of your cell phone the tune of a song? Did you pay attention when you walked into a store or a restaurant—because music was probably playing there, too. What about in the background of a TV show?

The fact is that in our culture, music is everywhere. The invention of digital music has only increased the constant availability of music to the masses. As of 2008, the latest iPod "Classic," with its 160 GB of storage, allows us to hold 40,000 songs in our pocket, or 2,000 hours of music listening.[1] That's three months of non-stop music if your iPod has really good batteries. Never more in the history of the world have God's children needed to understand why the music they listen to matters.

Musicians Say the WACKIEST THINGS

"Smoking, drinking, sex—why is it such a big deal?"
—Britney Spears[2]

The average teenager in America listens to nearly 1,750 hours of music per year![3]

Music and the Holy Ghost

Stephen D. Richardson, a stake president, wanted to teach the youth in his stake about the effects of music, so he decided to do a little experiment. He put plants in different parts of his house and made sure they received equal amounts of light and water. The only difference between the plants was the music they listened to. Plants listening to music? Yes! One group of plants listened 24/7 to a station that played alternative rock. The other group listened to classical music. The results? Interestingly enough, the plants that listened to classical music grew better and appeared healthier than those that listened to harder music.

Classical   Alternative

If music can affect plants, imagine how much more it can affect people. Have you noticed how music can affect how you feel? Maybe you have heard a patriotic song and had a feeling of national pride. Or perhaps you have been hurt emotionally and listened to loud, angry music to make the pain go away. Hopefully you have had the experience of listening to sacred music and feeling the presence of the Spirit.

One reason why the music we listen to is important is that music can and does affect how we feel; therefore, music affects our ability to recognize the Holy Ghost. *For the Strength of Youth* teaches, "Unworthy music may seem harmless, but it can have evil effects on your mind and spirit."[4] The prophets specifically tell us to "pay attention to how you *feel* when you are listening" to music.[5]

If you don't think music affects how you feel, ask yourself why movie producers spend so much time and money on the musical score. How different would the movie *Jaws* be if the theme song for *Mr. Rogers Neighborhood* pops on when the shark fin pops up?

> *It's a beautiful day in this neighborhood,*
> *A beautiful day for a neighbor . . .*
> *Hello, neighbor . . .* (as the shark opens his mouth on the unsuspecting victim)

That simple difference in music changes the moment from nail-biting suspense to laugh-out-loud comedy.

COUNT THE "VERY"S

"You are very, very, very, very, very, very foolish when you like to participate in music that is dark and noisy. Worthy inspiration cannot get through to you where you are. No matter how popular it may be or how much you want to belong, just remember that there are those angels of the devil using you."—Elder Boyd K. Packer[6]

DO TRY THIS AT HOME!

Remember those *Choose Your Own Adventure* books where you jumped to different pages in the book depending on what choice you made? Well, here's your chance to make some choices. You have a choice between turning to page 95 or 96 and reading a list of words. Choose just one, and then turn to page 98.

Musicians Say the WACKIEST THINGS

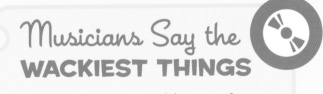

"So what if I'm smokin' weed onstage?" —Snoop Dogg[7]

A seminary student was asked, "Do you think the music you listen to affects you?"

"No," the seminary student responded. "It doesn't. For example, I got a new CD. When I first started listening to it, I had a really bad feeling inside. But I kept listening to the CD, and after awhile, the bad feeling went away."

WHOOPS!

The student had missed the point—the music he was listening to *did* affect him. He didn't realize it, but the bad feeling he had as the music was playing was the Spirit not dwelling with him. Over time, the student grew desensitized and did not even notice the loss of the Spirit.

On the positive side, if you listen to good music, it *increases* your ability to respond to the Spirit. An example is found in the Old Testament, in 1 Samuel 16. King Saul was being afflicted by an evil spirit that was not from God. The scriptures record that "David took an harp, and played with his hand: so Saul was refreshed, and was well, and the evil spirit departed from him" (JST 1 Samuel 16:23). The effect on our feelings and on the Spirit is the first reason why the music we choose to listen to matters so much.

Musicians Say the WACKIEST THINGS

"What happens someday if more people own my record than the Bible? Will that make me god because more people believe in me than him?" —Marilyn Manson[8]

BOUNDLESS POWER

"Music has boundless powers for moving families toward greater spirituality and devotion to the gospel. Latter-day Saints should fill their homes with the sound of worthy music."—The First Presidency[9]

Music Affects Our Actions

A second reason why the music you listen to matters is that music can affect your actions. Elder Gene R. Cook of the Quorum of the Seventy shared an experience that illustrates the power of music. He was on an airplane and happened to sit next to a world-famous rock star—Mick Jagger of the Rolling Stones.

Musicians Say the WACKIEST THINGS

"Is this chicken, what I have, or is this fish? I know it's tuna, but it says 'Chicken of the Sea.'" —Jessica Simpson[10]

After introducing himself, Elder Cook had a question for Mick Jagger. He said, "I have had the opportunity over the years to be with many young people all over the world. . . . Some of the young people I'm with tell me that rock music, the kind of music you and others are involved in has no real impact on them. . . . You've been in this thing for twenty years, I'd like to know—what's your opinion?"

Mick Jagger responded (and these were his exact words): "Our music is calculated to drive the kids to sex."

Elder Cook was shocked. But there it was, as plain as could be. This popular rock star said that the whole purpose of his music was to get people to be unchaste.[11]

"Our music is calculated to drive the kids to sex." —Mick Jagger

SURVEY SAYS

The *New York Times* reported on researchers who did a two-year study observing teenagers and music. The study showed that teenagers who were "exposed to the highest levels of sexually degrading lyrics were twice as likely to have had sex by the end of the study" as other teens.[12]

Musicians Say the WACKIEST THINGS

"I hurt myself today to see if I still feel." —Trent Reznor[13]

I (DON'T) WANT MY MTV

Researchers found that in 171 hours of MTV programming (that's less than 30 minutes a day for one year), there were:

1,548 sexual scenes

3,056 depictions of sex or various forms of nudity

2,881 verbal sexual references

1,518 uses of unedited profanities

3,127 bleeped profanities[14]

True Story!

Sadly, we have seen friends who have listened to music that encouraged negative behavior act on the teachings of those songs. One friend loved a song that was about shoplifting. He would always sing the chorus, which talked about walking right through the door with the stolen item. Before this young man was seventeen years old, he had already been in court for shoplifting. Did the music he listened to have an influence on his actions? There can be no doubt.

Music and Memory

A third reason why the music you listen to matters is that the lyrics you listen to affect how you think, whether you realize it or not. Can you fill in the blanks?

Oh come, all ye _____, joyful and triumphant. (Christmas hymn)

Everything I do, I do it _____ _____. (Bryan Adams)

I wish they all could be _____ girls. (The Beach Boys)

I still haven't found what ____ _____ for. (U2)

religious | Catholic | leader (now turn to page 98)

Even though some of these songs are older than you are (and some are even older than we are!), you probably knew the missing lyrics, didn't you? Isn't it amazing how the words just popped into your mind, as if they had been filed away from hearing the songs sung over and over? Numerous studies have shown that the human brain has an incredible ability to easily memorize words when they are put to music.[16]

Musicians Say the WACKIEST THINGS

"I have the same goal I've had ever since I was a girl. I want to rule the world." —Madonna[15]

HAVING TROUBLE MEMORIZING YOUR SCRIPTURE MASTERY VERSES?

Many teachers have put scripture mastery verses to music to help aid their students with memorization. If you want to download the songs to help you memorize the scriptures, go to http://ldswhy.com.

Music can easily get stuck in your head and stay there all day. This can be good or bad. One of John's children had been practicing a Christmas hymn each morning. One evening the child reported, "At school, I just sang that song in my heart and felt so happy."

Think of the impact of memorizing Primary songs or Church hymns and singing them to yourself every day:

"I Am a Child of God"
"We Thank Thee, O God, for a Prophet"
"I Love to See the Temple"
"I Believe in Christ"
"Teach Me to Walk in the Light"
"Love One Another"
"I Hope They Call Me on a Mission"
"Count Your Blessings"

DO YOU NEED A SLAP?

"Anyone who thinks there isn't a direct link between gangster rap, thug behavior and the problems that exist in inner city neighborhoods across this nation needs to be slapped!"—70s disco musician Gary "The G-man" Toms[17]

Musicians Say the WACKIEST THINGS

"I'm the type to swallow my blood 'fore I swallow my pride." —50 Cent[18]

Compare that with singing lyrics from some of the popular songs on the radio! (We wanted to include the lyrics of a recent #1 song but they were too suggestive.)

When we listen to good music, our thoughts and spirits will be uplifted throughout the day.

STOP DOWNLOADING IT AND START PLAYING IT

Music is better at enhancing early childhood development than computer use. Music training, specifically piano instruction, is far superior to computer instruction in dramatically enhancing children's abstract reasoning skills necessary for learning math and science.[19]

DO TRY THIS AT HOME!

Fill your iPod with free music! You can download hymns, EFY music, or seminary music at http://seminary.lds.org. You can also fill your iPod with talks from Church leaders or popular LDS speakers. Download the talks for free at http://lds.org; http://speeches.byu.edu; or http://byuradio.org.

TELL ME ONE MORE TiME!

Why Does the Music I Listen to Matter?

1. Music affects our emotions and our ability to feel the Holy Ghost.

2. Music affects our actions.

3. Song lyrics are easily memorized, and their message can influence us.

NOW that we have reviewed some of the *principles*, let's answer some of the questions regarding the *practices* connected to music:

Why can't I listen to a song that only has a couple of swear words if I hear worse than that every day at school?

Although you may *accidentally* hear foul or offensive language at school, there is a big difference between overhearing a swear word and deliberately joining in the conversation. Consider the following analogy: You are walking home when a bully comes along and beats you up. Although this would be sad, you may not be able to stop it from happening. But that doesn't mean you should start approaching bullies and picking fights with them.

Voluntarily listening to music with swearing in it is like picking fights with bullies. *For the Strength of Youth* tells us to "politely walk away"[20] if we are around people who use bad language. If we are seeking out music that contains swear words, we are not "walking away" from the foul language but actively choosing to make it a part of our life. Choosing to listen to songs with offensive swear words goes directly against the thirteenth Article of Faith, which tells us to "seek" out things that are "virtuous, lovely, or of good report or praiseworthy" (Article of Faith 1:13).

Why does it matter how loud my music is?

You mean besides the danger of hearing loss? ☺ Well, principle #1 in this chapter teaches that music affects our ability to feel the Holy Ghost. The Spirit is described many times as a "still small voice" that "whispereth" (D&C 85:6). If our music is too loud, it can affect our ability to be in tune to those subtle whisperings of the Holy Spirit. Sister Sharon G. Larsen, a former member of the Young Women general presidency, said in a general conference address, "There may be times the Spirit finds it difficult to help you because . . . maybe the message can't get through the loud music."[21] In fact, sometimes it is best to have no music on at all so that you can more easily listen to what the Spirit is teaching you.

Why should I listen to or sing the Church hymns?

Sometimes we focus on not doing bad things. As we look at the three main points in this chapter, listening to and singing the hymns provides a positive alternative for each point: Hymns will increase our ability to feel the Holy Ghost, inspiring music can improve our actions, and we can be uplifted by memorizing lyrics that teach eternal truths.

DO TRY THIS AT HOME!

(Continued from page 93)
Look at the following word and say the first thing that comes to your mind:
P_PE

If you chose page 95, you probably said "Pope." If you chose 96, you probably said "Pipe." What made the difference? The list of words you read primed your mind to think of something specific. If a few printed words affected your response, it should be obvious that music and lyrics will really affect your choices.

15 ch Why Are There Guidelines for Dancing?

Dancing is a universal way to communicate and express ourselves. As an art form, it stretches across cultures and time, and from the beginning it has proven to be both a blessing and a curse to God's children, depending on how it's used. *For the Strength of Youth* says, "Dancing can be fun. . . . However, it too can be misused."[1] Understanding why dancing is encouraged by the Lord, and why we need to be careful how we dance, are important truths for faithful Latter-day Saints to understand.

Everybody Dance Now!

Thou Shalt Dance . . . Really?

Why should we dance in the first place? Some might be surprised to discover that the Lord actually *encourages* us in the scriptures to dance. Consider the following verses: "To every thing there is a season, and a time to every purpose under the heaven. . . . A time to weep, and a time to laugh; a time to mourn, and *a time to dance*" (Ecclesiastes 3:1, 4; emphasis added).

"If thou art merry, praise the Lord with singing, with music, *with dancing*" (D&C 136:28; emphasis added).

"Let them praise his name *in the dance*" (Psalm 149:3; emphasis added).

Modern prophets even tell us to plan and attend wholesome dances.[2] Why would the Lord and his prophets encourage us to dance? There are many reasons, beginning with the fact that dancing can be a wonderful way to express gratitude, joy, and enthusiasm. King David even danced as a way to thank the Lord for a victory in battle (2 Samuel 6:14)!

Dancing is a part of many world cultures where it is used to celebrate and teach history and ethnic traditions, such as the Polynesian Haka warrior dance. Dancing was even a large part of the "Day of Celebration" that commemorated the 200th anniversary of the Prophet Joseph Smith's birth.

Dancing is also a way for people to show their athleticism and skills, such as ballroom dancing, tap dancing, clogging, and folk dancing. Ballet can express beauty and tell a story. Lately, dancing has even been encouraged for health reasons and weight loss.

Dancing is also used as a social event to meet other people and enjoy their company. Attending a dance can even be a great way to meet your future spouse. Marie K. Hafen, wife of Elder Bruce C. Hafen of the Seventy, shared the following: "We, my husband and I, had known each other two or three months before romance dawned on us. . . .

"I remember very well the night our friendship genuinely became something more—the night the top of our pyramid really sparked. We were dancing. Gradually, all else faded except the music, and the sense of moving together to the mellow tones of Nat King Cole. I just remember feeling a little zinging flare, like someone had struck a match."[4]

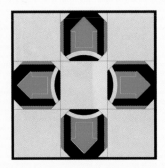

DANCE DANCE WEIGHT LOSS REVOLUTION

The video game *Dance Dance Revolution* (DDR) is so popular that it can be found in more than 2,000 arcades in malls and stores across America. In 2004, there were already more than 6.5 million home video game copies of DDR sold worldwide. Not only is dancing fun, it's a workout. Some people have made DDR their daily aerobic exercise. One person reported losing 95 pounds by adding DDR to her daily work-out routine.[3]

4 OUT OF 5 DANCERS RUN THE SERIOUS RISK OF GETTING MARRIED

On May 9, 1907, the *New York Times* published a European study of 1,097,503 people worldwide who were married or about to be married and asked them how they met their spouses. In five countries, over 80% of the people responded that they met at a dance (Germany, Switzerland, France, the United States, and Greece).[6]

You may not be ready to dance your way to an eternal companion right now, but even still, dancing can definitely help you have good, wholesome entertainment. *For the Strength of Youth* says, "Dancing can be fun and can provide an opportunity to meet new people."[5] So even if our moves are worse than a mechanical dancing Santa, we should stop being wallflowers and start dancing. It will help us properly express our emotions, celebrate culture, get some good exercise, and meet other people.

Do You Dance Like a Rigid Robot? . . . Sweet

DO TRY THIS AT HOME!

Dancing Can Have Wicked Purposes

Like the music we listen to, dancing can also be used "for wicked purposes."[7] Any time we use our bodies to express ourselves, we need to be conscious about what that expression makes other people think and feel. This is a major reason why we need to be careful how we dance.

The scriptures are full of examples about dancing being used for negative purposes. The children of Israel "corrupted themselves" (Exodus 32:7) in the wilderness by building a golden calf and dancing "naked" (or as the footnote explains, "or riotous, let loose"; see Exodus 32:25). In the Book of Mormon, the daughter of Jared used improper dancing to seduce King Akish. She said, "Behold, I am fair, and I will dance before him, and I will please him, that he will desire me" (Ether 8:10). Her worldly dancing caused Akish to lust after her and to be willing to do anything to have her, even implementing secret combinations and murder. Similarly, the daughter of Herodias used dancing to engineer the death of John the Baptist (see Matthew 14).

"When your bishop said to keep 'the standard works between us' I don't think he meant to include all the teachings of every prophet!"

BANNED!

Sometimes there isn't much difference between the immoral dancing of the daughter of Jared and the choreographed moves of some cheerleading squads. A Texas state representative has proposed a bill reducing state funding to any high school that allows their cheerleaders or dance squads to use "sexually suggestive" performances.[8] We shouldn't need legislation to control our dance squads . . . but we do need to be aware of the moves we are using and what they portray or suggest. Let's have the courage to not just sheepishly follow certain inappropriate dance trends and instead let our coaches know we can cheer and dance without being inappropriate.

Unfortunately, modern-day "freak dancing" and other inappropriate dance positions and moves have become a common occurrence at some school dances. In Doctrine and Covenants 59:6, the Lord said, "Thou shalt not . . . commit adultery . . . nor do anything like unto it." Many of these worldly kinds of dance moves are "like unto" sexual positions that definitely must be avoided. The modern prophets tell us, "When dancing, avoid full body contact with your partner. Do not use positions or moves that are suggestive of sexual behavior."[9]

It is also important to remember that not only should our dance moves be appropriate, but the whole environment of the dance should also "contribute to a wholesome atmosphere where the Spirit of the Lord may be present."[10] President Ezra Taft Benson asked, "Are [your] dances and music . . .

Napoleon Says: Keep Your Dance Moves Sweet by Dancing Like Me

virtuous, lovely, praise-worthy, and of good report, or do they represent a modern Sodom with short skirts, loud beat, strobe lights, and darkness?"[11]

QUIZ:
WHO SAID?

Match the quote with the prophet who said it.

A. Brigham Young

B. Joseph F. Smith

C. David O. McKay

D. Ezra Taft Benson

1. "My advice to [the youth] would be not to engage in . . . close and intimate contacts, including cheek to cheek dancing on the ballroom floor, whether it be at a Church dance, a public dance, or wherever it might be. I urge that they never do anything, on the dance floor or off the dance floor, that they would be ashamed to have their own fathers and mothers witness."[12]

2. "If you wish to dance, dance; and you are just as much prepared for a prayer meeting after dancing as ever you were, if you are Saints. . . . [However,] those who cannot serve God with a pure heart in the dance should not dance."[13]

3. "Those dances that require or permit the close embrace and suggestive movements . . . ought to be utterly prohibited."[14]

4. "I doubt whether it is possible to dance most of the prevalent fad dances in a manner to meet LDS standards."[15]

Answers: 1=D; 2=A; 3=B; 4=C

So go to dances and have a great time, but be sure to use dancing in the positive way the Lord intended us to and not as the immoral thing Satan can twist it into.

One young man said, "I was eighteen years old, just about to turn nineteen. I had already received my mission call and would be leaving in a few weeks. I went to a dance where I didn't know that many people. A girl asked me to dance and while we were dancing, she pulled me close to her. I could tell she wanted more than a simple dance. I realized that if I wanted to serve a mission, I needed to pull back. Avoiding 'dirty dancing' that night saved my mission."

TELL ME ONE MORE TiME!

Why Are There Guidelines for Dancing?

1. **Dancing can be used for good: It will help us properly express our emotions, celebrate culture, get some good exercise, and meet other people.**
2. **Dancing can be used for evil: Depending on the atmosphere and the moves used, it can lead us and others to have immoral thoughts and actions.**

NOW that we have reviewed some of the *principles*, let's answer some of the questions regarding the *practices* connected to dancing:

Why is freak dancing bad?

The modern prophets teach us, "Do not use positions or moves that are suggestive of sexual behavior."[16] "Freak dancing," or any dance moves that suggest sexual activity, can be used for wicked purposes, inviting temptation and immoral thoughts and desires.

Why should I go to Church dances?

One of the benefits of attending Church dances is that they are overseen by priesthood and youth leaders. Church dances are focused on sociality and fun, not sexuality and temptation. Some LDS dances require a "dance card" (given through an interview with the bishopric) or a temple recommend to enter, allowing you opportunity to meet other youth with your same standards. *For the Strength of Youth* teaches us to "plan and attend dances where dress, grooming, lighting, lyrics, and music contribute to a wholesome atmosphere where the Spirit of the Lord may be present."[17] Church dances provide an ideal setting where all of these factors are planned for and implemented so you can have an enjoyable dancing experience and keep the Spirit of the Lord.

Why should I still go to dances if I don't like dancing?

Dancing is a fun way to meet other people, get some exercise, celebrate your culture, and express yourself. Even if you don't like dancing, dances (especially LDS ones) are excellent places to meet other people with your same standards. And it's OK if you aren't comfortable dancing with someone of the opposite gender. Most youth dances have some sort of line dance where everyone can dance as a group and have a good time together. Remember that the Lord commanded the Saints to dance, and we can all benefit from busting a move every once in awhile.

Why Should I Use Clean Language?

John had the following experience that illustrates why it is so important to watch what we say. "One of my most embarrassing moments happened on my mission. I was serving in a singles' ward, and one day at church I noticed a woman arrive late to sacrament meeting. Her clothes were mismatched and her hair was extremely messy; she looked out of place. After the meeting, she ran to get out of the building before anyone could speak to her, but I ran faster. As we talked, I learned she was less-active and hadn't been to church for several years. I set up an appointment for my companion and I to meet with her the next week.

"I have to go to the bathroom."

"The day of our appointment, my companion and I went to the church to meet with the girl. When we arrived, the girl wasn't there yet, but I saw the Relief Society president and thought I should talk with her so that she could help fellowship the young woman we were going to meet with.

"'She's a little bit shy,' I said to the Relief Society president. 'She doesn't really have any friends here and doesn't fit in. Her clothes weren't that nice and her hair is kind of ratty. She was late for church and—'

"From behind me, I heard a female voice say, 'I was *not* late.' I turned around, and sure enough there was the girl. She had been there the whole time, but this time she was wearing nice clothes and her hair was combed. I didn't even recognize her.

"Time froze as I looked at her. Finally I said, 'I have to go to the bathroom,' and took off!

"I didn't mean to do anything wrong, but I realized that because I didn't watch what I said, I really hurt somebody's feelings."

We Will Be Judged by the Things We Say

In his great discourse to the Nephites, King Benjamin taught this truth: "If ye do not watch yourselves, and your thoughts, *and your words,* and your deeds . . . ye must perish. And now, O man, remember, and perish not" (Mosiah 4:30; emphasis added).

One reason why we should use good language is that part of our final judgment will include not only the things we have done, but also the things we have *said*. In Matthew 12:36, the Savior says, "Every idle word that men shall speak, they shall give account thereof in the day of judgment."

"Every idle word" means that we'll be held accountable for not only swear words, but also for words we say in joking or that we don't really mean. Sarcastic comments to younger siblings, a cruel text message, a prideful comment—they are all part of our final judgment.

On the positive side, every compliment given, every verbal expression of love, and every testimony of the gospel we share will also be part of our eternal evaluation. We should use good, clean language so that at judgment day the angels won't have to ask for earplugs as they review what we've said.

MIKED FOR ETERNITY

One of the latest trends in professional sports is to attach a small microphone to players and coaches so everyone can hear what they are saying during the game. We would do well to remember that we are all already "miked" for eternity.

Vocabulary and Intelligence

What we say not only affects our final judgment in the eternities, it also affects how other people judge us here and now. For better or worse, the words we use make an impression on others. Therefore, another reason why we should use good language is that our language reflects our character and intelligence. President Gordon B. Hinckley taught, "Failure to express yourself in language that is clean marks you as one whose vocabulary is extremely limited."[1]

YOU'RE NOT HIRED!

The following people were judged by the words they used on their job applications. Who would you hire?

• "Instrumental in ruining entire operation for a Midwest chain operation."

• "Physical disabilities include minor allergies to house cats and Mongolian sheep."

• "Please call me after five-thirty because I am self-employed and my employer does not know I am looking for another job."[2]

language ability = mental ability

Multiple studies have shown the relationship between language ability and mental ability.[3]

For the Strength of Youth says, "How you speak says much about who you are. Clean and intelligent language is evidence of a bright and wholesome mind."[4] People who tell racist or sexist jokes only reveal their own ignorant prejudices and bigotry. Those who put down others demonstrate disloyalty. On the other hand, people who compliment and congratulate others show that they are kind and thoughtful.

What We Say Affects Our Ability to Feel the Holy Ghost

President Henry B. Eyring taught, "We cannot hope to speak for the Lord unless we are careful with our speech. Vulgarity and profanity offend the Spirit. . . . You can decide—and you must—to change what you say even when you can't control what others say."[5]

For example, one morning Joseph Smith was translating the plates, and he got in an argument with his wife. When he went to translate the plates later that day, he found that he could not do it—the angry words he had spoken to his wife had robbed him of his ability to feel the Spirit. If we are not careful, the same thing can happen to us.[6]

The modern prophets have taught that our language will affect our spirituality:

"When you use good language, you invite the Spirit to be with you.

"Always use the names of God and Jesus Christ with reverence and respect. Misusing their names is a sin. Profane, vulgar, or crude language or gestures, as well as jokes about immoral actions, are offensive to the Lord."[7]

Encourage Others to Use Good Language: The Example of President Kimball

"In the hospital one day I was wheeled out of the operating room by an attendant who stumbled, and there issued from his angry lips vicious cursing with a combination of the names of the Savior. Even half-conscious, I recoiled and implored: 'Please! Please! That is my Lord whose names you revile.'

"There was a deathly silence; then a subdued voice whispered, 'I am sorry.'"—President Spencer W. Kimball[8]

CAN YOU CONTROL YOUR TONGUE?

Try to say "toy boat" ten times fast. Can you do it? What about saying "knapsack straps" ten times fast? Or the kicker, "Santa's short suit shrunk." James knew that it is hard to control the tongue. He wrote, "If any man offend not in word, the same is a perfect man. . . . The tongue is a fire. . . . Out of the same mouth proceedeth blessing and cursing. My brethren, these things ought not so to be" (James 3:2, 6, 10).

Sticks and Stones May Break Bones, But Words Will *Always* Hurt

The saying "Sticks and stones may break my bones, but words will never hurt me" isn't true. Broken bones heal over time, but words can continue to hurt throughout our lives. Perhaps that is why the scriptures frequently warn us to not speak unkindly about each other. Consider the following:

- "Let all . . . evil speaking, be put away from you." (Ephesians 4:31)
- "Speak evil of no man." (Titus 3:2)
- "Thou shalt not speak evil of thy neighbor." (D&C 42:27)
- "Cease to speak evil one of another." (D&C 136:23)

You have probably seen firsthand the effect words can have. An experience John had when he was fifteen is still etched in his memory. He says:

"We were having a teachers' quorum activity—driving around the city to make a movie. There were about seven teachers at the activity, and we were split up between two cars. One of the teachers who was there that night was Chris, a young man who had recently joined the Church. Chris was very nice, and also shy and significantly overweight.

"As we drove back to the Church, the car I was in went over a speed bump. The car bounced up and down, and it felt like it nearly smacked the ground. One of my friends said, 'It's a lucky thing Chris is in the other car. We would have smashed the ground for sure if he was in here!'

"And then we heard Chris's voice from the back seat, 'But I am in the car.'

"My heart ached for Chris that night. But the unkind words could not be unspoken. Maybe that comment was part of the reason Chris stopped coming to Church. I wish those words had never been said."

Have you noticed how babies learn to talk? They listen to everything around them and mimic what they hear. If you are having a problem with swearing, maybe you are hearing it too much in your music and media. Get rid of any CD or DVD and delete any file that "uses foul or offensive language."[9]

How many of us can still vividly remember something negative that somebody said to us? Let us never forget that what we say can hurt much more than any stick or any stone.

Kind Words Lift Spirits

It's amazing how kind words can help others. Have you ever felt sad or discouraged and then heard a compliment from somebody else? It feels great!

At the conclusion of Elder Neal A. Maxwell's mission, his mission president wrote a short note at the bottom of a letter to Elder Maxwell's bishop, complimenting the young missionary on his work. Elder Maxwell said, "It took President Eyre thirty seconds to write [the note], but it gave me encouragement for fifty years."[10]

Elder Maxwell also said, "We sometimes give needed physical cloaks to warm people and to cover them, and it is good that we do. How often do you and I also give what the scriptures call the 'garment of praise' (Isa. 61:3)? The 'garment of praise' is often more desperately needed than the physical cloak. In any case, as we all know, these needs are all around us, every day. There are so many ways we can 'lift up the hands which hang down, and strengthen the feeble knees' (D&C 81:5)."[11] One way to strengthen others is to speak kind words to them.

As in all things, our Savior is the supreme example of controlling the tongue. Often people justify using bad language when they are frustrated, upset, hurt, or being treated unkindly. None of these excuses held true for the Savior. After suffering unspeakable pain in the Garden of Gethsemane, he was captured by soldiers and mocked by the leaders of the people. Despite his suffering, we read that the Savior "held his peace" (Matthew 26:63), or as the footnote explains, "kept silent."

When we feel like lashing out at somebody in anger, swearing, taking the Lord's name in vain, or using any sort of foul language, remembering that majestic moment of our Savior's self-control should inspire us to follow his example.

WHICH AM I?

I watched them tearing a building down,
A gang of men in a busy town.
With a ho-heave-ho and a lusty yell,
They swung the beams and the sidewalls fell.

I asked the foreman, "Are these men skilled,
The kind you'd hire were you to build?"
He laughed and said, "Why, no indeed!
Just common laborers are all I need.
They can easily wreck in a day or two
What builders have taken years to do."

And I thought to myself as I went on my way:
"What part in the game of life do I play?
Am I a builder who works with care,
Measuring life by the rule and square?

Am I shaping my deeds to a well-made plan,
Patiently doing the best I can?
Or am I a wrecker who walkes the town,
Content with the labor of tearing down?"[12]

Read the following words out loud as fast as you can. Can you finish the list in five seconds? One trick though—don't say the color that the words spell, read the *color of ink* that the word is written in. Ready, set, go!

Red   Green

Yellow   Green

Red   Black

Blue   **Yellow**

Could you do it without making any mistakes? This activity shows that we tend to say the first thing that comes to mind—and that isn't always the right thing to say. The old saying "Think before you speak" is good counsel.

TELL ME ONE MORE TIME!

Why Should I Use Clean Language?

1. **God will judge us by the things we say.**
2. **How we speak reveals our intelligence and character.**
3. **What we say affects our ability to feel the Holy Ghost.**
4. **Sticks and stones may break bones, but words will hurt forever.**
5. **Kind words lift spirits.**

NOW that we have reviewed some of the *principles*, let's answer some of the questions regarding the *practices* connected to clean language:

Why shouldn't I gossip or talk behind people's backs?

Gossiping is a negative example of each of the five principles we discussed in this chapter. God will judge us for speaking ill of others. The scriptures teach we will be judged by "every *idle word,*" which footnote 36b suggests is "gossip" (Matthew 12:36; emphasis added). Gossiping reveals shallowness of character and will lessen our ability to feel the Spirit. By gossiping, we hurt others when we could be lifting them up. At a minimum, never say anything behind someone's back that you wouldn't say in front of them.

Why shouldn't I make fun of people, even if I'm joking?

Sometimes it can be hard to know when a joke is a joke. One young woman said, "This one guy would always rip on me and then say he was joking. I didn't say anything but his words really hurt." Perhaps that is why *For the Strength of Youth* says "do not insult others or put them down, even in joking."[13]

Why should I watch my tongue, even when playing sports?

It might seem like everybody swears playing sports, but in some ways that is the most important time to watch what we say. High-pressure situations in our life reveal our character. It is in those moments that we reveal who we really are. Also, you never know who can hear you, or who is reading your lips (such as your family or friends), and when your choice of language might disappoint them. When you control your mouth during intense situations (like sports), you show that you are truly in control of yourself and understand why you should use good language.

VIDEO BONUS

Watch a video of John teaching about the importance of our words at http://ldswhy.com

Write some "appreciation notes" that compliment friends or family members. Secretly put them in a place where you know they will be found.

DO TRY THIS AT HOME!

Why Should I Be Honest?

Raise your hand if you've never lied. If you aren't raising your hand right now, you just lied, so now we're all on the same page! Of all the commandments, "thou shalt not bear false witness" (Exodus 20:16) is probably the most frequently broken. Honesty covers every part of our lives, including our relationships with God and other people, and how we view ourselves. *For the Strength of Youth* says, "Be honest with yourself, others, and the Lord."[1] Understanding how dishonesty hurts our relationships answers the question about why we should be honest in all our dealings.

The Boy Who Cried Wolf: Dishonesty and Ourselves

It is ironic that we are most often dishonest in an attempt to save and help ourselves. Like all sin, dishonesty might temporarily appear to get us out of trouble, but in reality it only gets us into more trouble. No matter what the dishonesty is—lying, stealing, or cheating— eventually it all comes back to bite us in the end.[2]

Studies show that 20% of students in the United States started cheating in the first grade. Similarly, other studies reveal that currently in the U.S., 56% of middle school students and 70% of high school students have cheated.[3]

For example, those who cheat on tests, plagiarize papers, or copy assignments only cheat themselves out of knowledge and potential. Even if we are never caught by our teachers, our minds are caught in ignorance and darkness, and we may prevent ourselves from achieving further accomplishments.

Those who steal or shoplift might think they are getting something for free. But even if they aren't caught, they walk away with guilt and the worry that they will have to explain the new shirt or iPod to their parents.

Dad: "Honey, where did you get that iPod?"

Daughter: "Um, Jessica gave it to me. . . . She, like, had an extra one for her birthday and said I could have this one."

Dad: "That's nice of Jessica. I'll have to thank her for that next time she's over."

Daughter (in her mind): "Oh, man, I guess I can *never* have Jessica over here again, or I'm busted!"

Notice how one act of dishonesty led to another?

Of course, many times those who steal are caught and receive criminal penalties.

Interrogators use an effective tactic when interviewing suspects—they simply let them talk. They ask question after question, and more often than not, the lying suspect trips up, contradicting something they said earlier. This not only happens in formal interviews, but in daily conversations with friends and family. When we tell one lie, we need to cover it with a second and then another, and another, and another, until we can't remember what we have said and what we haven't. All too soon, it becomes

obvious we have lied, and those around us no longer trust us. These are just a few examples of how being dishonest doesn't help us and eventually hurts us.

"Honestly, Mom—I wasn't eating anything!"

Price Passed on to the Consumer: Dishonesty and Others

Prophets have taught that dishonesty not only hurts us but "usually hurts others as well."[4] Consider how many lives were devastated by the dishonesty in just one company.

THE PRICE OF ENRON'S DISHONESTY

Number of people who lost their jobs:

90,000 +

Loss in market value:

65 billion dollars

Number of employees who lost all their savings, children's college funds, and pensions:

Thousands[5]

Every year, theft costs stores almost 32 billion dollars.[6] Who pays that price? We do! When people steal clothes, everyone who buys clothes pays higher prices at the register.

When a father is dishonest and has an affair with another woman, who pays? Not just the father. His wife, their children, grandchildren, parents, neighbors, and friends *all* suffer feelings of betrayal, shame, guilt, loneliness, frustration, and anguish because of one person's dishonesty.

When one dishonest kid steals some personal items out of a neighbor's open garage, the entire neighborhood suddenly feels anxious and nervous, all because of one person's dishonesty. There can be no doubt that dishonesty hurts others—often the ones we care about the most. This is another reason why we should be honest.

The good news is that many people are honest. A passenger in a Los Angeles taxi cab left behind a brown bag with $350,000 worth in diamonds.

The honest taxi driver was Afghanistan-born Haider Sediqi, married with two children and his wife was pregnant with their third. He found the brown bag and discovered the diamonds along with a cell phone bill inside. He called the owner and returned the diamonds. Incredible! "Sediqi said keeping the loot never entered his mind, even though his wife loves diamonds and he dreams of opening a restaurant. 'God is up there,' he said Thursday as he waited outside an auto shop, where his cab was having its brakes fixed. 'He always watches.'"[7]

Struck Dead: Dishonesty and the Lord

We found many more inspiring stories of ordinary people who have blessed others with their honesty at http://honestyblog.com. You might want to check it out!

DO TRY THIS AT HOME!

After Christ's resurrection, the New Testament church lived the law of consecration and "had all things common" (Acts 2:44). That meant that they brought all they earned to the church and let it be divided among the members to meet each individual families' needs.

Ananias and Sapphira sold a piece of land for a certain amount of money. But when Ananias went to give the money to the apostle Peter, Ananias lied and told Peter that he had sold the land for less money. Peter said: "Why hath Satan filled thine heart to lie to the Holy Ghost, and to keep back part of the price of the land? . . . Why hast thou conceived this thing in thine heart? *thou hast not lied unto men, but unto God.* And Ananias hearing these words fell down, and gave up the ghost: and great fear came on all them that heard these things" (Acts 5:3–5; emphasis added).

There is a great truth in the midst of the lie of Ananias: We cannot lie to God. He "knows all the thoughts and intents of the heart" (Alma 18:32)—all that we ever do, see, hear, or think. Trying to lie to God is like playing hide-and-seek in the Sahara Desert. There is simply no place to hide.

When we are dishonest, we tend to want to hide from God by avoiding prayer, scripture study, and church. Dishonesty weakens our relationship with God and damages our spirit. We must remember that to be honest with the Lord is to be trusted by the Lord. Qualifying for God's trust is another reason why we must be honest with ourselves, others, and the Lord.

Playing hide-and-seek in the Sahara . . . What fun!

Honesty with Ourselves, Others, and the Lord

We have focused a lot on the negative consequences of dishonesty, but there is also a very positive flipside. When we are honest, we feel good about ourselves because we have integrity. Being honest allows others to trust us, and we develop healthier relationships. People frequently are offered jobs or higher positions at work because the employer knows they are honest. Perhaps most importantly, when we are honest, we strengthen our relationship with the Lord and allow him to guide our lives with confidence. Honesty truly is the best policy.

MOST PEOPLE ARE HONEST

A person did an experiment where he intentionally dropped 100 wallets throughout a city. Data was collected with the help of hidden cameras that recorded 100 random people in public places picking up these "lost" wallets. The idea was to see who would be honest and return the wallets and who would be dishonest and keep them. Seventy-four percent of the people returned the wallets.[9]

dishonest 26%

74% honest

DO TRY THIS AT HOME!

Try to be "perfectly honest" with yourself, others, and the Lord for a week (see Alma 27:27). What do you find changes in your life? Record your experience in your journal.

TELL ME ONE MORE TiME!

Why Should I Be Honest?

1. **Dishonesty hurts ourselves when we are caught in our web of lies and feel guilt and shame.**
2. **Dishonesty hurts innocent people.**
3. **Dishonesty hurts our relationship with God and causes us to lose the Spirit.**
4. **When we are honest, we feel better about ourselves, people trust us more, and we strengthen our relationship with God.**

NOW that we have reviewed some of the *principles*, let's answer some of the questions regarding the *practices* connected to honesty:

Why shouldn't I illegally download music, movies, or software?

Illegal downloading may not seem like stealing because you are not taking a physical item; however, the principle is the same. You wouldn't walk into a store and take a CD off the shelf and stick it under your shirt. Illegally downloading a copyrighted song at home is essentially the same thing because you are robbing the artist and the company that produced the music. Such theft robs you of your integrity, causes higher prices for everybody else, and makes you less receptive to inspiration from the Spirit.

Why shouldn't I copy my friend's homework assignment if I already know the material?

Good question. Based on the principles we've discussed in this chapter, how would you answer this question? Give us your answer at http://ldswhy.com.

Why is it wrong if I purposely leave out part of the truth, even though I'm not "lying"?

Suppose you saw a crime being committed. If the police asked you if you had seen anything, and you said yes but did not tell the police *everything* you saw, you would hurt the cause of justice. Similarly, leaving out parts of a story or not telling people the *whole* truth is generally a form of deception and therefore dishonest. Being honest is more than just *not lying,* it's also telling all the truth that needs to be told.

{}^{ch}18$ Why Should I Keep the Sabbath Day Holy?

The Lord has told us to "call the sabbath a delight" (Isaiah 58:13), but some people feel like Sunday is a restrictive day, a day when they *can't* do certain things. They might say, "Stuffy white shirts and ties, dresses and heels, shushes and hushes, talks and more talks, early-morning fast offerings and late-evening firesides, no shopping or dating or dancing. And this day is a 'delight'? Please tell us why!"

Rest and Rejuvenation

One of the reasons why we have the Sabbath is because there needs to be a designated day of rest. The Lord himself followed this pattern when he created the earth. After six days of creation, the Lord said, "And on the seventh day I, God, ended my work, and all things which I had made; and I *rested* on the seventh day from all my work" (Moses 3:2; emphasis added).

If the Lord took a break . . . we should too.

The Sabbath provides us with a day to rest from our daily work and worries. We can take a break from homework, deadlines, competitions, sports, performances, timecards, and all the other pressures we face during the week. "For verily this is a day appointed unto you *to rest from your labors*" (D&C 59:10; emphasis added). Our bodies need the physical rest and our souls need the spiritual rejuvenation that comes from taking a break from the demands of the world.

Brigham Young taught: "The Lord has directed his people to rest one-seventh part of the time, and we take the first day of the week, and call it our Sabbath. . . . We should observe this for our own temporal good and spiritual welfare. When we see a farmer in such a hurry, that he has to attend to his harvest, and to haying,

RESTING FROM HOME**WORK**

"I would counsel all students, if they can, to arrange their schedules so that they do not study on the Sabbath. If students and other seekers after truth will do this, their minds will be quickened and the infinite Spirit will lead them to the verities they wish to learn." —President James E. Faust[1] (What a promise!)

fence-making, or to gathering his cattle on the Sabbath day, as far as I am concerned, I count him weak. . . . Six days are enough for us to work."[2]

For the Strength of Youth promises that honoring the Sabbath day "will give you needed rest and rejuvenation."[3] Taking advantage of this rest is one reason why we should keep the Sabbath day holy.

A Day to Serve and Remember

There is a huge difference between resting from our labors on the Sabbath and taking a vacation. The Sabbath is a *holy* day, not a *holiday*. One of the reasons why we should keep the Sabbath holy and rest from our work is so that we will have time to do the Lord's work.

DO TRY THIS AT HOME!

This Sunday, try to "keep thyself unspotted from the world" (D&C 59:9) by avoiding watching worldly TV or doing any homework. Instead, focus your day on only doing spiritually productive things that bring you closer to Christ.

What are we worshipping on the Sabbath?

If we are keeping the Sabbath day holy and resting from our work, it's nearly impossible to claim that we are too busy to serve God or our fellow man. The Lord tells us that one of the purposes of the Sabbath is to "offer thine oblations and thy sacraments unto the Most High" (D&C 59:12). An oblation is "offerings, whether of time, talents, or means, in service of God and fellowman" (D&C 59:12, footnote 12b). If we rested on the Sabbath only by lounging around in pajamas and taking sporadic catnaps, we would not be keeping the day holy nor fulfilling its divine intentions. President Spencer W. Kimball said: "The Sabbath is a holy day in which to do worthy and holy things. Abstinence from work and recreation is important but insufficient. The Sabbath calls for constructive thoughts and acts, and if one merely lounges about doing nothing on the Sabbath, he is breaking it. To observe it, one will be on his knees in prayer, preparing lessons, studying the gospel, meditating, visiting the ill and distressed, sleeping, reading wholesome material, and attending all the meetings of that day to which he is expected. To fail to do these proper things is a transgression."[4]

Does this remind you of the Sabbath? It shouldn't!

Whether it's serving in our calling, going home teaching, having a nice long meal with the family, visiting Grandma, studying our scriptures, writing in our journal, talking to a friend or relative on the phone, baking cookies with siblings, or reading that really good book on why we should keep the commandments ☺, the Sabbath provides time to do all these spiritually uplifting things (and more) that might otherwise be overlooked in our busy schedules.

"Come visit, Sonny!"

Can I Get Baptized Again?

A primary reason why the Sabbath was created, and why we should keep it holy, is that it provides a day for us to rededicate ourselves to God and to remember the Savior's atonement by partaking of the sacrament.

We should keep the Sabbath day holy and attend our meetings so that we can partake of the sacrament and receive its cleansing effect. President Boyd K. Packer explained: "Generally we understand that, conditioned upon repentance, the ordinance of baptism washes our sins away. Some wonder if they were baptized too soon. If only they could be baptized now and have a clean start. But that is not necessary! Through the ordinance of the sacrament, you renew the covenants made at baptism. When you meet all of the conditions of repentance, however difficult, you may be forgiven and your transgressions will trouble your mind no more."[5]

A weekly baptism

Elder Dallin H. Oaks further taught: "Attendance at Church each week provides the opportunity to partake of the sacrament, as the Lord has commanded us. If we act with the right preparation and attitude, partaking of the sacrament renews the cleansing effect of our baptism and qualifies us for the promise that we will always have His Spirit to be with us."[6]

Elder Jeffrey R. Holland added, "Think for a moment how different our lives could be if through repentance we were made clean each and every Sabbath and could start each week absolutely pure, renewed, refreshed—totally confident of our standing before God."[7]

Each time we partake of the sacrament, in the spirit of repentance, we are cleansed from our sins and washed anew by the sanctifying power of the Holy Ghost (see 3 Nephi 27:20; 2 Nephi 31:17). The sacrament is specifically blessed to "sanctify . . . the souls of all those who partake of it" (D&C 20:77). This weekly cleansing is perhaps the purest reason why we should honor the Sabbath.

Understanding the cleansing effect of the sacrament also underscores why we must attend church and not simply study the scriptures in our homes or out in nature. President Spencer W. Kimball taught: "A man of my acquaintance remained home each Sabbath and justified himself by saying that he could benefit more by reading a good book at home than by attending the sacrament meeting and listening to a poor sermon. But the home, sacred as it should be, is not the house of prayer. In it no sacrament is administered; in it is not found the fellowship with members, nor the confession of sins to the brethren. The mountains may be termed the temples of God and the forests and streams his handiwork, but only in the meetinghouse, or house of prayer, can be fulfilled all the requirements of the Lord. And so he has impressed upon us that: 'It is expedient that the church meet together often to partake of bread and wine in the remembrance of the Lord Jesus' (D&C 20:75)."[8]

God might be in the mountains . . . but the ordinance of the sacrament isn't.

When we understand the blessings that are available to us, we have a powerful reason for why we should want to go to church and partake of the sacrament on Sunday.

Enjoying the rejuvenation that results from resting from our labors, finding the time to serve our fellow man, and accepting the cleansing power of the atonement through the sacrament is precisely why Isaiah called the Sabbath "a delight" (Isaiah 58:13) and why God commands us to keep it.

"Observance of the Sabbath is an indication of the depth of our conversion.

"Our observance or non-observance of the Sabbath is an unerring measure of our attitude toward the Lord personally and toward his suffering in Gethsemane, his death on the cross, and his resurrection of the dead. It is a sign of whether we are Christians in very deed, or whether our conversion is so shallow that commemoration of his atoning sacrifice means little or nothing to us."

—Elder Mark E. Petersen[9]

OUR CONVERSION IS MEASURED BY OUR SABBATH OBSERVANCE

TELL ME ONE MORE TiME!

Why Should I Keep the Sabbath Day Holy?

1. **The Sabbath provides us an opportunity to rest from the work and cares of the world.**
2. **Keeping the Sabbath day holy gives us the time and availability to serve God and others, to be with family and loved ones, and to complete spiritually uplifting activities that might otherwise be overlooked during the week.**
3. **Keeping the Sabbath day holy and attending Church each week allows us to partake of the sacrament and be "re-baptized" (so to speak) and receive spiritual cleansing and renewal through the Atonement and the sanctifying power of the Holy Ghost.**

NOW that we have reviewed some of the *principles*, let's answer some of the questions regarding the *practices* connected to the Sabbath day:

Why shouldn't I text message in sacrament meeting?

We have talked about how worthily partaking of the sacrament can be a second baptism. Would we text while being baptized? Probably not. Aside from the water ruining the cell phone, our actions would show a lack of focus, dedication, and humility during that sacred ordinance. Elder Dallin H. Oaks said, "Young people, [sacrament meeting] is not a time for whispered conversations on cell phones or for texting persons at other locations. When we partake of the sacrament, we make a sacred covenant that we will always remember the Savior. How sad to see persons obviously violating

that covenant in the very meeting where they are making it."[10] This principle holds true not only for texting, but also for any other activity that might divert our attentive worship during the ordinance of the sacrament.

Cont.

Much of fasting has to do with hunger—not just ours, but other people's hunger. For many who live in economically comfortable situations, being without food and feeling the pain of hunger is a rare experience. When the only trial regarding food for many Americans is deciding "*What* will I eat?", it becomes difficult to empathize and relate to the poor, whose daily question is "*Will* I eat?"

HELPING THE HUNGRY

"About 25,000 people die each day from hunger or hunger-related causes, most of them children."[9]

Voluntarily going without food for two meals for one day each month temporarily puts us in the same situation as those who involuntarily go without food for many meals each day. Elder Joseph B. Wirthlin explained, "When we fast, . . . we feel hunger. And for a short time, we literally put ourselves in the position of the hungry and the needy. As we do so, we have greater understanding of the deprivations they might feel."[10]

As we fast, we will feel an increased desire to help those who are hungry, and the Lord has prepared a perfect system for us to do so.

Inherent in fasting is the fact that we do not eat food during the time of our fast, usually for two complete meals.[11] Joseph Smith taught the Saints what to do with the food remaining from the fast when he said: "Let this be an example to all saints, and there will never be any lack for bread: When the poor are starving, let those who have, fast one day and give what they otherwise would have eaten to the bishops for the poor, and every one will abound for a long time. . . . And so long as the saints will all live to this principle with glad hearts and cheerful countenances they will always have an abundance."[12]

What an inspired way to care for the poor and the needy! Each time a fast offering is given to a bishop, he can use that money to help provide for the needs of the poor in his ward. And if there is more money than there is need in the ward, the money is passed on to the stake to help the poor within its boundaries. If more fast offerings are collected in the stake than are needed by its members, then it is passed on to the Church to be distributed across the world. What a beautiful system! It is truly inspired by the Lord, as it costs nothing more than a temporary sacrifice of food and the benefits reach so many. President Gordon B. Hinckley said: "The millions of dollars which are needed for this purpose [of caring for the poor] each year really cost no one anything. It is not a sacrifice for anyone to go without two meals a month and give the equivalent cost, and even more, to his or her bishop for the care of the needy.

"Think, my brethren, of what would happen if the principles of fast day and the fast offering were observed throughout the world. The hungry would be fed, the naked clothed, the homeless sheltered. Our burden of taxes would be lightened. The giver would not suffer, but would be blessed by his small abstinence. A new measure of concern and unselfishness would grow in the hearts of people everywhere. Can anyone doubt the divine wisdom that created this program which has blessed the people of this Church as well as many who are not members of the Church?"[13]

IF THE WEALTHIEST 20% OF PEOPLE IN THE WORLD FASTED . . .

The United Nations estimates that the cost to end world hunger *completely*, along with diseases related to hunger and poverty, is about $195 billion a year.[14]

$195,000,000,000 Cost to end world hunger per year.

$16,250,000,000 Cost to end world hunger per month.

$13.54 Cost per month to end world hunger if 1,200,000,000 (20% of world population) people fasted and gave fast offerings each month.

You cannot control whether 1.2 billion people fast or not, but you can control whether you do your part by giving a generous fast offering each month.

Some teenagers may think that they do not need to pay fast offerings because their parents pay a fast offering, or because they do not buy household groceries. But *For the Strength of Youth* says, "A proper fast day observance includes . . . giving a generous fast offering."[15] Isn't it interesting that this pamphlet for *youth* encourages the payment of fast offerings? The Lord expects even the youth to live their covenants and assist the poor.

The next fast Sunday, fast for a full twenty-four hours. Plan ahead of time to have something specific in mind to pray for. In addition, pay a generous fast offering—even if you still live at home!

DO TRY THIS AT HOME!

Blessings from Fasting

A third reason to obey the law of the fast (which includes paying a generous fast offering) is so the Lord will pour out blessings on those who fast. We should begin and end our fast with a prayer. Often during a fast we pray for something specific, something that we care about very much or for someone in need. Fasting is a way of showing the Lord that we really want something and are willing to sacrifice to obtain his help in receiving it.

A Missionary's Experience

One missionary shared the following experience of how fasting helped him receive an answer to a prayer. He said, "My companion and I had been working hard—and I mean *hard!*—for four weeks without any success. We decided to have a special fast for our area, and that month we gave a more generous fast offering than we had given before. In the following weeks, we felt impressed to fast again that we would be able to see people converted to the gospel. In the weeks after our special fast, we were able to teach and baptize people every week. This experience strengthened my testimony that when I fast and pray for something, the Lord will hear my prayers."

Isaiah promised that when we fast "the Lord shall answer; thou shalt cry, and he shall say, Here I am" (Isaiah 58:9).

Notice that when we fast, the Lord will be more likely to respond to our prayers. He says, "Here I am." We are also promised that through fasting, "the Lord shall guide thee continually" (Isaiah 58:11). He will guide us and we will feel an increased outpouring of the Spirit as we become more connected to him through our fast. What an incredible blessing to have the Lord hear and answer our prayers through a dedicated fast!

The next time fast Sunday rolls around, remember the blessings that come from living the law of the fast. They are even better than that bowl of cereal!

TELL ME ONE MORE TIME!

Why Should I Fast?

1. **Fasting helps us overcome sin as we learn how to control our appetites and passions.**
2. **Fasting helps us offer relief to the poor through the payment of fast offerings.**
3. **Fasting draws us closer to God and helps our prayers be answered.**

NOW that we have reviewed some of the *principles*, let's answer some of the questions regarding the *practices* connected to fasting:

Why does what time Church starts have little to do with how long I fast?

Sometimes people think that you should break your fast right after your church meetings, so if church starts at 9:00 AM you don't have to fast as long. That kind of thinking misses part of the purpose of the fast. Fasting means going without food or drink for two meals, and a full fast should last about twenty-four hours. Breaking your fast shouldn't be determined by when church ends, but by when you begin your fast. For example, eating four bowls of cereal at 11:59 PM Saturday night, and then eating "dinner" at 2:30 after church on Sunday would be a less-appropriate fast. It is not when church ends; it is when we last ate that should determine the end of our fast.

Why should I still pay fast offerings if my parents already pay?

One reason is because you can. Even if you don't have a job, there can be no doubt that you eat better than millions of others do. Paying fast offerings allows you—as a disciple of Christ—to help the poor and needy around you. A second reason is that to receive the full blessings of the fast, you need to pay fast offerings. Third, paying fast offerings when you are younger helps you develop a habit that will serve you well throughout your life.

Why should I have something I'm fasting for?

Earlier we quoted Isaiah 58, which says that when we fast the Lord will hear our prayers more easily. Fasting provides an excellent opportunity for us to ponder the needs we have and to turn to the Lord for help. If you don't have anything you need, find somebody who does and fast for them. This will give you a purpose for your fast and make it more meaningful than simply going without food or water. Some of the most beneficial fasts can be when you fast for others.

20ch Why Should I Pray Always?

We pray a lot! Personal and family prayer morning and night, prayers to open and close most church meetings and classes, prayers before Young Men and Women activities, prayers to bless the food (even if it is just donuts), prayers before we travel, prayers to begin a fast, and special prayers for ordinances such as baptism and the sacrament. Not to mention the fact that the Lord has told us to "pray *always*" (2 Nephi 32:9; emphasis added). The question then becomes, why should we pray always? Let's find out.

A 1995 study showed that LDS youth pray daily more than any other religion besides Jehovah's Witnesses, and that more than 90% of LDS youth pray at least sometime.[1]

Frequency of Prayer by Affiliation, Adolescents, 1995

Legend: Daily, Weekly, Monthly, Monthly, Never

Categories (left to right): Jehovah's Witness, Latter Day Saints, Holiness, Pentecostal, AME, AME Zion, CME, Assemblies of God, Christian Science, Adventist, Baptist, United Church of Christ, MUslim, Eastern Orthodox, Disciples of Christ, Other religion, Catholic, Other Protestant, Methodist, Presbyterian, Congregational, Lutheran, Episcopal, Buddist, Jewish, Baha'i, Quaker/Friends, Unitarian, National Baptist, Hindu, Don't Know

Source: National Longitudial Survey of Adolescent Health, 1995
Note: The Adventist, Congregational, Eastern Orthodox, Muslim, Christian Scientists and United Church of Christ affiliations each had less than 50 obversations.

Ask, and Ye Shall Receive

One reason why we should pray always is that many of the blessings God wants to give us depend on us asking for them first! Nephi said, "I know that God will give liberally *to him that asketh*" (2 Nephi 4:35; emphasis added). And Brigham Young taught, "By bowing down before the Lord to ask Him to bless you, you will simply find this result—God will multiply blessings on you temporally and spiritually."[2]

A PRAYER FOR YOUR HEALTH

According to a study by Centra State Hospital, "The psychological benefits of prayer may help reduce stress and anxiety, promote a more positive outlook, and strengthen the will to live."[3]

As the LDS Bible Dictionary teaches, "The object of prayer is not to change the will of God, but to secure for ourselves and for others blessings that God is already willing to grant, but that are made conditional on our *asking* for them."[4]

Why Should I Pray Always? • 129

If we only occasionally pray, it is certain that we are missing out on blessings God wants to grant us. We should pray *always* so that God may bless us *always*.

Pray Always . . . and Always Have His Spirit

One of the blessings of praying always is that the more we pray, the more in tune with the Spirit we become. Doctrine and Covenants 19:38 says, "Pray always, and I will pour out my Spirit upon you." The Lord also taught, "Ye receive the Spirit through prayer" (D&C 63:64).

Think of the many decisions we make every day. As we head out to school or work, before we perform in a play or participate in a sport, before we take a test or have an interview, or before we go on a date, we can pray and ask the Lord to bless us and guide us. If we do so, he has promised to bless us with the Spirit to direct us in our activities.

Hope u r pryng as mch as i c u txtng

In 2006, 1.2 *billion* text messages were sent. In some countries, the average teenager sends 60 text messages a day. Do we pray as much as we text?[5]

"ONE NATION, UNDER GOD . . . "

Did you know that an official prayer is offered before each session of the United States Congress? Go to http://chaplain.house.gov/archive/index.html to read the latest prayer offered for the U.S. Congress.

And did you know that the first Thursday of each May is designated as the national day of prayer?

National Day of Prayer

For the Strength of Youth says, "To help you become all that the Lord wants you to become, get on your knees each day and express to Him the desires of your heart. He is the source of all wisdom, and you need His help. He will hear and answer you."[6] When we pray always, we will have the guiding influence of God through the Holy Ghost in our lives each day.

That Ye May Come Off Conqueror

The Doctrine and Covenants provides another reason why we should pray always. "Pray always, that you may come off conqueror; yea, that you may *conquer Satan,* and that you may escape the hands of the servants of Satan that do uphold his work" (D&C 10:5; emphasis added).

One of the blessings of praying always is the spiritual strengthening that comes from being constantly connected with our Father in Heaven. When we are connected through prayer, God blesses us with the guidance of the Holy Ghost, which strengthens us and fortifies us against temptation.

Even the Savior prayed in his most trying hour in the Garden of Gethsemane. While atoning for the sins of the world, Jesus was struggling and he knelt down "and prayed, saying, Father, if thou be willing, remove this cup from me: nevertheless not my will, but thine, be done. And there appeared an angel unto him from heaven, *strengthening him*" (Luke 22:41–43; emphasis added).

For all of us who are striving and struggling to do what is right and need strengthening to overcome sin, there is little doubt why we should pray always.

SCRIPTURE SEARCH

Look up the following scriptures. What pattern do you notice?

- 3 Nephi 18:15
- 3 Nephi 18:18
- D&C 31:12
- D&C 61:39
- D&C 93:49

Recommit to having consistent personal prayer each day. Find ways that you can "pray always" throughout the day.

DO TRY THIS AT HOME!

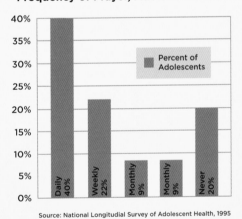

A four-year study by the University of North Carolina of 90,000 youth grades 7 through 12 found that 40% of the youth prayed daily.[7] Do you?

Frequency of Prayer, Adolescents 1995

Percent of Adolescents

- Daily 40%
- Weekly 22%
- Monthly 9%
- Monthly 9%
- Never 20%

Source: National Longitudial Survey of Adolescent Health, 1995

Pray Always to Know God

Joseph Smith taught, "It is the first principle of the gospel to know for a certainty the character of God"[8] and "I want you all to know Him . . . and be familiar with Him."[9] Another reason why we should pray always is that prayer helps us get to know our Heavenly Father. Prayer is a key that unlocks the door and opens a relationship with God. Bishop H. Burke Peterson taught, "Without prayer we will never really know our Heavenly Father or his Son, the Savior."[10]

Just as we stay in touch with our friends by texting, blogging, talking on the phone, or spending time with them, prayer allows us to spend time with our Heavenly Father. Through prayer we will feel his love for us, his knowledge of our life's details, and his care and concern for our personal problems, and we will know he is watching over and blessing us. Figuratively speaking, he is ready to visit our own homes and talk over dinner. He says, "Behold, I stand at the door, and knock: if any man hear my voice, and open the door, I will come in to him, and will sup with him, and he with me" (Revelation 3:20).

At judgment day, we do not want our Heavenly Father saying to us what was said to the foolish virgins, "Ye know me not" (JST Matthew 25:12). Praying always allows us to develop an intimate relationship with God so that when we see him, we will feel comfortable in his presence and "shall be like him" (Moroni 7:48).

VAIN REPETITIONS

See if you can fill in the blanks of these familiar prayers:

"Please bless this food that it will _____ _____ _____ _____ _____." (at an event with food)

"Please bless that ____ _____ ____ _____ ____ ____ _____ ____." (before leaving on a trip)

"We thank thee for the _____." (if it's raining)

"Please bless that we can take this lesson and _____ ____ ____ _____ _____ _____." (in a class)

"Please bless that all those who weren't here this week ____ _____ _____ _____." (after a meeting)

The Savior taught us to avoid using "vain repetitions" (Matthew 6:7) when we pray. It is difficult to feel close to God if we are simply rattling off memorized phrases without really thinking about them. The problem is not in the repetition of the prayer (after all, the sacrament prayer is repeated verbatim every Sunday), but in the vain repetition (meaning without real intent) of prayer. For us to feel close to God in prayer, the language and phrases we use must be said with sincerity and meaning.

Answers: Nourish and strengthen our bodies. No harm or accident will come upon us. Moisture (or rain). Apply it in our daily lives. Can come next week.

Yes, God Answers Every Prayer

Some people occasionally become frustrated because they feel that God does not answer their prayers. Please don't confuse God *answering* a prayer with God doing *what we want*. They are not the same thing. We could pray to God for a million dollars right now, and he would answer that prayer—the answer would probably be "No," but he would have answered.

If a child approached a parent and asked, "Mom, can we have ice cream for dinner?" The mother will (hopefully) say "No," not because she doesn't love her child, but because she does! It is not in the child's best interest to eat ice cream for dinner. But she still answered.

"Can I have ice cream for dinner?" Probably not, but you still got an answer.

Having our prayers answered is much the same. Sometimes in his wisdom the Lord tells us "No." Consider this testimony from Elder Gene R. Cook: "I believe that in the whole history of the world God has never failed to answer a humble, sincere prayer—no matter who offered it, whether male or female, young or old, weak or strong, member or nonmember. That's the way the Lord is. He is so kind. He is so anxious to respond. Of course, his answer might have been 'No.' Or he may have said, 'Yes, but not now.' Or he may have responded in a still, small voice that the person failed to hear. But answer he did."[11]

We also testify that God does hear and answer all prayers. Let's not allow our misunderstandings of how God answers our prayers to keep us from praying always.

TELL ME ONE MORE TIME!

Why Should I Pray Always?

1. **Prayer is an avenue for God to bless his faithful children with the righteous and needful things they ask for.**
2. **Praying always qualifies us to be led and guided by the Spirit.**
3. **Consistent prayer strengthens us against sin and temptation.**
4. **Prayer helps us get to know our Heavenly Father and develop an intimate relationship with him.**
5. **Prayers are *always* answered!**

NOW that we have reviewed some of the *principles*, let's answer some of the questions regarding the *practices* connected to prayer:

Why does it seem like sometimes I don't get an answer to my prayers?

If two sports teams are playing against each other, and they both pray that they will win, then one of them will not have their prayer "answered" (if that means they get exactly what they asked for). Sometimes God answers our prayers by saying "No" or "Wait." Doctrine and Covenants 46:30 says, "He that asketh in the Spirit asketh *according to the will of God; wherefore it is done even as he asketh*" (emphasis added). We need to make sure our requests are in harmony with what we feel spiritually prompted to pray for. Also, sometimes the Lord delays an answer because he wants us to exercise our agency and figure out the answer ourselves, instead of just asking him for the answer (see D&C 9:7–8). For an excellent talk on how prayers are answered, read Elder Richard G. Scott's talk "Using the Supernal Gift of Prayer."[12]

Why should I take off my hat and use words like "thee" and "thy" when I pray?

Words like "thee," "thou," and "thy" signal respect and honor. We take off our hat, use these words, and often kneel when we pray to show Heavenly Father that we respect, revere, and honor him. Although he is our loving Father, he is also the great God of the universe—and should be treated appropriately.

Why should I pray by myself if I pray with my family every day?

Family prayer is extremely important—yet one day you will be away from your family members, either for school, on a mission, or when you get married. If you have not already developed the habit of personal prayer, you may find it difficult to begin when you are on your own. In addition, you probably have many concerns that you would like help with, but that are private. Personal prayer is the time to pray for those personal things.

ch 21 Why Should I Study My Scriptures Daily?

"Kids, we need to turn around. I forgot something."

Have you ever forgotten something when you went on a trip? Perhaps a toothbrush? A pair of shoes? Maybe your camera? When the Book of Mormon prophet Lehi and his family fled Jerusalem and had been out in the wilderness for three days Lehi told his boys they needed to go back. That would be like driving from California to New York and right before you enter New York, your dad says, "Kids, we need to turn around. I forgot something."

You might say, "Whatever we left behind better be good!"

What did Lehi send his boys back for? He told them to go back for the *scriptures!* (see 1 Nephi 3:1–4). Would we have done the same? So that we don't make the mistake of leaving the scriptures behind in our lives, let's understand why the Lord gave his children scriptures and the commandment to study them daily.

Wise unto Salvation

The first reason we should study the scriptures is that they teach us the truths of the plan of salvation, which are necessary to know in order to become like God and live in his presence. The scriptures teach us the answers to the big questions of life: "Who, What, When, Where, and Why."

Ever Walked into the Middle of a Movie and Had No Clue What Was Happening?

According to Elder Boyd K. Packer, the scriptures are like the script to a movie or a play. They teach us what went on in act 1 (the pre-mortal life), what is happening in act 2 (earth life), and what will happen in the final scene, act 3 (after life).[1] If you want to make sense of the show, better get your script . . . ures!

From the scriptures we learn about the pre-mortal life, the creation of the world, the fall of Adam and Eve, sin, and death. The scriptures teach us right from wrong, truth from error, and how to follow the path to peace instead of traveling the miles of misery.

LOST: THE MULEKITES

The Nephites brought the scriptures to the promised land, but the Mulekites, another group that came to the Americas at the same time as Lehi, didn't. The result? "Their language had become corrupted . . . and they denied the being of their Creator" (Omni 1:17). The Mulekites lost their testimony of God and his plan because they lost their scriptures.

Most importantly, the scriptures teach and testify of the central figure of the plan of salvation, our Savior Jesus Christ. The scriptures contain the "fulness of the everlasting Gospel" (Joseph Smith–History 1:34). As the apostle Paul testified to his young friend Timothy: "From a child thou hast known the holy scriptures, which are able to make thee wise unto salvation through faith which is in Christ Jesus.

"All scripture is given by inspiration of God, and is profitable for doctrine, for reproof, for correction, for instruction in righteousness:

"That the man of God may be perfect, thoroughly furnished unto all good works" (2 Timothy 3:15–17).

The more we study the scriptures, the more we will know the truths of the plan of salvation and the teachings of Jesus Christ, which will lead us to eternal life through his name.

1.7

The Book of Mormon mentions the name of Christ in some form on average every 1.7 verses.[2] It truly is "Another Testament of Jesus Christ."

"I do not know of a better way to always remember [Christ] than to daily study the scriptures."—Elder David A. Bednar[3]

CHANGE YOUR ATTITUDE

"True doctrine, understood, changes attitudes and behavior.

"The study of the doctrines of the gospel will improve behavior quicker than a study of behavior will improve behavior. . . . That is why we stress so forcefully the study of the doctrines of the gospel."—President Boyd K. Packer[4]

Answers and Direction

On the hit television show *Survivor,* a group of contestants are deliberately marooned on a faraway island or country and expected to "survive" on their own under harsh conditions. One year, one of the contestants happened to be a faithful Latter-day Saint, Neleh Dennis. Each contestant was allowed *one* "luxury" item from home to take with them to the island. Some contestants brought footballs, or pillows to make things comfortable, but not Neleh. She brought her personal set of scriptures. "I knew that they would bring me comfort when times were tough," she said.[5] While others were seeking to make things *comfortable,* she was seeking for something *comforting.*

This story highlights another reason why we should study the scriptures on a daily basis. In addition to giving us comfort, the scriptures give us direction and guidance. Do you want to know what college to attend? The answer is in the scriptures. Do you want help to know how to do better at math? The answer is in the scriptures. Do you want to know what you should do about some friends who are being rude to you? The answer is in the scriptures. Do you want to know if you should break up with your sixteen-year-old boyfriend? Well, you should ☺ . . . but even if you didn't know that, the answer is in the scriptures. Nephi told us that if we feast on scriptures, "the words of Christ will tell you *all things* what ye should do" (2 Nephi 32:3; emphasis added).

Photo by Mark Johnson/Getty Images

Spiritual Survivor: Neleh Dennis knows true survival skills

"I NEED TO CUT YOU OFF!"

A junior high girl wondered if she should break up with her boyfriend or not. She heard her seminary teacher say that the scriptures had the answer to any question we might have, so she opened them up and turned to the Topical Guide under "B" for "boyfriend." There was no listing. She then turned to "D" for "dating" and once again, nothing. On a whim, she turned to "S" for "steady dating." Once again, blank. Frustrated, she opened her scriptures and started reading the allegory of the olive tree in Jacob 5. Do you think she found an answer to her dilemma there? As she read about this healthy tree being corrupted by a wild branch that had been brought in, she found her answer when the Lord of the vineyard said, "Let us pluck from the tree those branches whose fruit is most bitter . . . and this will I do that the tree may not perish" (Jacob 5:52–53).

The Spirit confirmed that she had found her answer! Excited, she read those verses to her unsuspecting boyfriend and then said to him, "Do you know what that means? I need to cut you off!" and she ended the relationship. The scriptures truly have the answers to our questions, even chapters like Jacob 5.

CLEAR CHANNEL

"Some of the clearest prompt-ings I have ever received have come while being immersed in the scriptures. They are a conduit for revelation. They teach us the language of the Spirit."—Sheri Dew[6]

Some people think that the scriptures are old, outdated, and boring, but that is simply because they don't know how to "liken all scriptures unto *[them]*, that it might be for *[their]* profit and learning (1 Nephi 19:23; emphasis added). The Old Testament is not only about God's dealings with the patriarchs from thousands of years ago, but it is also about God's dealings with us today. The Book of Mormon is not only about Lehi and Nephi and their family, but it is also about us and our family. The Doctrine and Covenants is not only about Joseph Smith and his revelations, but it is also about our problems and will provide us with our personal revelations. President Boyd K. Packer promised: "If [youth] are acquainted with the [scriptures], there is no question—personal or social or political or occupational—that need go unanswered. Therein is contained the fulness of the everlasting gospel. Therein we find principles of truth that will resolve *every confusion* and *every problem* and *every dilemma* that will face the human family or any individual in it."[7]

There are no problems that the scriptures will not give us direction and answers to if we will just search out the doctrines and principles and apply them in our lives. What a blessing!

DO **YOU** FEEL LIKE THE SCRIPTURES RELATE TO YOUR LIFE?

If you answered "Yes," you are in good company. In a 2004 study of 103 seminary students in Utah, those who felt that the scriptures related to them and held answers for their personal life read the scriptures 32.4% more than those who felt the scriptures did not relate to their life.[8]

DESPERATE FOR DIRECTION

By 2011, 444 million cell phones (almost one-third of all phones produced) will have GPS (Global Positioning System) in them to provide detailed directions.[9] Although this technology is convenient, a set of scriptures is much cheaper and never runs out of batteries.

A Promise: You Will Never Perish

Perhaps the most eternally powerful reason why we should make scripture study part of our daily lives is the following promise: Those who listen and obey the word of God, holding fast to it, will overcome the temptations of the adversary and make it to the celestial kingdom. In Nephi's explanation of his father Lehi's dream of the tree of life, he commented about the power of the rod of iron: "And they said unto me: What meaneth the rod of iron which our father saw, that led to the tree?

"And I said unto them that it was the word of God; and whoso would hearken unto the word of God, and would hold fast unto it, *they would never perish;* neither could the *temptations and the fiery darts of the adversary overpower them* unto blindness, to lead them away to destruction" (1 Nephi 15:23–24; emphasis added).

Why is it that those who daily immerse themselves in the scriptures will overcome temptation and "never perish"? Because when we immerse ourselves in the word of God, we are filled with the Spirit of God. Lehi said of his scripture study that "as he read, he was filled with the Spirit of the Lord" (1 Nephi 1:12). The Spirit acts as a shield and a protection against temptation, a strengthening influence against sin.

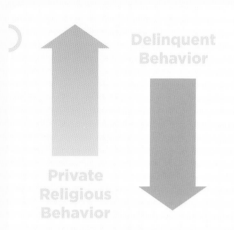

Researchers have found that "private religious behaviors, such as personal prayer, *personal scripture reading,* and fasting"[10] are better at minimizing delinquency than "public" religious behaviors. Stay close to the scriptures!

The Best Washing Machine in the House

"Reading the scriptures is the best washing machine for unclean or uncontrolled thoughts."
—President James E. Faust[11]

In order for these blessings of scripture study to take effect though, we must do more than occasionally glance at our scriptures, nibbling on a passage here or there. We must *"feast* upon the words of Christ" (2 Nephi 32:3; emphasis added).

Which Picture Better Represents Your Scripture Study?

Study the scriptures every day for one week. What differences did you notice spiritually? Did you find deeper insights to meaningful doctrines of the plan of salvation? Were you able to find direction to personal issues in your life? Record your experiences in your journal.

Don't leave the scriptures behind! They will bless our lives in many ways. With Lehi, we say, "Wherefore, it was wisdom in the Lord that we should carry [the scriptures] with us, as we journeyed in the wilderness towards the land of promise" (1 Nephi 5:22).

CELL PHONE VS. THE SCRIPTURES

We wonder what would happen if we treated the scriptures like we treat our cell phone? What if we . . .

- carried them around in our purses or pockets?
- flipped through them several times a day?
- turned back to retrieve them if we forgot them?
- used them to receive messages from the text?
- treated them like we couldn't live without them?
- gave them to kids as gifts?
- used them when we traveled?
- used them in case of an emergency?

And one more thing . . . the scriptures have no dropped calls!

Think of the direction Joseph Smith received because he went to the scriptures! But what if

this →

had been replaced with this →

He probably wouldn't have had the same experience! The direction we need is in the scriptures.

TELL ME ONE MORE TiME!

Why Should I Study My Scriptures Daily?

1. **The scriptures teach us the truths of the plan of salvation that we need to know in order to become like God.**
2. **The scriptures provide us with answers, comfort, and needed direction for any problem we face.**
3. **Those who daily study the word of God will overcome the temptations of the adversary and make it to the celestial kingdom.**

NOW that we have reviewed some of the *principles*, let's answer some of the questions regarding the *practices* connected to studying the scriptures daily:

Why is it so important that I study my scriptures every day?

First, it is much easier to maintain a habit if you do it consistently. Scripture study is no different. Furthermore, because scripture study is an important way to invite the Spirit into our lives, it is something we should do daily. Which day do we want to face without the Spirit to guide and direct us? Also, the more you read, the more you will be able to feel the power that comes from the words of the scriptures. Last, your spirit needs to be fed just like your physical body needs to be fed. What would happen to your body if you only ate once a week?

Why are the scriptures so hard to understand sometimes?

Some of the vocabulary in the scriptures is difficult to understand. The Bible was translated several hundred years ago and certain words that were commonly understood in the 1600s are not so common anymore. The good news is that the more you read the scriptures, the easier it becomes to understand them. Remember, the Holy Ghost knows what the scriptures mean, and he can help you understand. Joseph Smith said when he received the gift of the Holy Ghost, "Our minds being now enlightened, we began to have the scriptures laid open to our understandings,

Cont.

and the true meaning and intention of their more mysterious passages revealed unto us in a manner which we never could attain to previously, nor ever before had thought of" (Joseph Smith—History 1:74). The same can be true for you.

Why is it more important to study the scriptures for a set amount of time instead of a set amount of pages?

There is a difference between "reading" the scriptures and "studying" the scriptures. Nephi said we should "feast" on the scriptures (2 Nephi 32:3), and the Savior said we should, "search" them (John 5:39). Sometimes when we have a set number of pages to cover in our scriptures, we simply end up reading them without thinking, pondering, and praying about their meaning.

Ever read an entire chapter of scripture, closed the book, and couldn't remember what you just read? Us too! That usually is a result of "reading" and not "feasting." Perhaps that is why President Howard W. Hunter said, "There are some who read to a schedule of a number of pages or a set number of chapters each day or week. This may be perfectly justifiable and may be enjoyable if one is reading for pleasure, but it does not constitute meaningful study. *It is better to have a set amount of time to give scriptural study each day than to have a set amount of chapters to read.* Sometimes we find that the study of a single verse will occupy the whole time."[12]

22 Why Should I Pay Tithing?

MISSIONARY MOMENT WITH BONO

What would you say if you asked Bono to pay tithing and he said, "The God I believe in isn't short of cash, mister!" Better read this chapter if you're not even sure why he should pay tithing.

Photo by George Pimentel/Getty Images

At a concert on December 20, 1987, Bono, lead singer of the famous rock band U2, voiced a concern he had about paying money to churches. During a song, he said to the crowd, "Well, the God I believe in isn't short of cash, mister!"[1] And you know what . . . Bono's right! The great God of heaven who created the entire universe does not *need* our money. Since God commands and controls all the elements of the earth and since God knows all, he could simply reveal to the prophet where a number of mineral or oil deposits were located and have the Church buy up the land and ka-ching! The Church would have all the money it needs. No, God isn't short of cash. So why are we asked to pay tithing? Perhaps a Church history story will help us understand.

When Hyrum Smith's widowed and poor wife Mary Fielding Smith came to the tithing house to pay tithing despite her poverty, William Thompson, a tithing clerk, told her she didn't need to pay. Mary quickly answered, "William, you ought to be ashamed of yourself. Would you deny me a blessing? If I did not pay my tithing I should expect the Lord to withhold His blessings from me. I pay my tithing, not only because it is a law of God, but because I expect a blessing by doing it."[2] Tithing is not for God, it is for us.

Let's take a look at why we should pay a full tithe and the blessings we can expect from our obedience.

The Windows of Heaven

The first reason why we should pay tithing is that the Lord will bless us both temporally and spiritually if we do. Simply stated: Blessings come to those who pay tithing. The Lord himself promised, "Bring ye all the tithes into the storehouse, that there may be meat in mine house, and prove me now herewith, saith the Lord of hosts, if I will not open you the windows of heaven, and pour you out a blessing, that there shall not be room enough to receive it.

The Lord promises more blessings than we can receive. I don't know about you, but we've got a lot of room for blessings, so those must be some pretty *big blessings!*

"And I will rebuke the devourer for your sakes, and he shall not destroy the fruits of your ground; neither shall your vine cast her fruit before the time in the field, saith the Lord of hosts" (Malachi 3:10–11).

President Gordon B. Hinckley taught that those who pay their tithing would "always have food on their tables, they would always have clothing on their backs, and they would always have a roof over their heads."[4] There are many the world over who want nothing more than those simple blessings promised by a prophet.

President Spencer W. Kimball listed some of the specific temporal blessings that can come from paying tithing: "The Lord has promised that he will open the windows of heaven when we are obedient to his law [of tithing]. He can give us better salaries, he can give us more judgment in the spending of our money. He can give us better health, he can give us greater understanding so that we can get better positions. He can help us so that we can do the things we want to do."[5]

STUDIES SHOW THAT CHARITABLE GIVING MAKES YOU WEALTHIER

Giving to charity can make you wealthier. "Imagine you have two families that are exactly the same. . . . The only difference is that the first family gives $100 more to charity than the second family. It turns out that first family will earn, on average, $375 more than the nongiving family."[3] If giving to any charity produces this result, giving to the Lord will do even more!

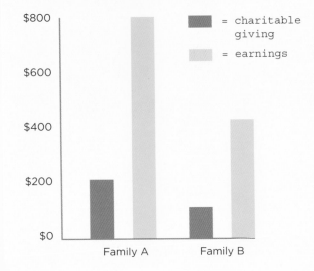

Paying tithing qualifies you for more than just temporal blessings. President Gordon B. Hinckley taught: "The Lord will open the windows of heaven according to our need, and not according to our greed. If we are paying tithing to get rich, we are doing it for the wrong reason. The basic purpose for tithing is to provide the Church with the means needed to carry on the Lord's work. The blessing to the giver is an ancillary return, and that blessing may not be always in the form of *financial or material benefit*."[6]

Elder Robert D. Hales explained, "Like the outward physical ordinances of baptism and the sacrament, the commandment to pay tithing requires temporal sacrifice, which ultimately yields great *spiritual* blessings."[7]

Two young men were talking about an upcoming ward trip to the temple to perform baptisms for the dead.

"I'm not going," Jeff said.

"Why not?" Tom asked.

"Because I haven't paid my tithing."

Jeff let a few dollars of unpaid tithing keep him from going to the temple. Missing those spiritual blessings was definitely not worth the money.

One of the spiritual blessings that we can receive from paying tithing is the blessing of increased faith. As President Gordon B. Hinckley taught, "Tithing is not a matter of money so much as it is a matter of faith."[8] It takes faith to believe that we will be blessed for paying tithing—especially if money is tight. But paying tithing allows us the opportunity to have our faith strengthened, and to be blessed both temporally and spiritually.

LAME ROBBERS

Have you heard the stories about robbers who made simple mistakes and were caught? Here are some of our favorites:

- A man was arrested for trying to hold up a bank without a weapon. He used his thumb and finger to simulate a gun—but he forgot to keep his hand in his pocket. Oops!

- A man walked into a store, pulled out a gun, and said he was robbing the place. Then he pulled a trash bag mask over his face, but he'd forgotten to cut eyeholes in the mask.

- A man walked into a store, put a $20 bill on the counter and asked for change. When the clerk opened the cash drawer, the man pulled a gun and demanded all the cash in the register. The man took it and fled—leaving the $20 bill on the counter. The total amount of cash he got from the drawer? Fifteen dollars.[9]

These examples of theft are pretty lame, and it's easy to laugh at these robbers. But the Lord has told us that not paying tithing is the same as robbing him (see Malachi 3:8; 3 Nephi 24:8). Any excuse we make for not paying our tithing will surely sound just as lame to the Lord.

What's in Your Heart?

One of the great spiritual conflicts we face is between loving the material things of the world and loving the Lord. The first commandment to come down from Mount Sinai was "Thou shalt have no other gods before me" (Exodus 20:3). This gives us another reason why we should pay tithing—because it shows the Lord we love him more than we love the worldly possessions that our tithing money could buy.

There is a common saying that "Nothing is closer to a man's heart than his wallet." In many ways, that is true . . . and tithing tests what truly is in our heart. President Joseph F. Smith said, "By this principle [of tithing] the loyalty of the people of this Church shall be put to the test. By this principle it shall be known who is for the kingdom of God and who is against it."[10]

Do you remember the story of the rich young man from the New Testament? An apparently very righteous, and also very rich, young man approached the Savior to ask an important question: What must the young man do to obtain eternal life? The Savior answered: "Thou knowest the commandments, Do not commit adultery, Do not kill, Do not steal, Do not bear false witness, Defraud not, Honour thy father and mother.

"And he answered and said unto him, Master, all these have I observed from my youth.

"Then Jesus beholding him loved him, and said unto him, One thing thou lackest: go thy way, sell whatsoever thou hast, and give to the poor, and thou shalt have treasure in heaven: and come, take up the cross, and follow me.

GIVING IN THE UNITED STATES

In a 2002 study of American generosity, the average American gave 2.3% ($1,065) of their income to charitable organizations. Utah led the nation in charitable donations with an average of 5.1% per person ($2,109), almost double the national average.[11]

"And he was sad at that saying, and went away grieved: for he had great possessions.

"And Jesus looked round about, and saith unto his disciples, How hardly shall they that have riches enter into the kingdom of God!

"And the disciples were astonished at his words. But Jesus answereth again, and saith unto them, Children, how hard is it for them that trust in riches to enter into the kingdom of God!" (Mark 10:19–24).

Truly, for those who trust in riches and love them more than they love God, it will be hard for them to enter the kingdom of God. Paying tithing is one way to show God that we love him and his kingdom more than any earthly possessions that money can buy (see Jacob 2:18).

Fire Insurance

Another famous promise regarding paying tithing is found in Doctrine and Covenants 64:23, which states, "Behold, now it is called today until the coming of the Son of Man, and verily it is a day of sacrifice, and a day for the tithing of my people; for he that is tithed shall not be burned at his coming."

Some people refer to this promise as "fire insurance" because of the statement that if we pay our tithing, we won't be burned at the Second Coming. But tithing is more than an insurance policy. It is chance to change the way we live. It is our obedience to the commandments (including the commandment to pay tithing) that will prevent us from burning in the last days.

For example, if we pay a full tithe we will be active in the Church. President Thomas S. Monson said, "I will give you a formula which will guarantee to a large extent your success in [always being active in the Church]. It is simple. It consists of just three words: Pay your tithing."[13]

Put Your MONEY Where Your MOUTH Is

"I want to say this much to those who profess to be Latter-day Saints—if we neglect our tithes and offerings we will receive the chastening hand of the Lord. We may just as well count on this first as last. If we neglect to pay our tithes and offerings we will neglect other things and this will grow upon us until the spirit of the Gospel is entirely gone from us, and we are in the dark, and know not whither we are going."—President Brigham Young[12]

On the other hand, many who do not pay tithing fall into inactivity. President Gordon B. Hinckley taught, "We lose so very many converts to inactivity. I am confident they will not remain active in the Church unless they pay an honest tithing."[14]

To Build the Kingdom of God . . . Literally

One of most important reasons why we should pay our tithing is that we can directly contribute today to building up God's kingdom here on the earth. Anthony once used a piano to teach this principle to one of his classes. He says, "Before class started, I moved the piano across the room from where it was usually positioned. On the board I wrote, 'The piano shall roll forth to fulfill its destined position!' I told the class to watch as that prophecy was fulfilled. And, as I suspected, they all sat there and just looked at the piano.

"I said out loud, 'Roll forth, piano! Fulfill your destiny!' Once again, nothing.

"Finally, after a minute or two of awkward silence, a few students stood up and pushed the piano back where it belonged. The students learned the lesson: Pianos, just like the kingdom of God on earth, don't move forward and fulfill their destinies by themselves."

In a similar way, the Church doesn't just magically move forward. It takes work, and the reality is that work takes money. It takes money to build temples and churches and seminary buildings. It takes money to pay for things like air conditioning, computers, paper, markers, and the thousand other things that we use and need in the Church. Think about it—your tithing dollar could have been used to help purchase the microphone at the Conference Center (someone's dollar did)!

When you pay your tithing you "push the piano" (so to speak) and literally move the work of the Lord forward through your contribution.

WHAT IS TITHING USED FOR ANYWAY?

- "Constructing temples, chapels, and other buildings.
- "Providing operating funds for the Church.
- "Funding the missionary program.
- "Preparing materials used in Church classes and organizations.
- "Performing temple work, family history, and many other important Church functions.
- "Education [such as seminary and institute and church schools and universities].

"Tithing does not pay local Church leaders. They serve without receiving payment of any kind other than the spiritual blessings from providing service."[15]

President Gordon B. Hinckley told the story of a young woman in Brazil who faced a difficult decision. She was working and attending school at the same time. To complete her school curriculum, she needed to take a series of tests, which were very expensive. If she didn't pay for them, she would forfeit the entire year of school she had just completed. When she received her paycheck, she did not have enough money to cover her basic living expenses, pay tithing, *and* pay for the tests. Acting on faith, she paid her tithing first. Within a few days, she learned that her employer had decided to pay for all of her education—which not only paid for the upcoming tests, but also the tuition for the rest of her college classes.[16] This young woman, like many others who pay tithing faithfully, was richly blessed for her obedience.

DO TRY THIS AT HOME!

If you do not already pay a full tithe, start doing so today and watch for the blessings the Lord has promised to those who faithfully pay their tithing.

WOULD PAYING TITHING MAKE ME HAPPIER?

Givers

Non-givers

"People who give some amount of money every year are 43% more likely than nongivers to say they're very happy people."—Arthur C. Brooks[17]

TELL ME ONE MORE TiME!

Why Should I Pay Tithing?

1. **Paying tithing qualifies us for increased blessings, both temporally and spiritually.**
2. **Through the payment of tithes we are able to show the Lord that we love him more than we love the worldly possessions that our tithing money could buy.**
3. **Our obedience to paying our tithing is "fire insurance" for the Second Coming and will help us remain active in the Church.**

4. Through the payment of tithes, we contribute to the literal building up of God's king-dom by helping to pay for Church buildings and materials and other expenses to help move the Church forward.

NOW that we have reviewed some of the *principles*, let's answer some of the questions regarding the *practices* connected to tithing:

Why does God need me to pay tithing if he can just create gold or money?

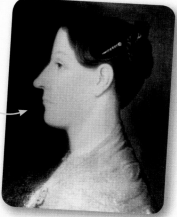

You don't pay tithing because God needs it—you pay tithing because *you* need it. Reread the story about Mary Fielding Smith from the beginning of this chapter for a review of this principle.

Why do some people who pay tithing still not have a lot of money?

Paying tithing does not mean that you will automatically become wealthy. Specific blessings have been promised to those who pay a full tithe: food, clothing, and shelter. But big-screen plasma televisions are not neces-sarily part of the promised blessing. Also, many of the blessings we receive from paying tithing are spiritual in nature. However, there is no doubt that any person is better off paying tithing than they would be without paying tithing.

Why can't I enter the temple if I don't pay tithing?

Elder Robert D. Hales answered this question when he said, "The strict observance of the law of tithing not only qualifies us to receive the higher, saving ordinances of the temple, it allows us to receive them on behalf of our ancestors. When asked whether members of the Church could be baptized for the dead if they had not paid their tithing, President John Taylor, then of the Quo-rum of the Twelve, answered: 'A man who has not paid his tithing is unfit to be baptized for his dead. . . . If a man has not faith enough to attend to these little things, he has not faith enough to save himself and his friends.' Tithing develops and tests our faith. By sacrificing to the Lord what we may think we need or want for ourselves, we learn to rely on Him. *Our faith in Him makes it possible to keep temple covenants and receive eternal temple blessing.*"[18]

"Our lime still lies there."

Lorenzo Hill Hatch lived near Nauvoo in the 1840s. He was in the process of building a home and was laying a foundation of limestone and wood when he and his brother received word from Church leaders to evacuate the area. Mobs had resumed their persecution of the Saints. Of the experience, Lorenzo simply said, "Our lime still lies there," meaning that when the call from Church leaders came, he obeyed immediately, leaving behind the materials for the foundation of his house. Lorenzo's record of his experience has influenced many of his descendants to leave behind material things to follow the counsel of the prophet.[1]

Prophets have long taught that members of the Church should record their lives in a journal. The Lord himself said, "For I command all men . . . that they shall write the words which I speak unto them" (2 Nephi 29:11) and to "write the things which ye have seen and heard" (3 Nephi 27:23).

President Wilford Woodruff's journal was more than 7,000 pages long! Many of Joseph Smith's teachings were recorded by President Woodruff, and his journal is the only reason we have them.

Your Journals Will Help You Recognize God's Blessings

One reason why we should keep a journal is because when we remember the things that the Lord has done for us, gratitude and contentment fill our hearts and we recognize more easily God's blessings to us in our daily lives. President Henry B. Eyring once taught: "How can you and I remember, always, the goodness of God . . . ?

". . . You could have an experience with the gift of the Holy Ghost today. . . . As you write an entry in your book of remembrance . . . ask yourself, 'How did God bless me today?' If you do that long enough and with faith, you will find yourself remembering blessings. And sometimes, you will have gifts brought to your mind which you failed to notice during the day, but which you will then know were a touch of God's hand in your life."[2]

When President Spencer W. Kimball was called to be President of the Church, his records included 33 journals!

President Spencer W. Kimball, a prolific journal writer himself, taught, "Keeping journals reminds us of blessings. Those who keep a book of remembrance are more likely to keep the Lord in remembrance in their daily lives. Journals are a way of counting our blessings."[3]

Journals and Inspiration

Another reason why we should keep a journal has to do with the process of revelation. The Lord inspires us through his Spirit, and if we will write down those heaven-sent impressions, he will give us more inspiration. That is why it is critical for us to take notes during gospel classes and talks, during our scripture study, and during times of quiet pondering after prayer.

Elder Richard G. Scott shared the following experience he had with this principle: "I visited [a] Sunday school class. . . .

"In that environment, strong impressions began to flow. . . . I wrote them down. . . .

". . . I continued to write the feelings that flooded into my mind and heart as accurately and as faithfully as possible. After each powerful impression was recorded, I pondered the feelings I had received to determine if I had accurately expressed them in writing.

". . . I prayed, reviewing with the Lord what I thought I had been taught by the Spirit. When a feeling of peace and serenity confirmed what I had sought, I thanked Him for the guidance given. I was then impressed to ask if there was yet more that I could be given to understand. I received further impressions. . . . When that last, most sacred experience was concluded, I had received some of the most precious, specific personal direction one could ever hope to obtain in this life."[4]

To receive an additional outpouring of the Spirit as we record what we learn is another reason why we should keep a journal.

JOURNAL WRITING IS GOOD FOR YOUR HEALTH

In one study, researchers found that those who wrote daily about good experiences increased their positive outlook on life and decreased their chances for illness.[5] Amazing, but true!

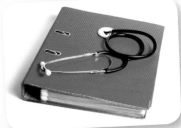

Your Journals Will Help Others

Some might say, "I've never done anything great or inspiring so there is no need for me to keep a journal."

To them President Kimball said, "People often use the excuse that their lives are uneventful and nobody would be interested in what they have done. But I promise you that if you will keep your journals and records, they will indeed be a source of great inspiration to your families, to your children, your grandchildren, and others, on through the generations. Each of us is important to those who are near and dear to us—and as our posterity reads of our life's experiences, they, too, will come to know and love us."[6]

Did you notice the promises in that paragraph? You life will be extremely important to your children and grandchildren—perhaps even to other people you will not even meet in this lifetime. For example, your descendants might want to know how you felt when a new prophet was called, how you dealt with trials and temptation, and how you gained your testimony. They will want to know what you learned from your scripture study, how God answered your prayers, and hundreds of other things about you. Don't rob your children and grandchildren of the chance to get to know you! It's possible that your journal may save the spiritual lives of some of your descendants.

WRITTEN PROOF: SHE HAD THE HOTS FOR ME IN 7TH GRADE

Anthony Says:

Luckily for me, my wife, Cindy, faithfully kept a journal when she was a teenager. We grew up near each other and attended junior high and high school together. Although we never dated during that time, I teased her that she had a crush on me. One day after we were married, we were thumbing through her journals. To our surprise, we found this random entry on page 53 of her seventh-grade journal:

> Oct 23, 1989 Monday
>
> Today was fun!! We had an assembly on "Drug Free Youth" it was good this week is on Critical issues! Anyways I like Tony Sweat hes is really nice! Also tonight for family night we wrote about Grandparents.

There it was in permanent ink: "I like Tony Sweat"! Irrefutable, written proof! Even though my wife might not be thankful she kept *that* detailed of a journal, I sure am.

BE YOUR REAL SELF

When keeping your journal, tell the truth about your life and focus on the positive, but don't embellish your stories or edit out your mistakes because you are afraid of other people thinking you aren't perfect. Nephi was told to make a "full account" of his history (1 Nephi 9:2). The books of First and Second Chronicles in the Old Testament are primarily copies of First and Second Samuel. One main difference is that the writer of Chronicles decided to edit out the mistakes made by the Israelites, like King David's murder of Uriah and King Solomon's immorality and apostasy.

How grateful we are that we can learn from David's mistakes by reading about them in Samuel! Sometimes it is beneficial to know that people we admire weren't perfect either and made mistakes. It gives us hope that we can overcome our own imperfections. And sometimes learning about their mistakes helps teach us what *not* to do.

So when you keep your journal, be sure to focus on your real self—imperfections and all.

President Henry B. Eyring talked about how he had had several small experiences that testified to him of how the Lord loved him and cared about his family. Then a prompting from the Lord came to him: "I'm not giving you these experiences for yourself. Write them down."

President Eyring followed that counsel and for years afterward wrote daily about how he had seen the hand of the Lord in his life that day. Years later, his children read those experiences and were greatly blessed.[7]

The Lord is giving us small and simple experiences right now that will bless us and our descendants if we choose to record them. Will you?

DO TRY THIS AT HOME!

Take the twenty-day journal writing challenge. For the next twenty days write in a notebook, a journal, or on your computer. If you don't know what to write, start by listing two or three blessings that you are grateful for, or an experience you had that day that showed the Lord's hand in your life.

BOYS: TOO TOUGH FOR A "DIARY"?

Attention, boys! Do you not keep a journal or a diary because it seems too feminine for your masculine nature? If so, may we offer a suggestion? Title your journal "The Manly Book of Experiences." You can even bind it in rawhide or dried bark. There, that will toughen it up. No more excuses, boys, you need to keep a record too.

THE MANLY BOOK OF EXPERIENCES

TELL ME ONE MORE TIME!

Why Should I Write in a Journal?

1. **Keeping a journal will help us recognize God's blessings.**
2. **The more we record our impressions, the more the Spirit will teach us.**
3. **Keeping a journal will help others who read it.**

Cont.

NOW that we have reviewed some of the *principles*, let's answer some of the questions regarding the *practices* connected to journals:

Why shouldn't I just write down the "good" stuff in my journal?

When you write, be sure to write down the true challenges and experiences you have in your real life—both good and bad. Sometimes reading through someone's struggles helps you admire them more because you see how they overcame challenges. And it can be helpful for you to look back through your journal to see how the Lord blessed you during difficult times.

Why should I take notes during Church meetings and scripture study?

Elder David A. Bednar said, "Recording what we learn and writing about what we think and feel as we study the scriptures helps us to revisit the same spirit that brought the initial insight or revelation and invites even greater understanding than was originally received. Recording our learnings and writing about our thoughts and feelings is another form of pondering and of always remembering him and is an invitation to the Holy Ghost for continued instruction."[8]

Why can't I have my blog, scrapbook, or video recordings count as my journal?

Easy—you can!

24 ^{ch} Why Should I Be Grateful?

Do you have a pet peeve? Something that really bugs you? Maybe it's people who have private conversations on their cell phone in public places, or people not changing the toilet paper roll when it is empty, or the dreaded "bed-head."

Do you think the Lord has pet peeves? We think he might. Doctrine and Covenants 59:21 says, "And in nothing doth man offend God, or against none is his wrath kindled, save those who confess not his hand in all things, and obey not his commandments."

Two things that offend God the most, that really kindle his wrath, are ingratitude ("confess[ing] not his hand") and disobedience. That's bad news for some members of the Church because Joseph Smith said that "one of the greatest sins of which the Latter-day Saints would be guilty is the sin of ingratitude."[1] Let's learn why we should be grateful so that we don't offend God and kindle his wrath.

REASON NUMBER 3,243 TO BE GRATEFUL

You are not being chased by a lion. (Somebody, somewhere in the world, probably is!)

Counting Your Blessings—It's More Than Just a Song

You've heard the hymn "Count Your Blessings," but did you know studies show that literally counting your blessings increases your emotional health? In a scientific experiment, researchers had three different groups of people: one group wrote for twenty minutes each day about things they were grateful for; the second group wrote about things they were angry about; and the third group did nothing.[2] Guess which group was happiest? If you guessed the

gratitude   happiness

first group, congratulations, keep reading this chapter. If not, go straight to the telestial kingdom and be grateful you're not going to outer darkness. (Just kidding, you can keep reading too).

DO TRY THIS AT HOME!

Write a list of 100 things you are thankful for. Too many? Then try writing down:

- 10 living people you are grateful for.
- 10 people who have died you are grateful for.
- 10 physical abilities you are grateful for.
- 10 material possessions you are grateful for.
- 10 things about nature you are grateful for.
- 10 things about today you are grateful for.
- 10 places on earth you are grateful for.
- 10 modern-day inventions you are grateful for.
- 10 foods you are grateful for.
- 10 things about the gospel you are grateful for.

Guess what? A list of 100 blessings doesn't even begin to scratch the surface of all the things God has given you that you could possibly be grateful for.

Count 100 of Your Blessings

Elder Joseph B. Wirthlin said gratitude "is a quality I have found in every happy person I know."[3] Think about that. Do you know any happy person who is *not* grateful?

He might be lacking some gratitude!

Being Grateful Leads to More Blessings

There are many blessings that come from being grateful for the good things we enjoy. *For the Strength of Youth* says, "Live with a spirit of thanksgiving and you will have greater happiness and satisfaction in life."[4]

Elder Wirthlin also taught that gratitude will make you "more likable and more at peace."[5]

The Lord himself promised, "He who receiveth all things with thankfulness shall be made glorious; and the things of this earth

REASON NUMBER 6,923 TO BE GRATEFUL

Some time in your life you have tasted chocolate. (Millions of people never have.)

shall be added unto him, even an hundred fold, yea, more" (D&C 78:19).

Elder Marvin J. Ashton shared a specific blessing that can come from gratitude. He taught, "The best way to get your family members active in the Church or to become members is to tell them 'thank you' for all they do to support you and tell them how much you love them."[6] This promise is especially helpful to those who have family members who are not members of the Church.

Another blessing of gratitude is that it increases our ability to see. For example, what do you see in the picture below?

Chances are you probably noticed the dark flowers first. That's normal because, as Elder Joseph B. Wirthlin said, "Our minds have a marvelous capacity to notice the unusual."[8] But there is a problem! Elder Wirthlin pointed out that unfortunately, "The opposite is true as well, the more often we see the things around us—even the beautiful and wonderful things—the more they become invisible to us.

"That is why we often take for granted the beauty of this world—the flowers, the trees, the birds, the clouds—even those we love.

". . . Because we see things so often, we see them less and less."[9]

Did you notice the blue sky in the picture? The beautiful clouds? The mountains in the background? The dozens of flowers that *weren't* discolored? There are so many beautiful things to be grateful for, and as we practice being grateful, we will notice them more and more.

Consequences of Ingratitude

It seems obvious, but when we are grateful, we avoid the consequences of ingratitude. When people are not grateful they tend to complain, and that isn't good for anyone. A story from the Old Testament illustrates this point. The Israelites were wandering in the wilderness and even though the Lord had delivered them from slavery and given them manna to eat, they were not grateful. Notice what happens: "And when the people complained, it displeased the Lord: and the Lord heard it" (Numbers 11:1).

So the Lord hears when we complain, and he does not like it. As a result of Israelites' complaining, a fire swept through the camp and many people died. Throughout the scriptures we see examples of people forgetting to thank the Lord and choosing to complain instead. Often, as in the case of the Israelites, the Lord sends the people trials so that they will humble themselves and remember him. Remember, ingratitude offends God (see D&C 59:21), and while the Lord may not cause a fire to come down on those who complain, ingratitude and complaining have plenty of other consequences.

I'D BE HAPPY IF . . .

Some people have a hard time being grateful for what they have. They say, "I'd be happy *if only I had* (fill in the blank—a new car, an iPod, good hair, etc.). Or like the girl who says, "When I'm 16, I'll be happy." Then she turns 16 and says, "When guys start asking me out, I'll be happy." And then guys start asking her out and she says, "When I get a boyfriend, I'll be happy." Then she gets a boyfriend and says, "When I can *break up* with my boyfriend, I'll be happy," and so it goes. If we say, "I'll be happy when . . . " the happiness may never come. But when we are grateful, we invite happiness to come into our lives immediately.

NIKE OR ADIDAS? NEITHER, THEY'RE GOODYEAR

Some people aren't happy because they don't have the latest style of shoes. Let's be grateful we *have* shoes.

Anthony Says:

When I was in Bolivia, I was amazed to see that the Andean Indians cut up leftover tires and turned them into sandals. These Bolivians were so grateful for "tire sandals"! One man even told me they were guaranteed for 50,000 miles.☺

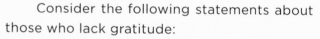

Consider the following statements about those who lack gratitude:

"Where there is an absence [of gratitude], there is often sadness, resentment, and futility."—Elder Joseph B. Wirthlin[11]

"Many a family, many a marriage is broken because of a lack of appreciation. . . . Too many times I have heard people say, 'My marriage was terminated primarily because my husband (or wife) didn't appreciate anything I ever did for him. No matter what I did, there was no thanks!'"—Elder Marvin J. Ashton[12]

"Absence of gratitude is the mark of the narrow, uneducated mind. It bespeaks a lack of knowledge and the ignorance of self-sufficiency. It expresses itself in ugly egotism and frequently in wanton mischief. . . .

"Without [gratitude], there is arrogance and evil."—Elder Gordon B. Hinckley[13]

The good news is we can avoid the consequences of ingratitude because gratitude is entirely in our control. We might not be able to make the varsity team, or be elected student body president. We might not get asked out on dates, or have the biggest muscles (we speak from personal experience). But we can control whether we have a grateful attitude or not.

REASON NUMBER 10,003 TO BE GRATEFUL

Indoor plumbing!
(Need we say more?)

PERSPECTIVE

Some get mad when they look at their plate
And only see food which taste they really hate
Others are thankful and ever so nice
Even if their plate contains just a handful of rice.
Some complain their car is too slow
Saying "I've got things to do, I've got to go, go, go!"
Others are grateful for a bicycle that is old
They treasure it like precious gold.

TELL ME ONE MORE TIME!

Why Should I Be Grateful?

1. **When we *aren't* grateful, we offend God.**
2. **Counting our blessings helps us be more positive and happy.**
3. **Being grateful brings additional blessings.**
4. **When we complain and are ungrateful, the Lord may give us additional problems to help us recognize the blessings we do have. Other negative consequences also come with ingratitude.**

NOW that we have reviewed some of the *principles*, let's answer some of the questions regarding the *practices* connected to gratitude:

Cont.

Why should we thank God for blessings before asking for more blessings?

When you stop to think about it, Heavenly Father has already given us everything. In a way it can seem greedy to ask for more without considering all that we already have. Expressing our gratitude in prayer is an important part of truly acknowledging our thanks to God for the blessings we have received before we ask for more.

Why should I be grateful if there is so much I don't have?

You know the question: "Is the glass half-full or half-empty?" Yes there are probably lots of things that you do not have—but what about all the things that you *do* have? One of the keys to a successful life is to learn to focus less on what you want and more on being grateful for what you have.

Why is saying "thank you" a sign of an educated person?

As part of his classic six "B's" talk, President Gordon B. Hinckley said, "Be grateful. . . . The habit of saying thank you is the mark of an educated man or woman."[14] Why would he say that? Because when we thank others, we recognize and understand our dependence on others. Think of the food you eat . . . someone grew it. Think of the clothes you wear . . . someone made them. Think of the house you live in . . . someone built it and paid for it. Think of everything you know . . . someone taught it to you at some point. All we have and all we are is partly dependent on others. That is why President Hinckley said, "Express appreciation to everyone who does you a favor or assists you in any way"[15] because it shows your true awareness of the world around you.

25^{ch} Why Should I Honor My Parents?

We'll give you **5,475** reasons why we should honor our parents. Not sure what they are? Here's a hint:

That's right—on average your parents changed your diapers **5,475** times. Do you think that was enjoyable for them? Do you think they were excited to change your diapers? Chances are, you have never even thanked them! Those diapers alone ought to be reason enough to say, "Yes, Mom," and do the dishes whenever she asks.

As compelling a reason as diapers may be, there are even better reasons why we should honor our parents.

A Commandment with a Promise

One reason why we should honor our father and mother is that we are promised that we will live longer if we do. The apostle Paul wrote, "Honour thy father and mother; (which is the first commandment with promise)" (Ephesians 6:2). What does that mean, "the first commandment with promise"?

Of the Ten Commandments that God gave to Moses, only one came with a stated promise: the fifth commandment, which says, "Honour thy father and thy mother: *that thy days may be long* upon the land which the Lord thy God giveth thee" (Exodus 20:12; emphasis added). The scriptures don't spell out exactly how it is that your days will be long, but common sense dictates that those who honor their parents will probably live longer than if they didn't.

Parents Say	Honoring Them	Not Honoring Them	Choice that will help you live longer
Don't touch the stove	Don't do it	Give that burner a big kiss!	Honoring parents
Look both ways before crossing the street	Look twice	Run across the street without looking	Honoring parents
Obey traffic laws	Drive the speed limit	Burn rubber, baby!	Honoring parents
Don't do dumb stuff	Use wisdom	Jump off a second-story roof	Honoring parents

Elder Russell M. Nelson shared the following experience that shows one example of how honoring parents could have led to a longer life: "Several years ago, I was invited to give an important lecture at a medical school in New York City. The night before the lecture, Sister Nelson and I were invited to dinner at the home of our host professor. There he proudly introduced us to an honor medical student—his beautiful daughter.

"Some weeks later, that professor telephoned me in an obvious state of grief. I asked, 'What is the matter?'

"'Remember our daughter whom you met at our home?'

"'Of course,' I replied. 'I'll never forget such a stunning young lady.'

"Then her father sobbed and said, 'Last night she was killed in an automobile accident!' Trying to gain composure, he continued: 'She asked permission to go to a dance with a certain young man. I didn't have a good feeling about it. I told her so and asked her not to go. She asked, "Why?" I simply told her that I was uneasy. She had always been an obedient daughter, but she said that if I could not give her a good reason to decline, she wanted to go. And so she did. At the dance, alcoholic beverages were served. Her escort drank a bit—we don't know how much. While returning home, he was driving too fast, missed a turn, and careened through a guardrail into a reservoir below. They were both submerged and taken to their death.' . . .

"This experience will not have been in vain if others can listen and learn from it. Children, honor your parents."[2]

By the Numbers: What Have Your Parents Done for You?

200,000. That's the number of dollars the U.S. Department of Agriculture estimates it costs to raise you.[1] With that kind of money, your parents could have bought a condo on the beach, 200 plasma TVs, 10,000 DVDs, or 400,000 bags of candy—but they got you instead!

Besides a longer life, other important blessings come to those who honor their parents. Speaking of this commandment, President Gordon B. Hinckley said, "I think it is such a great commandment from the Lord. If it were only observed more widely, there would be far less misery in the homes of the people. Instead of backbiting, accusation, argument, there would be appreciation and respect and quiet love."[3]

HONOR

The word "honor" means much more than to just "obey" our parents. Think about the word "honor" in the following contexts and how they apply to honoring our parents:

If you were told to *honor* the flag, what would you do?

What does it mean to *honor* a promise?

If you were told to *honor* someone in a speech, what would you say about them?

"Honor thy father and mother" also implies respect, reverence, honesty, and bringing praise to them.

The Savior said, "The works which ye have seen me do that shall ye also do" (3 Nephi 27:21). In other words, the Savior has invited us to follow his example.

The Savior gave us the ultimate example of honoring his parents as he hung on the cross. Think of the excruciating pain the Savior must have felt. The previous twenty-four hours had been torture and misery and now he was suffering one of the cruelest deaths possible. Yet even still, he honored his mother. The scriptures record, "Now there stood by the cross of Jesus his mother. . . . When Jesus therefore saw his mother, and [John, the Apostle], he saith unto his mother, Woman, behold thy son! Then saith he to the disciple, Behold thy mother! And from that hour [John] took her unto his own home" (John 19:25–27).

Even in that moment of supreme agony, Jesus was concerned about what would happen to his mother after he died. He showed honor to her by making sure her needs were met.

HONORING YOUR PARENTS

"There come thundering to our ears the words from Mount Sinai: 'Honour thy father and thy mother.' . . .

"How do you honor your parents? I like the words of William Shakespeare: 'They do not love that do not show their love.' There are countless ways in which you can show true love to your mothers and your fathers. You can obey them and follow their teachings. . . .

"Be honest with your mother and your father. One reflection of such honesty with parents is to communicate with them. Avoid the silent treatment. . . . If you are [late], make a telephone call. . . .

"Don't wait . . . before you say, 'I love you, Mother; I love you, Father.' Now is the time to think and the time to thank. I trust you will do both. You have a heritage; honor it."—President Thomas S. Monson[4]

2,920 hours of sleep per year

2,320 hours of sleep per year

Before you were born   After you were born

Respect and Love

No matter how you look at it, our parents have made untold, uncounted sacrifices for us. Even if they aren't perfect parents, they are probably doing the best they can. The least we can do is honor them for all they have done for us by treating them with the kindness and obedience, respect and love they deserve.

Elder M. Russell Ballard taught, "You do not have the right ever to be disrespectful to your mother or your father. Period. If you haven't had that taught to you before, write it in your journal and in your minds and hearts right now. Write down that I said you do not have the right to be ugly, to raise your voice, to slam doors, to scream or holler within the walls of your own home. Young people, you do have the right to be heard. If you are having difficulty getting your mother and your father to listen to you, in a calm manner just ask: 'Mom and Dad, I've got a different feeling about a matter. Can we set a time to talk about it?'"[5]

DO TRY THIS AT HOME!

The next time your parents ask you to do something, say, "Yes! I will do it right away." (And then do it!)

WHAT ABOUT SIBLINGS?

Some might wonder, do I have to be nice to my siblings too? In a word—yes! Why? President Ezra Taft Benson said, "Your most important friendships should be with your own brothers and sisters and with your father and mother."[6] You might find this hard to believe, but trust us—as time goes on, the friendships that will matter the most to you are the ones you have with your parents and siblings. Thirty years from now they will be the people you most likely talk to on a consistent basis, not your junior high and high school friends. Family relationships are the ones that have been (or can someday be) bound together in the temple for eternity.

TELL ME ONE MORE TIME!

Why Should I Honor My Parents?

1. **Honoring your parents is the first commandment with a stated promise—a longer life.**
2. **The Savior set the example for us of honoring parents.**
3. **Our parents have changed diapers, made meals, lost sleep, and done countless other things for us, the least we can do is honor them by showing kindness and obedience.**

NOW that we have reviewed some of the *principles*, let's answer some of the questions regarding the *practices* connected to honoring our parents:

Why shouldn't I talk back to my parents?

We already gave you 5,475 reasons why. If that's not enough, see the quote by Elder Ballard on page 164.

Why is honoring my parents more than simply obeying them?

The commandment from the Lord is to *honor* our parents—which includes obedience. But as President Ezra Taft Benson said, "To honor and respect our parents means . . . that we love and appreciate them and are concerned about their happiness. . . . We treat them with courtesy. . . . We seek to understand their point of view. Certainly obedience to parents' righteous desires and wishes is a part of honoring."[7]

Why should I listen to my parents even if I think they are wrong?

This is a tough question. After reading this chapter, what do you think the answer is? Send us your response and read other answers from teens at http://ldswhy.com.

26 ch Why Is It So Important I Gain an Education?

What would you think if you received this offer in the mail?

Successful Couch Potato shows you how to . . .

Make Big Money sitting on your couch watching T. V. doing "mindless" work!

Tempting, right? After all, who doesn't want to make "big money" while watching TV? But seriously—do you really believe you'll get rich doing "mindless" work? The fact is, success in life doesn't usually go to those who are lazy or uneducated; it goes to those who set worthwhile goals and work hard to achieve them.

Intelligence and the Resurrection

One of the main reasons why getting a good education is so important is rooted in the plan of salvation: God wants us to become like him . . . and he knows everything. Nephi's brother Jacob taught us, "[God] knoweth *all* things, and there is not anything save he knows it" (2 Nephi 9:20; emphasis added). Can you imagine a god who doesn't know science or history? A creator who doesn't grasp human anatomy? Can you envision a king and ruler of the universe who doesn't understand government? Since we hope to one day become like God, we must gain all the knowledge we can. That is why the Lord said: "Whatever principle of intelligence we attain unto in this life, it will rise with us in the resurrection. And if a person gains more knowledge and intelligence in this life through his diligence and obedience than another, he will have so much the advantage in the world to come" (D&C 130:18–19).

The Lord wants us to learn about all kinds of subjects; in fact, he has commanded us to learn about them. Notice the different fields of knowledge he commands us to learn about in the following verses: "Things both in heaven and in the earth, and under the earth; things which have been, things which are, things which must shortly come to pass; things which are at home, things

THE FACT THAT YOU'RE READING THIS BOOK IS A GOOD SIGN

Do you like to read? Good! Studies have shown that those who have high levels of proficiency in reading are more likely to graduate from high school and to pursue higher education.[1]

which are abroad; the wars and the perplexities of the nations, and the judgments which are on the land; and a knowledge also of countries and of kingdoms—That ye may be prepared in all things" (D&C 88:79–80).

There are not many things that we will be able to take with us from this life to the next life. We won't be able to take our clothes, awards, cars, money—not even our cell phones (how cruel!). But our knowledge will stay with us for eternity and what we learn will rise with us in the resurrection. After all, "the glory of God is intelligence" (D&C 93:36).

EVEN WHEN SCHOOL ENDS, LEARNING SHOULDN'T

"Learning is not just for one set of people or for one time of life. It is a basic activity for all mankind. We are on earth to learn—first of all the principles of salvation, and then the secrets of the world. . . .

"[When I was younger] I did not often think of my learning as a religious activity, [but] it clearly was, in the sense that I came to value the inherent goodness in people, to appreciate the world around me, to see the fruits of unselfish cooperation, to increase my sense of self-worth, and to feel I had a capacity to be of service to others."—Camilla Kimball[2]

Education and Remuneration (If You're Educated, You'll Know What That Means)

Another reason why pursuing an education is so important is because the level of your education is directly connected to how much money you can expect to earn to provide for yourself or your family. An interesting account of this principle is found in the Book of Mormon when Amulon, one of the priests of King Noah, was captured by the Lamanites. The king of the Lamanites appointed Amulon and the other priests to be teachers of the people. Notice

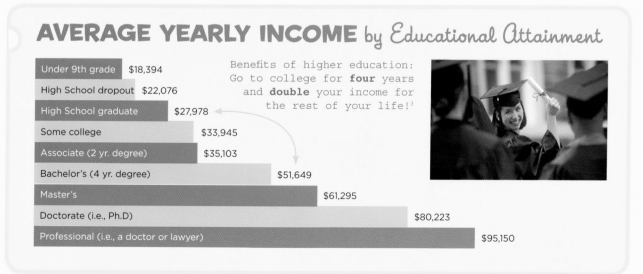

AVERAGE YEARLY INCOME by Educational Attainment

Educational Attainment	Average Yearly Income
Under 9th grade	$18,394
High School dropout	$22,076
High School graduate	$27,978
Some college	$33,945
Associate (2 yr. degree)	$35,103
Bachelor's (4 yr. degree)	$51,649
Master's	$61,295
Doctorate (i.e., Ph.D)	$80,223
Professional (i.e., a doctor or lawyer)	$95,150

Benefits of higher education: Go to college for **four** years and **double** your income for the rest of your life![3]

MANY TALK THE TALK, BUT ONLY 18 IN 100 WALK THE COLLEGE GRADUATION WALK[4]

100 Ninth Graders	100
Graduate High School on Time	67
Directly Enter College	38
Graduate College Within 6 Years	18

what the scriptures say: "And thus the language of Nephi began to be taught among all the people of the Lamanites . . . [and] they taught them that they should keep their record, and that they might write one to another" (Mosiah 24:4, 6).

What was the result of this education, this teaching of "the language of Nephi"? "And thus the Lamanites began to increase in riches" (Mosiah 24:7).

Education led to increased prosperity, even in the year 120 BC!

A good education will help you be self-reliant and provide temporally for your family. Remember these words from President Gordon B. Hinckley: "[The] world will in large measure pay you what it thinks you are worth, and your worth will increase as you gain education and proficiency in your chosen field. . . . There can be no doubt, none whatever, that education pays. Do not short-circuit your lives. If you do so, you will pay for it over and over and over again."[5]

DO TRY THIS AT HOME!

Visit http://besmart.com and explore the insights this web site has to offer on preparing for higher education.

Building Our Minds and Building the Kingdom

If education was only about money, it might seem a little shallow and selfish. But education has to do with much more than just temporal things like money; it also has spiritual purposes. Another reason why getting a good education is important is that it will allow us to better serve the Lord in building up his kingdom. President Hinckley explained: "The Lord . . . wants you to train your minds and hands to become an influence for good as you go forward with your lives. And as you do so and as you perform honorably and with excellence, you will bring honor to the Church, for you will be regarded as a man or woman of integrity and ability and conscientious workmanship."[6]

Consider Elder Russell M. Nelson. As a young man he studied hard and became a successful heart surgeon. During his career he developed new techniques for performing heart surgery that have blessed people throughout the world. He was such a skilled surgeon that when a famous

Chinese opera star needed heart surgery, Chinese officials flew Elder Nelson to China to perform the surgery. Think of how this created opportunities for Elder Nelson and other Church officials to talk with leaders in China! Because Elder Nelson chose to excel in his educational training, he helped open doors for the Church that might not have been opened otherwise. He also performed life-saving heart surgery on President Spencer W. Kimball, extending his life so he could serve as prophet and seer of the Church.[7]

FYI: Most university application deadlines are in January or February the year *before* you want to go to college. Don't wait until the summer after high school to apply!

You don't have to be a heart surgeon for your education to open doors and further the kingdom. In fact, you can be a teenager. In the Old Testament, there were four young men—Daniel, Shadrach, Meshach, and Abed-nego—who were given "knowledge and skill in all learning and wisdom" (Daniel 1:17). Because of Daniel's knowledge, he was able to interpret King Nebuchadnezzar's dream and teach him about God's kingdom (see Daniel 4). In addition to Daniel and Elder Nelson, we have seen computer technicians, plumbers, accountants, teachers, lawyers, and many other professionals use their skills to assist the Church with specific challenges, all of which helped the work of the Lord move forward.

"According to a 2006 *U.S. News and World Report* survey, BYU–Hawaii is the most internationally diverse campus in the United States, with more than 74 countries represented."[8]

Education and Motherhood

Education will help move the kingdom of God forward in the home just as much as it will in the workplace. Concerning the greatest of all professions, that of a mother and a

"We want our women to be well educated, for children may not recover from the ignorance of their mothers." —President Spencer W. Kimball[9]

homemaker, President Kimball taught: "It's been said that, 'When you educate a man, you educate an individual; but when you educate a woman, you educate a whole family.' We want our women to be well educated, for children may not recover from the ignorance of their mothers."[10]

Good mothers are actually multi-professionals. They need to know economics, first-aid, psychology, history, math, science, English, music, art, government, interior design, gardening, and religion—just to name a few. All these varied disciplines (and more) will be put to use by a mother as she makes her home and teaches her children. Think of how many different fields of knowledge a good mother needs to know in order to raise a strong family! And since the Church needs strong families, a mother's education is essential to move the kingdom of God forward.

A MAJOR REASON TO ATTEND COLLEGE

You can study what you are interested in. There are more than 100 different majors to choose from at most universities, ranging from accounting to zoology.

The Key to Opportunity

"I forgot to make a back-up copy of my brain, so everything I learned last semester was lost."

Another reason why it is so important to get a good education is because education opens doors that otherwise would remain closed. President Gordon B. Hinckley said that, "Education is the key to opportunity."[11] All of us have natural abilities and amazing potential within us, and education helps bring out and refine those capacities that will allow us to become our best self.

Education is one of the "small and simple things" (Alma 37:6) that makes a huge difference in what we will be able to do in our lives. President Hinckley compared education to a switch point on a railroad.

At the switch point between tracks, the distance is small—just a few inches. But over time, the two tracks lead to dramatically different places. Education is one of the switch points of life. At times it may seem that quitting school to work full-time or focusing on a social life over education are more attractive options. But over the long haul of life, the choice to pursue the very best education you can will lead you down a much more meaningful road of opportunity and experiences.[12]

One reason why seminary and institute are so important is the daily spiritual strengthening that comes from hearing the word of God and feeling the influence of the Holy Ghost.

Some seminary students were asked to respond to the following question: "If you had to give one reason to someone who is not taking seminary as to why they should enroll, what would you say?" The answers were overwhelmingly *Spirit*-based. Read just a sample:

Visit the web site seminary .lds.org. You can download posters, songs, and scripture mastery verses. You can also see where the closest institute is to where you live.

- "As you keep attending seminary, your spirituality and faith will grow. Seminary is a place where this is guaranteed to happen."—11th-grade girl
- "Seminary is peace and respite for the soul. Nowhere else do I feel the Spirit as clearly and profoundly as in seminary."—10th-grade boy
- "Being in seminary and having the great lessons gives you the Spirit to carry with you all day."—9th-grade girl
- "In the middle of our fight against sin, [seminary] is a pit stop. Seminary will . . . make you stronger; it will give you the courage to stand up; it will give you the Spirit to trust; it will give you the faith to believe."—11th-grade boy

Elder L. Tom Perry said that seminary and institute "will put a shield of protection around you to keep you free from the temptations and trials of the world. . . . I know of no better place for the young people of the Church to gain a special knowledge of sacred things than in the institute and seminary programs of the Church."[6]

LDS TEENS TOP POLLS National Study Credits Seminary and Institute with Righteousness of LDS Youth

A four-year study of U.S. teens and religion at the University of North Carolina found that LDS teens were less likely to participate in behaviors such as pre-marital sex, smoking marijuana, or viewing pornography than their peers of other religions. The researchers explained the difference by saying, "It probably has to do with *daily religious training* through high school [i.e., seminary]. . . . Daily engagement with people of their own faith, that's an amazing corrective to tip the balance."[7]

"Circles of Exaltation"

In 1968, Elder Spencer W. Kimball gave another profound reason why we should enroll in seminary and institute. On the chalkboard, he drew four circles in a vertical column with an arrow connecting each circle to the one above it. In the top circle, he wrote "Eternal Life," which is the purpose and goal of this life. Take a look at what Elder Kimball wrote in the second and third circles. What do you think he wrote in the fourth circle? The one that would best help youth achieve a mission, eternal marriage, and eternal life?

Circles of Exaltation

Eternal Life

↑

Eternal Marriage

↑

Mission

↑

Seminary and Institute

He said, "What shall we put in it? Well, there is only one thing to put there, and that is *the seminary and institute program*. . . . I am convinced that the seminaries and institutes can do much to get young people into the mission field and into temple marriage and, finally, into exaltation. This program is that perfect agency in the Church."[8]

Perhaps one reason the seminary and institute programs are credited for getting people onto the path of exaltation is due to the daily sacrifice required for attendance.

For each seminary class taken, there is a sacrifice—of sleep, time, or school credit—that is required. Those who enroll and attend are more likely to serve missions and marry in the temple—not only because of the increased knowledge and spirituality they gain, but also because *they are willing to sacrifice.*

A young woman who sacrifices her sleep will be willing to sacrifice to serve her neighbor. A young man who is willing to sacrifice an hour of his day to learn the gospel will find it easier to sacrifice two years of his life to teach the gospel. This spirit of sacrifice can permeate your life and lead you toward the circle of exaltation.

DO TRY THIS AT HOME!

If you are not currently enrolled in seminary or institute, enroll now! If you are enrolled, make an effort to maximize what you gain from your classes. Come early, bring your scriptures, take notes, participate, and pray for yourself and the teacher.

100		
90	**96**	**98**	**96**
80		
70		
60		
50		
40		
30		
20		
10		
	Received Temple Endowments	Of those Endowed, % Married in Temple	Male Graduates Served Missions

"The Church periodically checks the pulse and measures the progress of the institute programs. This last year an institute study revealed the following: of those graduating from institute, 96 percent received temple endowments; 98 percent of those receiving their endowments had their marriages performed in the temple; 96 percent of the men graduating from institute served missions."—Elder L. Tom Perry[9]

A Modern-day School of the Prophets

Another reason why we should enroll in seminary and institute is that we will never again have such a concentrated period of our lives dedicated to being taught and learning the gospel.

In the early days of the Church at Kirtland, Ohio, Joseph Smith established a weekday religious training class for the leading elders called "The School of the Prophets." Here, the elders were instructed in the things of eternity during the week as preparation for their call to be sent out into the world as missionaries. This school produced some of the greatest missionaries and leaders of the early Church. In our day, President Hinckley has called the programs designed to assist the youth of the Church in learning the gospel, "the schools of the future prophets."[10]

Did you know President Thomas S. Monson is a graduate of West High Seminary in Salt Lake City, Utah?

Youth who attend seminary have a concentrated opportunity to formally learn the gospel. It would take almost *four years* of attending a weekly Sunday School class to equal the amount of time dedicated to studying the gospel in *nine months* of seminary. Only during our teenage and young adult years do we have this rare opportunity for such focused gospel instruction.

COMBAT TRAINING

Can you imagine going to war unprepared and untrained? Basic training for a U.S. Marine is a twelve-week process of preparation, culminating in a 54-hour test of combat challenges and problems called "The Crucible."

Weekday religious education will help prepare us in the basic doctrines, principles, and history of the restored gospel. In seminary and institute we can master important scriptures. We will be trained on how to search, analyze, and apply the word of God in our lives. Our abilities to express and verbalize our thoughts, feelings, and experiences about the gospel will increase, thereby making us more effective tools in the hands of the Lord.

President Gordon B. Hinckley said, "Our great program of Church education moves forward. The work of training students through the seminary and institute program is constantly being enlarged. . . . We urge all for whom it is available to take advantage of it. We do not hesitate to promise that your knowledge of the gospel will be increased, your faith will be strengthened, and you will develop wonderful associations and friendships."[11]

How You Doin'?

Speaking of "associations and friendships"—look at all those wonderful people who share your same standards!

Seminary and institute classes are a great place to meet, associate with, date, and eventually marry someone who loves the Lord.

TELL ME ONE MORE TiME!

Why Should I Attend Seminary and Institute?

1. **We need daily spiritual strengthening to combat the evil influences that surround us on all sides.**
2. **Seminary and institute help us through the "circles of exaltation."**
3. **Those who sacrifice to attend seminary and institute are more likely to sacrifice for the Lord in all other areas of their life in order to achieve the goals of a mission, temple marriage, and exaltation.**
4. **We will never again have such a concentrated period of our lives dedicated to being taught and learning the gospel.**
5. **We are able to make friends and associate with people who share our same standards and beliefs.**

NOW that we have reviewed some of the *principles*, let's answer some of the questions regarding the *practices* connected to seminary and institute:

Why is seminary more important than any other school class?

Each school subject is important. Math, science, even physical education all have an important role. But only in seminary will you learn the doctrine of Christ and the preparation you need for eternal life. Elder John A. Widstoe said, "It is a paradox that men will gladly devote time every day for many years to learn a science or an art; yet will expect to win a knowledge of the gospel, which comprehends all sciences and arts, through perfunctory glances at books or occasional listening to sermons. The gospel should be studied more intensively than any school or college subject."[12]

Why is it so important that I enroll in all four years of seminary?

Each year of seminary is devoted to a different book of scripture. You can't skip the Old Testament—it is the foundation of all scripture. The New Testament teaches of the life of the

Savior—can't miss that class. The Book of Mormon is the most correct of any book on earth! And in the Doctrine and Covenants you will learn more about how the only true Church on the earth was restored. None of those are topics that can be missed! Additionally, as principle #1 of this chapter teaches, we need additional spiritual strengthening during all our years at school, not just one or two of them.

Why is institute just as important as seminary?

One reason seminary is so important is that it helps you through the high school years and prepares you for one of the most important decades of your life—your 20s. You attend institute while you are *in* your 20s, and that continued religious education will guide you as you make some of the most important decisions in your life.

28 ch Why Should I Serve a Mission?

Although this chapter is primarily geared toward young men, many of the principles discussed also apply to young women who desire to serve full-time missions.

When a baby boy is born to faithful members of the Church, there is the hope he will eventually serve a mission. There are even little missionary name tags that some young boys wear to Church.

FUTURE MISSIONARY

WE'LL BRING THE WORLD HIS TRUTH

As a matter of fact, it is not just *hoped* that a young man will serve a mission, he is *commanded* to serve a mission. President Spencer W. Kimball said: "A mission is not just a casual thing. . . . Neither is a mission a matter of choice any more than tithing is a choice, any more than sacrament meeting is a choice, any more than the World of Wisdom is a choice. Of course, we have our agency, and the Lord has given us choices. . . . We can go on a mission or we can remain home. But every normal young man is as much obligated to go on a mission as he is to pay his tithing, attend his meetings, keep the Sabbath day holy, and keep his life spotless and clean."[1]

Understanding why young men are commanded to serve a mission and why they should fulfill that divine obligation is instrumental in persuading a greater number of young men to become known as "Elder."

WHAT ABOUT YOUNG WOMEN AND MISSIONS?

"There seems to be growing in the Church an idea that all young women as well as all young men should go on missions. We need some young women. They perform a remarkable work. They can get in homes where the elders cannot. . . .

"I wish to say that the First Presidency and the Council of the Twelve are united in saying to our young sisters that they are not under obligation to go on missions. I hope I can say what I have to say in a way that will not be offensive to anyone. Young women should not feel that they have a duty comparable to that of young men. . . .

"A mission is not necessary as part of their lives."—President Gordon B. Hinckley[2]

"We need more missionaries. The message to raise the bar on missionary qualifications was not a signal to send fewer missionaries but rather a call for parents and leaders to work with young men earlier to better prepare them for missionary service and to keep them worthy of such service. All young men who are worthy and who are physically and emotionally able should prepare to serve in this most important work."—President Gordon B. Hinckley[3]

As of December 31, 2007, there were 52,686 full-time missionaries serving in the world[4]—but many more could be serving. The Lord needs all worthy young men to serve a mission. Will you be number **52,687?**

The Best Investment

A few young men worry about serving a mission because they are afraid of missing out on some things. Some ask, "What if I fall behind in school? What about all the social opportunities I'll miss? What about the money I could make? What if the girl I like marries someone else?" (Oh, that would *never* happen! ☺) Those are all legitimate concerns, but the blessings of serving a mission far outweigh the sacrifices asked of you. President Gordon B. Hinckley gave the following promises to those who faithfully served missions. See how many you can count: "I promise you that the time you spend in the mission field, if those years are spent in dedicated service, *will yield a greater return on investment than any other two years of your lives.* You will come to know what dedication and consecration mean. You will develop powers of persuasion which will bless your entire life. Your timidity, your fears, your shyness will gradually disappear as you go forth with boldness and conviction. You will learn to work with others, to develop a spirit of teamwork. The cankering evil of selfishness will be supplanted by a sense of service to others. You will draw nearer to the Lord than you likely will in any other set of circumstances. You will come to know that without His help you are indeed weak and simple, but that with His help you can accomplish miracles.

"You will establish habits of industry. You will develop a talent for the establishment of goals of effort. You will learn to work with singleness of purpose. What a tremendous

WANT TO GET RICH?

$1,000,000+

$18,000

Stock Market   Savings Account

If you invest $10,000 today in the stock market, and you earn an average of 8% interest per year, in 60 years you'll have more than a million dollars. If you take that same $10,000 and put it in a savings account earning 1% interest, in 60 years you'll have about $18,000. Which seems like a better investment to you? In a similar way, serving a mission is *by far* the best investment on your time that you can make!

foundation all of this will become for you in your later educational efforts and your life's work. Two years will not be time lost. It will be skills gained.

"You will bless the lives of those you teach, and their posterity after them. You will bless your own life. You will bless the lives of your family, who will sustain you and pray for you.

"And above and beyond all of this will come that sweet peace in your heart that you have served your Lord faithfully and well. Your service will become an expression of gratitude to your Heavenly Father.

"You will come to know your Redeemer as your greatest friend in time or eternity. You will realize that through His atoning sacrifice He has opened the way for eternal life and an exaltation above and beyond your greatest dreams.

"If you serve a mission faithfully and well, you will be a better husband, you will be a better father, you will be a better student, a better worker in your chosen vocation."[5]

We counted *twenty-two* incredible blessings! There can be no doubt about the blessings available to us as we serve a mission.

AN HUNDREDFOLD *Anthony Says:*

When I was about to leave for my mission, I had four things that I cared deeply about that I was afraid to leave behind: A girl that I hoped to marry, an opportunity to play college basketball, my own black Labrador dog that I loved, and I had a new black Jeep Wrangler. I decided to take a picture of all four of those things together to take with me. So I parked my Jeep in front of my basketball hoop, had my girlfriend and my dog climb in the front seats, and I snapped a photo.

In the MTC, I put the picture right above my bed. One day, our branch president came into our room and asked me about the picture. I explained it was of the four things I cared about the most, to which he responded, "You know what's funny, Elder Sweat? You're going to lose all four of those things on your mission." Needless to say . . . I didn't think it was funny. I thought to myself, "Why would God make me *lose* what I love if I am serving him?"

It didn't take long before the branch president's prophecy began to come true. Five months into my mission I learned my dog had died of a sudden seizure. Six months into my mission things ended with the girl at home. The basketball skills and recruiting letters quickly left me. And to top it off, my Jeep was eventually sold to my best friend. Luckily, I came across this promise from the Savior: "Verily I say unto you, There is no man that hath left house, or brethren, or sisters, or father, or mother, or wife, or children, or lands, for my sake, and the gospel's, but he shall receive an *hundredfold* now in this time, houses, and brethren, and sisters, and mothers, and children, and lands, with persecutions; and in the world to come eternal life" (Mark 10:29–30; emphasis added).

Upon returning home from my mission, I was led to and married my wife, Cindy, whom I love with all my heart. Instead of playing basketball, I get to teach for a living, which has brought me more joy and opportunities than hoops ever did. Instead of a dog, I have five beautiful children (can't even compare that one). And instead of a beautiful Jeep Wrangler . . . I have a minivan that seats seven! Yeah, baby! (OK, so I am still waiting for that promise to be fulfilled . . . but it will be.)

I found the Savior's promise to bless those who sacrifice for the gospel "an hundredfold" to be true, and so will you.

Elder Richard G. Scott made his decision to serve a mission after he graduated from college. One of his professors told him that if he went on a mission it would be a waste of his education—that everything he had learned would be obsolete by the time he returned. Nevertheless, Elder Scott served a mission. When he returned, he was hired to work in the Naval Nuclear Program. A few months after he began his new job, he was given a list of people he was responsible for. On that list was the same professor who had discouraged him years before. The professor was now working *three levels below* Elder Scott.

In summarizing his mission, Elder Scott said: "All that I now hold dear in life began to mature in the mission field. Had I not been encouraged to be a missionary, I would not have the eternal companion or precious family I dearly love. I am confident that I would not have had the exceptional professional opportunities that stretched my every capacity. I am certain that I would not have received the sacred callings with opportunities to serve for which I will be eternally grateful. My life has been richly blessed beyond measure because I served a mission."[7]

There can be no doubt that serving a mission *helped* not *hindered* Elder Scott. A mission is an investment that pays over and over.

Start now to prepare for your missionary service by studying the Book of Mormon, *Preach My Gospel*, and saving money so that you can serve.

DO TRY THIS AT HOME!

A MISSION WILL MAKE YOU A MAN

Before the Mission	After the Mission
You can shave with two tweezer plucks.	You have a 5 o'clock shadow by 4 o'clock.
You can wear a size 14 collared shirt (that's still too big).	You're at least a 16 because you actually have an Adam's apple.
Your suit is pressed and your shoes are shined.	Your suit is worn at the elbows and too small. Your shoes are considered "holy."
Some scripture pages are still stuck together because that page has never been read. (There's a book called Habbakuk?)	Each page is marked and underlined. The binding is broken, and you have empanada juice stains on the book of Habbakuk because you read it so much at lunch.
Letters from your mom at home.	Text messages from your companion's girlfriend now that you are home.

The Seed of Abraham—It Is Who You Are

Anciently God made a covenant with Abraham and his descendants. They were given posterity, priesthood, and a promised land. In return, the descendants of Abraham accepted certain responsibilities. The Lord said to Abraham, "Thou shalt be a blessing unto thy seed after thee, that in their hands *they shall bear this ministry and Priesthood unto all nations*" (Abraham 2:9; emphasis added).

Elder David A. Bednar explained, "The phrase 'bear this ministry and Priesthood unto all nations' refers to the responsibility to proclaim the gospel of Jesus Christ and to invite all to receive by proper priesthood authority the ordinances of salvation."[8] In other words, those who are the seed of Abraham have the duty to teach the gospel to others.

> ## WE ARE THE SEED OF ABRAHAM.
> ### ELDER DAVID A. BEDNAR[9]

Elder David A. Bednar further explained, "Missionary work is a manifestation of our spiritual identity and heritage. . . .

"You may enjoy music, athletics, or be mechanically inclined, and someday you may work in a trade or a profession or in the arts. As important as such activities and occupations can be, they do not define who we are. First and foremost, we are spiritual beings. *We are sons of God and the seed of Abraham.*"[10]

> ## EVERY WORTHY YOUNG MAN SHOULD FILL A MISSION.
> ### PRESIDENT SPENCER W. KIMBALL[11]

President Joseph F. Smith had a vision in which he saw the "noble and great ones who were chosen in the beginning to be rulers in the Church of God. *Even before they were born,* they, with many others, received their first lessons in the world of spirits and were prepared to come forth in the due time of the Lord *to labor in his vineyard for the salvation of the souls of men*" (D&C 138:55–56; emphasis added).

So no matter who you are, if you hold the priesthood, your foremost commitment and duty is to share the gospel with others. It is what you were born to do.

Did you know the scriptures talk about having beautiful feet? In Mosiah 15:16 it says, "How beautiful upon the mountains are the feet of those that are still publishing peace!" That verse doesn't necessarily mean that missionaries have beautiful feet, but it does mean that those who teach the gospel (those who publish peace) are blessed!

Do you have beautiful feet?

You Can Bless Others Eternally

Perhaps the most important reason why we should serve a mission is that a mission gives us the opportunity to share the life-changing message of the gospel of Jesus Christ. Think how many blessings are ours because we enjoy the privilege of having the restored gospel of Jesus Christ in our lives! Our efforts in serving as missionaries can be eternal—and they can spread throughout generations.

President Gordon B. Hinckley told the story of a missionary who left his mission discouraged. This missionary felt he had accomplished nothing. "I baptized one man in the backwoods of Tennessee," the missionary said. "He didn't know enough or have enough sense to wear shoes. And that's all I've done. I have wasted my time and my father's money."

THE RIPPLE EFFECT

Have you ever seen what happens to a still pond when a drop of water hits it? From that one spot, ripples flow in all directions until they cover the entire area. Similarly, by touching one person's life through missionary work, unknown thousands can end up being blessed by the gospel.

The mission president later checked on that man and found that he had been ordained a deacon. Later he received the Melchezidek Priesthood and was made branch president. Eventually the man moved to Idaho and had many children, and his children eventually served missions. The mission president said, "I have just completed a survey which indicates, according to the best information I can find, that over 1,100 people have come into the Church as a result of the baptism of that one man by a missionary who thought he had failed."[13]

A great scriptural example of this same ripple effect is the Book of Mormon prophet Abinadi. From what we know in the scriptures, Abinadi did not baptize anyone before he was put to death by King Noah. But he was able to change the life of one of Noah's priests, Alma. Abinadi's one convert, Alma, became one of the great Nephite prophets (see Mosiah 17–18). And the rest of the Book of Mormon deals primarily with Alma's descendants and their effect upon the Nephite and Lamanite civilizations. Think of all that happened from one man—Abinadi—bearing his testimony and teaching the gospel!

Similarly, we may never know the monumental effect our missionary work may have. But by changing even one person's life with the blessings of the gospel, we can have a large impact in moving the kingdom of God forward.

No Greater Joy

The Lord promised, "And if it so be that you should labor all your days in crying repentance unto this people, and bring, save it be one soul unto me, how great shall be your joy with him in the kingdom of my Father! And now, if your joy will be great with one soul that you have brought unto me into the kingdom of my Father, how great will be your joy if you should bring many souls unto me!" (D&C 18:15–16).

PREPARE TO CONSECRATE TWO YEARS OF YOUR LIVES TO THIS SACRED SERVICE. THAT WILL IN EFFECT CONSTITUTE A TITHE ON THE FIRST TWENTY YEARS OF YOUR LIVES.

PRESIDENT GORDON B. HINCKLEY[14]

President Brigham Young taught, "When men enjoy the spirit of their missions and realize their calling and standing before the Lord and the people, it constitutes the happiest portions of their lives."[15] Elder Orson F. Whitney promised, "There is no joy that can compare with that of a missionary who has been made the instrument for the salvation of a soul."[16] And President Ezra Taft Benson testified, "I have tasted the joy of missionary work. There is no work in all the world that can bring an individual greater joy and happiness."[17]

As returned missionaries, we both testify that there is an incomparable and indescribable joy that comes to the souls of those who have faithfully consecrated part of their life to serving the Lord as a full-time missionary. The only way you'll know is when you go.

And We Thought 18 or 24 Months Was a Long Time . . .

In August of 1852, a special conference was held in the old tabernacle on Temple Square. President Heber C. Kimball opened the conference by announcing that brethren would be called on missions.

"The missions we will call for during this conference are, generally, not to be very long ones; probably from *three to seven years* will be as long as any man will be absent from his family." Ninety-eight names were then read of men who were to leave as soon as possible.[18]

TELL ME ONE MORE TiME!

Why Should I Serve a Mission?

1. It's the best investment you can make during the early years of your life.

2. **For young men, as part of the seed of Abraham, you have a priesthood responsibility to serve. Additionally, you covenanted to serve before you were born.**
3. **You can change a person's life eternally by sharing the blessings of the gospel.**
4. **There is no greater joy than in helping others come unto Christ.**

NOW that we have reviewed some of the *principles*, let's answer some of the questions regarding the *practices* connected to serving missions:

Why do we need a raised bar for missionary standards?

The world in which we live is increasingly more complex and demanding. Missionaries need to be prepared in order to meet the intellectual, physical, and spiritual challenges a mission brings. Equally important, we need stronger missionaries with deeper testimonies so that they can carry the gospel to many more people.

Why can't I just serve a mission when I am older with my spouse instead of when I am 19?

Serving a mission later with your spouse is a great idea. But what about all the opportunities you will have to serve in the Church between the ages of 20 and 60? It is estimated that a missionary gains the equivalent of 30 years of Church service experience during a full-time, two-year mission. Think of how much more qualified you will be to serve the Lord for the rest of your life when you are a returned missionary in your early twenties!

Also, if you choose not to follow the prophet by serving a mission now, that decision might put your life on a different track so that by the time you are 60, you *won't* actually serve a mission, even though you think it's a good idea now.

Why do boys have to serve a mission and girls don't?

The answer is that missionary work is an assignment that belongs primarily to priesthood holders. President Gordon B. Hinckley stated, "Missionary work is essentially a priesthood responsibility. As such, our young men must carry the major burden. This is their responsibility and their obligation.

"We do not ask the young women to consider a mission as an essential part of their life's program. . . . To the sisters I say that you will be as highly respected, you will be considered as being as much in the line of duty, your efforts will be as acceptable to the Lord and to the Church whether you go on a mission or do not go on a mission."[19]

29 ch Why Should I Repent Now and Not Later?

You've heard the saying, "Never put off till tomorrow what you can do today." Unfortunately, one of the flaws of our human nature is that many times we would rather put off till *next week* what we could do today. President Spencer W. Kimball said, "One of the most serious human defects in all ages is procrastination, an unwillingness to accept personal responsibility *now*."[1]

Procrastination TEMPTATION

Put this book down and go get some food!

NEWSFLASH! Procrastinators Are Procrastinating Even More!

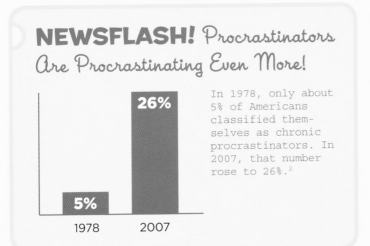

26%

5%

1978   2007

In 1978, only about 5% of Americans classified themselves as chronic procrastinators. In 2007, that number rose to 26%.[2]

How many times have we known we needed to do something, but waited until the last minute to get it done? If a teacher assigns a two-page essay that is due in two months, how many of us wait until the night before or sadly, the morning it is due, (or even worse, sometimes during first period) to get it done? If the essay will only take a few hours to complete, why not do it early?

One reason could be that we don't feel the *need* to get it done right away. We know that it would be nice to get it done early, but it isn't necessary. This procrastination problem is prevalent, not only in school life, but in spiritual life as well. An evil influence whispers to us that although we know the Church is true, our youth is the time to be wild. The adversary would have us think that, although the "spiritual homework" will come due, it is such a long way off, and we can always take care of it later.

Such erroneous statements come as thoughts like, "I can get serious about the gospel and about my spirituality before my mission" or "I can start living righteously in college, when I am ready for marriage." One of the worst procrastinating statements is "I know I shouldn't do this, but . . . I can always repent later." Understanding the atonement of Jesus Christ will help us to see why it is a blessing to repent as early as possible and to not procrastinate living righteously.

"Repentance is a great blessing, but you should never make yourself sick just so you can try out the remedy."
—Elder M. Russell Ballard[3]

Helping your mom can wait. Call your friends!

Replacing Pain with Peace

None of us, except our Savior Jesus Christ, has lived a life without sin. Paul teaches us that "all have sinned, and come short of the glory of God" (Romans 3:23). Throughout this book we have outlined many standards and commandments, and perhaps you have found yourself saying, "I don't keep that commandment very well" or "Man, I failed living up to that standard." Don't get discouraged! Our Heavenly Father understood that we would all fail to measure up in some way; therefore, he planned for and provided a Savior to redeem us from our fallen state and, conditioned upon our repentance, to cleanse us from our sins. That is the good news of the gospel—we can be forgiven! As a matter of fact, that is the best news.

We were not sent here to be perfect, but to "come unto Christ, and be perfected in him" (Moroni 10:32). The true test of life is not whether we will make any mistakes (because, unfortunately, we all make many of those), but if we will repent and let the Atonement cleanse our souls and heal our hearts. That leads us to the first and primary reason why we should repent now

"TOUGH ON SINS"

Have you ever seen those commercials where a laundry detergent promises to get rid of any stain? Isaiah promised, "Come now, and let us reason together, saith the Lord: though your sins be as scarlet, they shall be as white as snow; though they be red like crimson, they shall be as wool" (Isaiah 1:18). The Lord has promised complete forgiveness to those who do what is required and truly repent.

and not later: The atonement of Jesus Christ not only can cleanse us from our sins, but it can also heal our hearts of the pain, sorrow, guilt, and despair that is caused as a result of sin. We should repent *now* so that we can enjoy the true peace that the Atonement can provide, instead of carrying around guilt and pain for what we have done for years. Alma the Younger testified of the spiritual relief that can come to our souls from almost the moment we begin the repentance process. He said about his own repentance: "And oh, what joy, and what marvelous light I did behold; yea, my soul was filled with joy as exceeding as was my pain!

"Yea, I say unto you, my son, that there could be nothing so exquisite and so bitter as were my pains. Yea, and again I say unto you, my son, that on the other hand, there can be nothing so exquisite and sweet as was my joy" (Alma 36:20–21).

The replacement of pain with joy through the Atonement is one of the primary reasons why we should repent now and not later in life.

Procrastination TEMPTATION

Don't do your homework— watch some TV!

Gone Is the Guidance

In the introduction to *For the Strength of Youth,* the First Presidency says: "We promise that as you keep these standards and live by the truths in the scriptures, you will be able to do your life's work with greater wisdom and skill and bear trials with greater courage. *You will have the help of the Holy Ghost.*"[4] Another reason why we shouldn't willfully sin and plan to repent later is because then we will lose the guidance of the Holy Ghost and the blessings that come from obedience.

For example, if a young man begins committing serious sins when he is sixteen, can he come back to full fellowship later in his life and still make it to the celestial kingdom? Yes, conditioned upon his repentance, it is possible! So why should this young man strive to not make mistakes and to avoid willful rebellion when he is sixteen? Because he will miss out on many blessings during his rebellious years, including the guiding influence of the Holy Ghost in making critical decisions.

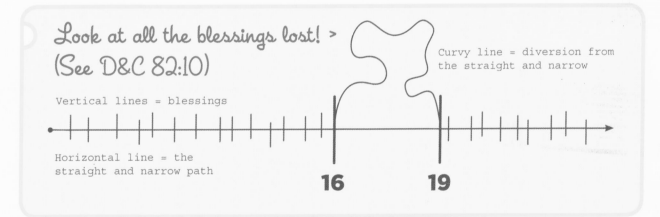

Look at all the blessings lost! >
(See D&C 82:10)

Curvy line = diversion from the straight and narrow

Vertical lines = blessings

Horizontal line = the straight and narrow path

16 **19**

The Decade of Decision

Our teenage years and early twenties are what Elder Robert D. Hales has called the "decade of decision."[5] Think of the major decisions a young man or woman makes between the ages of 15 and 25! This timeframe is generally when we decide what our likes and dislikes are, what type of high school student we will become, if and where we will to go to college, if and when we will serve a mission, what career we will pursue, and most important, whom we will marry! Often these decisions build upon a previous decision; therefore, poor decisions made early will affect our ability to make good decisions later.

Our 20s, the decade of decision

We might end up in our 40s and 50s having missed out on opportunities and experiences that could have been ours but weren't because we had lost the guidance of the Spirit during the decade of decision. Our youth is such a critical time that we must have the constant guidance of the Holy Ghost to "enlighten [our] mind[s]" (D&C 6:15) as we make life-altering decisions.

We need to repent now to qualify for the guidance of the Holy Ghost, so that our decade of decision can be classified as a decade of *inspired* decisions.

The Downward Spiral of Sin

Another reason why we need to repent immediately is that it makes it easier to stay on the path of righteousness. If we wait to repent, the easier it is to stray from the straight and narrow path and the harder it is to find our way back.

Frequently, as people commit sin they begin a downward spiral in which they successively commit more and more grievous sins. Consider the story of David and Bathsheba found in 2 Samuel 11. David ultimately committed adultery and murder, but those sins came after smaller ones. Had David repented immediately after those first sins, he could have avoided the severe consequences that later came into his life.

Procrastination **TEMPTATION**

How about you take the trash out *after* you take a nap.

WHEN IS IT EASIEST TO STOP?

Suppose we are going to roll a bowling ball down a ramp. Your job is to stop the bowling ball from rolling away. But you can only touch the ball with a yard stick. Where will you put your stick to stop the ball?

If we were actually doing this experiment (and hey, you might want to try it!), you would discover that the best time to stop the ball is at the top of the ramp, long before the ball starts rolling. Similarly, the best time to repent is immediately, long before things spin out of control.

"ITH'S TOO METHY"

Anthony Says:

Each week my kids have to clean their toy room. If they stay on top of it each week it doesn't take too long on a Saturday morning to clean up the mess they made during the week. There was a stretch of time where, for some reason or another, my kids skipped cleaning for about three weeks. The playroom was a disaster. Toys were strewn about like a hurricane had hit.

I sent them down to the playroom to clean it up and told them I would check on them in about thirty minutes. When the time had elapsed, I went down to see the progress. To my surprise, the room hadn't been touched. I found my six-year-old daughter sitting in the middle of the chaos, surrounded by toys, and asked her why nothing had been cleaned up yet.

She looked at me, and with tears in her eyes, threw back her head and said with her little lisp, "Ith too methy! I don't know where to sthtart!"

Overwhelmed, my little girl had looked around the room that had gotten out of hand and had given up without trying because it just seemed like too much work.

Similarly, some of us have made a mess of our lives, procrastinating our repentance and waiting to clean up our life until "later." Sadly, we find that when the time comes to straighten things up, our lives are in such a mess, we don't know where to begin to clean up our lives. Consequently we lose hope, and never make our way back.

Procrastination
TEMPTATION

On a level of 1 to 10, what is your procrastination level?—or would you like to decide later?

President Spencer W. Kimball taught, "Sin is intensely habit-forming and sometimes moves men to the tragic point of no return. . . . As the transgressor moves deeper and deeper in his sin, and the error is entrenched more deeply and *the will to change is weakened,* it becomes increasingly near-hopeless, and he skids down and down until either he does not want to climb back or he has lost the power to do so."[6]

We must repent quickly to avoid the downward spiral of sin.

DO TRY THIS AT HOME!

ZYXW

How fast can you recite the alphabet? If you're fast, you can probably do it in less than four seconds. But what about reciting the alphabet *backward?* How fast can you do that? Go ahead—try it! The lesson here is that it is hard to change deeply ingrained habits. When you're used to saying the alphabet a certain way, doing it any different is hard! If we get in a habit of sinning, it can be difficult to change that pattern. Another reason why it is better to repent now and not later!

"As a Thief in the Night"

Perhaps the ultimate reason why we should not procrastinate our repentance is the simple fact that nobody knows when the Second Coming will be, nor when they will die and "be brought to stand before the bar of God, to be judged of him" (Mosiah 16:10). Although statistically most people live a relatively long time, many people face death quickly and unexpectedly. Our error lies in the assumption that "it won't happen to me"—death happens to everyone.

Knowing that the end could come at any moment should immediately change our procrastinating perspective. If your teacher assigned you a two-page essay and said, "I might call for it anytime. I won't tell you when it is due. I might ask you to turn it in tomorrow, maybe next week, or maybe at the end of the year, but I will call for it." What would you do, especially if your entire grade rested on that one paper?

Suddenly, the thought of completing it right away would quickly move from nice to necessary, if only for our own mental well-being. If we remained unprepared, we would fear walking into class each day, hoping that the teacher would not call for the paper. What a fearful way to live life! This unprepared feeling is similar to

CRAB KILLER *John Says:*

When I was in the fourth grade, my class went to the ocean and I found some tiny crabs. Even though there was a sign that said, "Do not remove any animal life from the beach," I put some crabs into my lunch box and took them home. At home, I put the crabs in a big bowl of water and watched them swim around. But soon they stopped swimming.

I was worried and asked my mom what I should do. She told me that since the crabs were from the ocean, they needed to be in salt water. So I dumped some salt into my bowl, but it was too late—the crabs were dead. I was a crab killer.

I felt so guilty. About eighteen months later, I went in for an interview with the bishop to receive the Aaronic priesthood. At the end of the interview, Bishop McDonald asked me, "Is there any sin in your life that should have been cleared with priesthood authority that hasn't been?"

I thought of the crabs, and my heart began to pound. I broke down in his office.

Between sobs, I explained the whole story. Looking back, I'm not sure that was the kind of sin that I needed to confess to the bishop, but after confessing to the bishop, I felt so much cleaner inside. The burden of guilt was gone.

If we have a sin weighing on our mind, it is best to talk about it with the bishop. That way we won't have to bear the burden alone.

The Lord has commanded that we "*confess . . . and forsake*" our sins (D&C 58:43; emphasis added).

Is there a sin that you need to repent of? One you should confess to your bishop? Don't procrastinate!

"that awful fear of death which fills the breasts of all the wicked" (Mormon 6:7). Nobody wants to live their life in fear, unprepared like the foolish virgins who scrambled to find the oil of spirituality that would have come from repentance (see Matthew 25:1–13).

The fact is, we do not know when we will die, nor when the Lord will return. "Watch therefore, for ye know neither the day nor the hour wherein the Son of man cometh" (Matthew 25:13). By repenting now, and not later, we will be prepared for our spiritual final exam, whenever it comes.

Remember these words from Elder Henry B. Eyring: "'Now' can seem so difficult, and 'later' appear so much easier. The truth is that today is always a better day to repent than any tomorrow."[7]

TELL ME ONE MORE TiME!

Why Should I Repent *Now* and Not *Later?*

1. When we delay repentance, we lose years of blessings and the guidance of the Holy Ghost.
2. We need to repent early so the Spirit will guide us during the "decade of decision," which is a critical time in our lives to make important decisions.
3. If we procrastinate our repentance, we might find ourselves so far off the path of righteousness that we can't find our way back or that we have lost the spiritual strength to do so.
4. We do not know when we will die or when the Second Coming will be. When we delay repentance, we run the terrible risk of finding ourselves unprepared to stand before our Savior.

NOW that we have reviewed some of the *principles*, let's answer some of the questions regarding the *practices* connected to repentance:

Cont.

Why should I talk to my bishop about certain sins?

As illustrated in the "crab killer" story, confession to the bishop brings peace. If you have a problem with something that is addictive, such as pornography, the bishop can provide you with additional support in helping you overcome your addiction. The bishop will also help you through the repentance process and ensure you are ready to make sacred covenants. The Lord has said that to repent of serious transgression we need to confess our sins both to the Lord and to our priesthood leaders (see Mosiah 26:29).

Why do I need the Savior's atonement to truly repent? Isn't being "sorry" the same thing?

Being sorry when we sin is definitely an important part of repentance—but just being sorry cannot make up for everything we have done wrong nor can it change our hearts. For example, if you say an unkind word to someone, you can be sorry, and you can say sorry, but can that truly make up for the hurt they felt? Through the Atonement, that pain and suffering that we could never heal *can* be healed. It is also significant to recognize that people can be "sorry" for many reasons (such as getting caught or being punished), but that doesn't necessarily equal repentance. Paul taught, "For godly sorrow worketh repentance to salvation . . . but the sorrow of the world worketh death" (2 Corinthians 7:10). "Godly sorrow" means we feel sorrow because we have offended God and we desire to change and be forgiven, and that is only possible through the Atonement.

Why is repentance a positive commandment and not a negative one?

Repentance simply means "change" toward God, or improvement—and the fact that you can change is extremely positive! Elder Jeffrey R. Holland said, "*Repentance* is not a foreboding word. It is following *faith,* the most encouraging word in the Christian vocabulary. Repentance is simply the scriptural invitation for growth and improvement and progress and renewal. You can change! You can be anything you want to be in righteousness."[8]

Conclusion: Sometimes We Do Not Need to Know *Why*

We have spent the pages in this book explaining some of the very important whys concerning the Lord's commandments. We hope it has helped you see some of the powerful reasons for the directions God has given his children. But before concluding the book, we felt it was important for you to understand that there are times that we don't need to know why. In fact, some kinds of "why" questions are not even good to ask.

"Why" in Times of Trial

For example, chances are you've had your fair share of problems. In times of trial, we sometimes might ask, "Why me?" But Elder Richard G. Scott explained that this is not a good question. He said, "When you face adversity, you can be led to ask many questions. Some serve a useful purpose; others do not. To ask, Why does this have to happen to me? Why do I have to suffer this, now? What have I done to cause this? will lead you into blind alleys. It really does no good to ask questions that reflect opposition to the will of God. Rather ask, What am I to do? What am I to learn from this experience? What am I to change? Whom am I to help? How can I remember my many blessings in times of trial? Willing sacrifice of deeply held personal desires in favor of the will of God is very hard to do. Yet, when you pray with real conviction, 'Please let me know Thy will' and 'May Thy will be done,' you are in the strongest position to receive the maximum help from your loving Father."[1]

Notice that Elder Scott suggests that some why questions can be changed around.

Not . . .	But . . .
Why me?	What should I learn?
Why is this happening now?	Whom can I help?
Why isn't this problem fixed?	What does the Lord want me to do?

When it comes to personal trials, we may never know in this life why we have them. Elder Lance B. Wickman of the Seventy shared a tender story about his five-year-old son who suddenly contracted a deadly disease. After several days of intensive care, his son passed away. It would have been easy for Elder Wickman to ask, "Why did this have to happen to us?" But instead he taught, "Do not ever doubt the goodness of God, even if you do not know 'why.' . . .

The Lord has said simply, 'My ways [are] higher than your ways, and my thoughts than your thoughts' (Isaiah 55:9). As the Son's will was 'swallowed up in the will of the Father' (Mosiah 15:7), so must ours be.

"Still, we mortals quite naturally want to know the why. Yet, in pressing too earnestly for the answer, we may forget that mortality was designed, in a manner of speaking, as the season of unanswered questions. . . . I believe that mortality's supreme test is to face the 'why' and then let it go, trusting humbly in the Lord's promise that 'all things must come to pass in their time' (D&C 64:32)."[2]

My thoughts are not your thoughts.

Elder Robert D. Hales suffered several heart attacks and endured other health challenges. In spite of, or perhaps because of these difficulties he said, "I have come to understand how useless it is to dwell on the *why*s, *what if*s, and *if only*s for which there likely will be given no answers in mortality. . . . The questions Why me? Why our family? Why now? are usually unanswerable questions. These questions detract from our spirituality and can destroy our faith. We need to spend our time and energy building our faith by turning to the Lord and asking for strength to overcome the pains and trials of this world and to endure to the end for greater understanding."[3]

"Why" and Revelation

The Lord has given reasons why for many of his commandments, several of which we have discussed in this book. However, there is a difference between general commandments that have been given to God's children and *personal revelation.* Many times revelation does not come with a reason why. The Holy Ghost will give us direct impressions and instructions but will *not* always give us a reason why we should follow them. Perhaps there isn't time to tell us why, or maybe we wouldn't understand the reason. Possibly, the Lord wants to test our faith to see if we trust him. There is always a reason behind the Lord's decisions, but sometimes he won't tell us.

A classic scriptural example of this is in the first few chapters of the Book of Mormon. Nephi was told to make two sets of records. Upon making the second set, Nephi said, "Wherefore, the Lord hath commanded me to make these plates for a wise purpose in him, *which purpose I know not*" (1 Nephi 9:5; emphasis added). When completing the Book of Mormon, the prophet Mormon was prompted to insert these small plates of Nephi, even though they covered the same historical time period abridged in the Book of Lehi. When Mormon received this unusual instruction, he said,

"And I do this for a wise purpose; for thus it whispereth me, according to the workings of the Spirit of the Lord which is in me. And now, I do not know all things; but the Lord knoweth all things which are to come; wherefore, he worketh in me to do according to his will" (Words of Mormon 1:7).

Both Nephi and Mormon had no idea why they were prompted to take this course of action regarding the small plates of Nephi, and perhaps they never knew why in their entire lives. But to us the reason is clear—the Lord knew the fate of the first 116 pages of the Book of Mormon and prepared a way so the information would not be lost forever (see D&C 3; 10).

Just like Mormon including the small plates of Nephi, sometimes the reason why will be made known to a later generation and not to us!

Elder David A. Bednar explained, "Let me use a rather simple example to illustrate this lesson. We are walking along, and the impression comes to turn left. We do not know why. 'Ye receive no witness until after the trial of your faith' (Ether 12:6). After we have turned left, after we have proceeded along that pathway, then perhaps we gain some insight that answers the question of why. Revelation is a *what* and a *conclusion;* it is not a *why* and an *explanation.* So there are many things that, frankly, cannot be fully explained to the satisfaction of the rational mind.[4]

FOLLOWING THE RULES
John Says:

At one point in my mission, we received a rule that whenever somebody missed an appointment with us that we should put a Church pamphlet on their doorstep with our phone number on it.

One afternoon, a fourteen-year-old young man named Jeff missed an appointment with us. We both felt that Jeff might not be interested in meeting with us, but we still went back to our car and, following the rules, took a pamphlet back to his door.

When we got to his door, we were surprised to see Jeff open it! It turned out that he had been asleep, and had been awakened by our knocking, but had not yet made it to the door. He invited us in, and we taught him the first discussion.

That was the first of many discussions with Jeff McGee. Later he and his father were baptized. And that would be a good story by itself, but there's more.

Fourteen months later I was a returned missionary madly in love with Lani Olsen. The only problem was that she wasn't in love with me. In fact, she had just put our relationship "on hold" for a week. (I didn't know what that meant either.) The only bright spot that week was that I talked with one of my former companions and we made plans to drive back to Denver to witness Brother and Sister McGee be sealed in the temple to each other and to Jeff.

But at the last minute, my former companion backed out so Lani decided to come with me to Denver, where we spent time with the McGees and many other people I had shared the

gospel with. Lani said that it was in seeing me with those converts and former investigators that she fell in love with me. And six months later, we were sealed to each other.

As I look back on this story, if somebody were to say to me, "Why do you have to put a pamphlet on the door?" I would say, "So I could get Lani to fall in love with me!"

Now that wasn't the reason why we were given the rule. As we have said, the personal whys in your life are not always clear—but when we obey, even without knowing why, blessings come—after the trial of our faith.

President Thomas S. Monson tells of driving down a road and feeling impressed to stop at a less-active member's house. He didn't know why, but he followed the prompting. When he knocked on the door, a woman answered and said, "All day long I have been hoping somebody would call. How did you know today is my birthday?"[5]

Knowing the reason why was not important to President Monson, he simply did what he was prompted to do. If we expect to be given a why for every prompting that comes, we will be disappointed and may miss out on many tender blessings.

Follow the Example of Adam

In the Introduction, we wrote about Adam when he was cast out of the Garden of Eden. He was told to make sacrifices, *"and after many days an angel of the Lord appeared unto Adam, saying: Why dost thou offer sacrifices unto the Lord? And Adam said unto him: I know not, save the Lord commanded me"* (Moses 5:6; emphasis added).

Although the angel did give Adam a reason, it is important to note that Adam followed the commandment *for many days* without knowing the reason why. There will be many times in life when we are told by the Spirit or by the Lord's prophets to do something and for many days, perhaps for many years, there will not be a reason why.

One of our purposes here on earth is to develop faith in the Lord Jesus Christ. "Without faith it is impossible to please [God]" (Hebrews 11:6). Joseph Smith taught that faith is "the *principle of action* in all intelligent beings,"[6] and sometimes the Lord wants us to *act* without knowing the

"Faith, to be faith, must walk to the edge of the light and then a few steps into the darkness."

reason why. As Elder Boyd K. Packer taught: "Faith, to be faith, must center around something that is not known. Faith, to be faith, must go beyond that for which there is confirming evidence. . . . Faith, to be faith, must walk to the edge of the light, and then a few steps into the darkness. If everything has to be known, if everything has to be explained, if everything has to be certified, then there is no need for faith. Indeed, there is no room for it."[7]

We hope that you know more whys as a result of reading this book and that you feel a desire to keep the commandments more fully. We also hope that you will have faith in the Lord and the courage to move forward, even when you do not know the reason why.

Together we testify that God, our Heavenly Father, really does live. He knows you personally. Jesus Christ is our Savior. Joseph Smith truly saw Heavenly Father and Jesus Christ in 1820, and from that time to the present we have had prophets on the earth. We testify that the kingdom of God was restored to the earth again through the Prophet Joseph Smith. We testify that a life centered on the teachings of Jesus Christ and keeping his commandments is the only way to have true happiness and peace in this life, and eternal life in the world to come. When we listen to the Lord and his prophets, we are blessed and protected. We pray that these blessings will be yours as you strive to live the teachings of the gospel of Jesus Christ.

Notes

INTRODUCTION: WHY ASK "WHY"?

1. Charles Didier, "The Message of the Restoration," *Ensign,* November 2003, 73; emphasis in original.
2. This really happened! See http://www.mirror.co.uk/news/topstories/2008/02/07/kamil-kaplan-the-man-who-threw-the-baby-from-blaze-flat-speaks-out-89520-20311324/ and http://www.cnn.com/2008/WORLD/europe/02/04/germany.fire/index.html for the news photos and story.
3. Richard G. Scott, CES Symposium on the Doctrine and Covenants and Church History, 11 August 1998, 2; emphasis added.
4. Gordon B. Hinckley, "Words of the Prophet: Daughters of the Almighty," *New Era,* November 2003, 6; emphasis added.
5. David A. Bednar, "Teach Them to Understand," Ricks College Campus Education Week Devotional, 4 June 1998; emphasis added.
6. Julie B. Beck, "For the Strength of Youth: A Conversation with the Young Women General Presidency," *Ensign,* October 2007, 13-14; emphasis added.
7. Boyd K. Packer, CES Symposium on the Doctrine and Covenants and Church History, 10 August 1993, 3; emphasis added.
8. Glenn L. Pace, "Morality," Ricks College Devotional, 24 September 1991, 1.
9. Richard L. Evans, in Conference Report, April 1962, Third Day—Morning Meeting, 97.
10. See Joseph Smith, *The Teachings of the Prophet Joseph Smith,* comp. Joseph Fielding Smith (Salt Lake City: Deseret Book, 1976), 256-57.
11. Boyd K. Packer, in Conference Report, April 1963, 107.

CHAPTER 1: WHY SHOULD I KEEP THE COMMANDMENTS?

1. Shankar Vedantam, "Science Confirms: You Really Can't Buy Happiness," *Washington Post,* 3 July 2006, A2.
2. Joseph Smith, *The Teachings of the Prophet Joseph Smith,* comp. Joseph Fielding Smith (Salt Lake City: Deseret Book, 1976), 256-57; emphasis added.
3. Bruce C. Hafen, "The Waning of Belonging," *Ensign,* October 1989, 69.
4. U.S. Department of Justice Prison Report, http://www.ojp.usdoj.gov/bjs/prisons.htm.
5. Medicinenet.com, http://www.medterms.com/script/main/art.asp?articlekey=8575.
6. Ezra Taft Benson, quoted in Donald L. Staheli, "Obedience—Life's Great Challenge," *Ensign,* May 1998, 82; emphasis added.
7. *For the Strength of Youth* (Salt Lake City: The Church of Jesus Christ of Latter-day Saints, 2001), 42.

CHAPTER 2: WHY SHOULD I LISTEN TO AND FOLLOW THE PROPHET?

1. Joseph Smith, *The History of the Church,* edited by B. H. Roberts, 2d ed. 7 vols. (Salt Lake City: The Church of Jesus Christ of Latter-day Saints, 1932-51), 5:85.
2. Joseph Smith, quoted by Wilford Woodruff, in Conference Report, April 1898, 57.
3. "The Family: A Proclamation to the World," *Ensign,* November 1995, 102.
4. "Same-Sex Marriage," http://en.wikipedia.org/wiki/Same-sex_marriage.
5. "The Family: A Proclamation to the World," *Ensign,* November 1995, 102.
6. Bruce R. McConkie, "Stand Independent above All Other Creatures," *Ensign,* May 1979, 93.
7. Ibid.
8. See Jon Krakauer, *Into Thin Air: A Personal Account of the Mt. Everest Disaster* (New York: Villard, 1997).
9. Joseph Smith, quoted by William G. Nelson, in "Joseph Smith, the Prophet," *Young Woman's Journal,* December 1906, 543.
10. Wilford Woodruff, *Discourses of Wilford Woodruff,* edited by G. Homer Durham (Salt Lake City: Bookcraft, 1946), 212-13.
11. Harold B. Lee, "Closing Remarks," *Ensign,* January 1974, 128.

CHAPTER 3: WHY DOES IT MATTER WHO MY FRIENDS ARE?

1. *For the Strength of Youth* (Salt Lake City: The Church of Jesus Christ of Latter-day Saints, 2001), 12.

2. See Philippe G. Schyns and Aude Oliva, "Dr. Angry and Mr. Smile," *Cognition* 69 (1999): 243–65. Photo courtesy of Philippe Schyns.

3. Quoted in Brent L. Top and Bruce A. Chadwick, *10 Secrets Wise Parents Know* (Salt Lake City: Deseret Book, 2004), 83.

4. See Brent L. Top and Bruce A. Chadwick, "Helping Teens Stay Strong," *Ensign,* March 1999, 27–34.

5. Thomas S. Monson, "Pioneers All," *Ensign,* May 1997, 94–95.

6. Gordon B. Hinckley, "Stay on the High Road," *Ensign,* May 2004, 113–14.

7. *For the Strength of Youth*, 12.

8. Ibid., 13.

9. Ibid., 12.

10. Henry B. Eyring, "Hearts Bound Together," *Ensign,* May 2005, 77.

11. *For the Strength of Youth*, 12.

12. Ibid.

CHAPTER 4: WHY SHOULD I KEEP THE WORD OF WISDOM?

1. Larissa Hirsch, "Smoking," August 2007, http://www.kidshealth.org/teen/drug_alcohol/tobacco/smoking.html. Photos courtesy of American Lung Association.

2. "Social effects of alcohol abuse," http://www.helpguide.org/mental/alcohol_abuse_alcoholism_signs_effects_treatment .htm#effects.

3. See "Smoking," http://en.wikipedia.org/wiki/Image:Cancer_smoking_lung_cancer_correlation_from_NIH.svg.

4. James E. Enstrom, "Health practices and cancer mortality among active California Mormons," *J. Natl. Cancer Inst.* 81, no. 23 (6 December 1989): 1807–14.

5. Heber J. Grant, in *Teachings of the Presidents of the Church: Heber J. Grant* (Salt Lake City: The Church of Jesus Christ of Latter-day Saints, 2002), 192.

6. Brigham Young, in *Teachings of the Presidents of the Church: Brigham Young* (Salt Lake City: The Church of Jesus Christ of Latter-day Saints, 1997), 212.

7. http://www.drawyourline.com/harms/effects-on-the-brain. Photos of brain scans by Dr. Daniel Amen, http://www.amen clinic.com.

8. See "Consequences of Underage Alcohol Use," http://ncadi.samhsa.gov/govpubs/rpo992/.

9. The NHSDA Report, "Academic Performance and Youth Substance Use," 6 September 2002, http://www.oas.samhsa .gov/2k2/academics/academics.htm.

10. Anonymous, "Addiction Is," 16 September 2001, http://addictionis.org/.

11. Boyd K. Packer, "The Word of Wisdom: The Principle and the Promises," *Ensign,* May 1996, 19.

12. George Albert Smith, *The Teachings of George Albert Smith,* ed. Robert K. McIntosh (Salt Lake City: Deseret Book, 1996), 103.

13. Grant, in *Teachings of Presidents of the Church: Heber J. Grant*, 192–93.

14. Joseph F. Smith, in *Teachings of Presidents of the Church: Joseph F. Smith* (Salt Lake City: The Church of Jesus Christ of Latter-day Saints, 1998), 324.

15. For an expanded discussion on this question and a great story about alcohol and eating manure, see "Questions and Answers," *New Era,* June 2008, 16–17.

16. Quoted in "Policies and Procedures," *New Era,* May 1972, 50.

17. See Thomas J. Boud, "The Energy Drink Epidemic," *Ensign,* December 2008, 49–52. See also Russell Wilcox, "Energy Drinks: The Lift That Lets You Down," *New Era,* December 2008, 30–33.

18. See James O'Keefe and Joan O'Keefe, *The Forever Young Diet and Lifestyle* (New York: Andrews McMeel, 2006), 233.

19. Thomas S. Monson, "True to the Faith," *Ensign,* May 2006, 19.

20. See Sharon Worcester, "Energy Drink Trends Alarm Some; No Data Back Safety," *Family Practice News,* 1 February 2007, 1.

CHAPTER 5: WHY SHOULDN'T I PIERCE OR TATTOO MY BODY?

1. Gordon B. Hinckley, "'Great Shall Be the Peace of Thy Children,'" *Ensign,* November 2000, 52.
2. See Timothy A. Roberts and Sheryl A. Ryan, "Tattooing and High-Risk Behavior in Adolescents," *Pediatrics* 110, no. 6 (6 December 2002).
3. See "Tattoo," http://en.wikipedia.org/wiki/Tattoo.
4. Harold B. Lee, "Be Loyal to the Royal Within You," in *Speeches of the Year: BYU Devotional and Ten-Stake Fireside Addresses* 1973 (Provo: BYU Press, 1974), 92.
5. *For the Strength of Youth* (Salt Lake City: The Church of Jesus Christ of Latter-day Saints, 2001), 15.
6. David A. Bednar, "Quick to Observe," BYU Devotional, 10 May 2005, 3–4.
7. David A. Bednar, "Heartfelt and Willing Obedience," BYU-I Campus Education Week Devotional, 27 June 2002; emphasis added.
8. Anna Swan, "Tattoo Statistics," 16 May 2006, http://www.associatedcontent.com/article/31975/tattoo_statistics .html?cat=7.
9. Nicor, "Tattoo," http://en.wikipedia.org/wiki/Tattoo.
10. "Tattoo," http://en.wikipedia.org/wiki/Tattoo; emphasis added.
11. Dallin H. Oaks, "Repentance and Change," *Ensign,* November 2003, 37, 39.

CHAPTER 6: WHY SHOULD I DRESS MODESTLY?

1. *For the Strength of Youth* (Salt Lake City: The Church of Jesus Christ of Latter-day Saints, 2001), 14–15; emphasis added.
2. Thomas S. Monson, "Peace, Be Still," *Ensign,* November 2002, 53.
3. http://www.yourdictionary.com/modesty.
4. Robert D. Hales, "Modesty: Reverence for the Lord," *Ensign,* August 2008, 35.
5. *For the Strength of Youth,* 16.
6. Dallin H. Oaks, "The Aaronic Priesthood and the Sacrament," *Ensign,* November 1998, 39.
7. Jeffrey R. Holland, "'This Do in Remembrance of Me,'" *Ensign,* November 1995, 68.
8. Dallin H. Oaks, "Pornography," *Ensign,* May 2005, 90; emphasis added.
9. Jill C. Manning, *What's the Big Deal about Pornography?* (Salt Lake City: Shadow Mountain, 2008), 82.
10. Jeffrey R. Holland, "To Young Women," *Ensign,* November 2005, 29–30; emphasis added.
11. *For the Strength of Youth,* 14.
12. Ibid., 15.

CHAPTER 7: WHY SHOULD I BE SEXUALLY PURE?

1. *For the Strength of Youth* (Salt Lake City: The Church of Jesus Christ of Latter-day Saints, 2001), 25.
2. David E. Sorensen, "You Can't Pet a Rattlesnake," *Ensign,* May 2001, 41.
3. *For the Strength of Youth,* 24.
4. Ibid.
5. Ezra Taft Benson, "The Law of Chastity," *New Era,* January 1988, 4–5.
6. *For the Strength of Youth,* 26.
7. Ibid.
8. See *For the Strength of Youth,* 27.
9. *For the Strength of Youth,* 25.
10. Gordon B. Hinckley, "Some Thoughts on Temples, Retention of Converts, and Missionary Service," *Ensign,* November 1997, 51.
11. Benson, "The Law of Chastity," 5.
12. *For the Strength of Youth,* 17.

13. Jeffrey R. Holland, "Personal Purity," *Ensign,* November 1998, 76.

14. Richard G. Scott, "Making the Right Choices," 13 January 2002, http://speeches.byu.edu/reader/reader
   .php?id=605&x=61&y=5.

15. Holland, "Personal Purity," 76.

16. *For the Strength of Youth,* 15.

17. Holland, "Personal Purity," 76.

18. Gordon B. Hinckley, "To the Women of the Church," *Ensign,* November 2003, 115.

19. *For the Strength of Youth*, 36.

20. Ibid.

21. Gordon B. Hinckley, address to CES religious educators, February 2003, 3. See also D&C 10:5.

22. See Lawrence K. Altman, "Sex Infections Found in Quarter of Teenage Girls," *The New York Times,* 12 March 2008,
   http://www.nytimes.com/2008/03/12/science/12std.html.

23. See Fragile Families Research Brief, *Parents' Relationship Status Five Years after a Non-Marital Birth,* no. 39 (June
   2007): 1–4, http://www.fragilefamilies.princeton.edu/briefs/ResearchBrief39.pdf.

24. "Out of Wedlock Pregnancy Fact Sheet," http://firstthings.org/page/research/out-of-wedlock-pregnancy-fact-sheet.

25. "The Family: A Proclamation to the World," *Ensign,* November 1995, 102.

26. Benson, "The Law of Chastity," 5.

27. *For the Strength of Youth*, 27.

28. Ibid.

29. Ibid., 26.

30. "The Family: A Proclamation to the World," 102.

31. See Holland, "Personal Purity," 75–78.

CHAPTER 8: WHY SHOULDN'T I DATE UNTIL I'M 16?

1. International Communications Research National Omnibus Survey, "Parents of Teens and Teens Discuss Sex, Love, and
   Relationships: Polling Data," April 1998, http://www.icrsurvey.com/Study.aspx?f=Teenpreg.html.

2. *For the Strength of Youth* (Salt Lake City: The Church of Jesus Christ of Latter-day Saints, 2001), 24.

3. Carrie P. Jenkins, "Making Moral Choices," *BYU Today,* April 1985, 39.

4. Bruce Monson, "Speaking of Kissing," *New Era,* June 2001, 36.

5. Spencer W. Kimball, *The Miracle of Forgiveness* (Salt Lake City: Bookcraft, 1969), 223.

6. See Kate Fogarty, "Teens and Dating: Tips for Parents and Professionals," University of Florida IAF Extension, http://edis
   .ifas.ufl.edu/fy851.

7. See Claudia Wallis and Kristina Dell, "What Makes Teens Tick," *Time* Magazine, 10 May 2004, http://www.time.com/
   time/magazine/article/0,9171,994126-1,00.html.

8. *For the Strength of Youth*, 2.

9. See Deborah A. Cohen et al. "When and Where Do Youths Have Sex?" *Pediatrics* 110, no. 6 (December 2002): 2.

10. See Monson, "Speaking of Kissing," 36.

11. See Cohen, "When and Where Do Youths Have Sex?" 2.

CHAPTER 9: WHY SHOULDN'T I STEADY DATE IN HIGH SCHOOL?

1. Spencer W. Kimball, "President Kimball Speaks Out on Morality," *Ensign,* November 1980, 96; emphasis added.

2. Bruce Monson, "Speaking of Kissing," *New Era,* June 2001, 36.

3. *For the Strength of Youth* (Salt Lake City: The Church of Jesus Christ of Latter-day Saints, 2001), 27.

4. Gordon B. Hinckley, "A Prophet's Council and Prayer for Youth," *New Era,* January 2001, 13; emphasis added.

5. Spencer W. Kimball, *Teachings of Spencer W. Kimball,* edited by Edward L. Kimball (Salt Lake City: Bookcraft, 1982),
   287–88; emphasis added.

6. Larry Elder, "Kids, Guns, and Dr. Phil," *WorldNetDaily,* 28 November 2002; emphasis added, http://www.worldnetdaily .com/news/article.asp?ARTICLE_ID=29811.

7. Spencer W. Kimball, *The Miracle of Forgiveness* (Salt Lake City: Bookcraft, 1969), 66; emphasis added.

8. See *Adolescent Brain Development: Vulnerabilities and Opportunities,* edited by Ronald E. Dahl and Linda Patia Spear (New York: The New York Academy of Sciences, 2004).

9. John Fetto, "First Comes Love," *American Demographics,* 1 June 2003, http://findarticles.com/p/articles/mi_m4021/ is_5_25/ai_102102599/pg_1.

10. Kate Fogarty, "Teens and Dating: Tips for Parents and Professionals," University of Florida IAF Extension, http://edis .ifas.ufl.edu/fy851.

11. Ibid.

12. "Inside the Teenage Brain: Interview: Deborah Yurgelun-Todd," http://www.pbs.org/wgbh/pages/frontline/shows/ teenbrain/interviews/todd.html. Photo courtesy of Dr. Deborah Yurgelun-Todd.

13. Ibid.

14. *For the Strength of Youth*, 24.

15. Kimball, "President Kimball Speaks Out on Morality," 96; emphasis added.

16. Hinckley, "A Prophet's Council and Prayer for Youth," 13.

17. Ezra Taft Benson, "To the Young Women of the Church," *Ensign,* November 1986, 82–83; emphasis added.

18. Anonymous, http://dearelder.com/index/inc_name/dear_john_display/. Read more "Dear John's" at the same site.

CHAPTER 10: WHY SHOULD I GET MARRIED IN THE TEMPLE?

1. Gordon B. Hinckley, "Don't Drop the Ball," *Ensign,* November 1994, 48.

2. Lorenzo Snow, *The Teachings of Lorenzo Snow,* comp. Clyde J. Williams (Salt Lake City: Bookcraft, 1984), 1.

3. "The Family: A Proclamation to the World," *Ensign,* November 1995, 102; emphasis added.

4. Eliza R. Snow, "O My Father," in *Hymns of The Church of Jesus Christ of Latter-day Saints* (Salt Lake City: The Church of Jesus Christ of Latter-day Saints, 1985), no. 292.

5. Catherine Ross, *Journal of Marriage and the Family,* quoted in Linda J. Waite and Maggie Gallagher, *The Case for Marriage* (New York: Doubleday Publishing, 2000), 47.

6. Linda J. Waite and Maggie Gallagher, *The Case for Marriage* (New York: Doubleday Publishing, 2000), 67.

7. Ibid., 99.

8. Dallin H. Oaks, "'The Great Plan of Happiness,'" *Ensign,* November 1993, 75.

9. Joseph F. Smith, *Gospel Doctrine* (Salt Lake City: Deseret Book, 1971), 275.

10. Spencer W. Kimball, *Marriage and Divorce* (Salt Lake City: Deseret Book, 1976), 28.

11. Spencer W. Kimball, *The Teachings of Spencer W. Kimball,* ed. Edward L. Kimball (Salt Lake City: Bookcraft, 1982), 297.

12. See "Temples of the World," http://www.lds.org/temples/chronological/0,11206,1900–1,00.html.

13. Jeffrey R. Holland, "Helping Those Who Struggle with Same-Gender Attraction," *Ensign,* October 2007, 43–44.

CHAPTER 11: WHY SHOULD I WANT TO HAVE CHILDREN WHEN I'M MARRIED?

1. "TIME'S Man of the Year," http://history1900s.about.com/library/weekly/aa050400a.htm.

2. Neal A. Maxwell, "The Women of God," *Ensign,* May 1978, 10–11.

3. Ibid., 10.

4. Ezra Taft Benson, "America at the Crossroads," *New Era,* July 1978, 38.

5. Spencer W. Kimball, "Privileges and Responsibilities of Sisters," *New Era,* January 1979, 43–44.

6. E. T. Sullivan, quoted in Gordon B. Hinckley, "These, Our Little Ones," *Ensign,* December 2007, 5–6.

7. Brigham Young, in *Journal of Discourses,* 26 vols. (Liverpool: Latter-day Saints' Book Depot, 1854–86), 19:72.

8. N. Eldon Tanner, in Conference Report, October 1973, 127.

9. See "Statistics of a Fatherless America," http://www.paternita.info/America/fatherless-america.pdf.

10. See Walter E. Williams, "Population Control Nonsense," 19 February 1999, http://www.gmu.edu/departments/economics/wew/articles/99/Population-Control.htm.

11. M. Russell Ballard, "The Sacred Responsibilities of Parenthood," *Ensign,* March 2006, 28–29.

12. "The Family: A Proclamation to the World," *Ensign,* November 1995, 102.

13. Quoted in Russell M. Nelson, "Our Sacred Duty to Honor Women," *Ensign,* May 1999, 38.

14. Susan W. Tanner, "Strengthen Home and Family," 2004 Spring President's Message, March 2004, http://www.lds.org/pa/display/0,17884,7039–1,00.html.

15. Some ideas taken from Teresa McEntire, "Top 10 Benefits of Having Children," 29 September 2006, http://parenting.families.com/blog/top-10-benefits-of-having-children.

16. Anonymous, http://sofinesjoyfulmoments.com/humor/kidprvrbs.htm.

17. Gordon B. Hinckley, "'Great Shall Be the Peace of Thy Children,'" *Ensign,* November 2000, 50.

18. Boyd K. Packer, "Building up a Righteous Posterity," *Worldwide Leadership Training Meeting,* 9 February 2008, 7–8.

19. "The Family: A Proclamation to the World," 102.

20. Young, in *Journal of Discourses,* 4:56.

CHAPTER 12: WHY CAN'T I WATCH WHATEVER I WANT?

1. Henry B. Eyring, "We Must Raise Our Sights," CES Symposium, Brigham Young University, 14 August 2001, 1; emphasis added.

2. See "NOAA Scientists Able to Measure Tsunami Height from Space," 10 January 2005, http://www.noaanews.noaa.gov/stories2005/s2365.htm. Photos courtesy of DigitalGlobe Inc.

3. Ad copy for iPod Classic, http://www.apple.com/ipodclassic; emphasis added.

4. Stefanie Olsen, "Teens and Media: A Full-Time Job," 7 December 2006, http://news.cnet.com/2100–1041_3–6141920.html.

5. *For the Strength of Youth* (Salt Lake City: The Church of Jesus Christ of Latter-day Saints, 2001), 17.

6. Parents Television Council, "Facts and TV Statistics," http://www.parentstv.org/PTC/facts/mediafacts.asp.

7. See Randal Wright, 25 *Mistakes LDS Parents Make and How to Avoid Them* (Salt Lake City: Deseret Book Distributors, 2007), 95.

8. See Malcolm Gladwell, *Blink: The Power of Thinking without Thinking* (New York: Little Brown & Company, 2005), 53–55.

9. See Committee on Communications, "Media Violence," *Pediatrics* 95, no. 6 (June 1995).

10. See "Addictive Behaviors," http://www.commonsensemedia.org/parent_tips/healthsurvivalguide/addictivebehaviors.php.

11. Russell M. Nelson, "Addiction or Freedom," *Ensign,* November 1988, 8; emphasis added.

12. Dallin H. Oaks, "Pornography," *Ensign,* May 2005, 88.

13. *For the Strength of Youth*, 17.

14. Ibid.

CHAPTER 13: WHY SHOULDN'T I VIEW PORNOGRAPHY?

1. Gordon B. Hinckley, "Some Thoughts on Temples, Retention of Converts, and Missionary Service," *Ensign,* November 1997, 51.

2. "2006 and 2005 Pornography United States Industry Revenue Statistics," from "Internet Pornography Statistics," compiled by Jerry Ropelato, http://internet-filter-review.toptenreviews.com/internet-pornography-statistics.html.

3. *For the Strength of Youth* (Salt Lake City: The Church of Jesus Christ of Latter-day Saints, 2001), 17.

4. Ibid.

5. "Pornography," in *True to the Faith* (Salt Lake City: The Church of Jesus Christ of Latter-day Saints, 2004), 117.

6. Dallin H. Oaks, "Pornography," *Ensign,* May 2005, 89.

7. D. Todd Christofferson, "A Sense of the Sacred," 7 November 2004, 4–5, http://speeches.byu.edu/reader/reader.php?id=8555.

8. "Pornography Time Statistics," from "Internet Pornography Statistics," compiled by Jerry Ropelato, http://internet-filter-review.toptenreviews.com/internet-pornography-statistics.html.

9. "Internet Pornography Statistics," compiled by Jerry Ropelato, http://internet-filter-review.toptenreviews.com/internet-pornography-statistics.html.

10. "Pornography," in *True to the Faith*, 118.

11. Oaks, "Pornography," 88.

12. *For the Strength of Youth*, 17.

13. "The Odds of Dying From . . ." National Safety Council 2004, http://www.nsc.org/research/odds.aspx.

14. See Janis Wolak, Kimberly Mitchell, David Finkelhor, "Unwanted and Wanted Exposure to Online Pornography in a National Sample of Youth Internet Users," *Pediatrics* 119, no. 2 (February 2007).

15. *For the Strength of Youth*, 19.

16. Thomas S. Monson, "Pornography, the Deadly Carrier," *Ensign*, July 2001, 2.

17. "Women and Pornography," from "Internet Pornography Statistics," compiled by Jerry Ropelato, http://internet-filter-review.toptenreviews.com/internet-pornography-statistics.html.

18. See James Dobson, *Life on the Edge* (Nashville, Tenn.: Word Publishing, 1995), 192–200.

19. Hinckley, "Some Thoughts on Temples, Retention of Converts, and Missionary Service," 51.

20. See Jill C. Manning, *What's the Big Deal about Pornography?* (Salt Lake City: Shadow Mountain, 2008), 39–40.

21. See Manning, *What's the Big Deal about Pornography?* 26–27.

22. "Study Proves 'Pornography Is Harmful,'" 12 March 2002, National Foundation for Family Research and Education (NFFRE), http://www.lifesitenews.com/ldn/2002/mar/02031203.html.

23. *For the Strength of Youth*, 19.

24. "Pornography ruined their lives, say inmates," *Church News*, 21 April 2007, Z07.

25. Thomas S. Monson, "True to the Faith," *Ensign*, May 2006, 18–19.

26. *For the Strength of Youth*, 17.

27. Monson, "Pornography, the Deadly Carrier," 3.

28. "Pornography," in *True to the Faith*, 118.

CHAPTER 14: WHY DOES THE MUSIC I LISTEN TO MATTER?

1. See ad copy for iPod Classic, http://www.apple.com/ipodclassic/.

2. Britney Spears, quoted in Michelle Tauber, "Britney's Big Break," *People Magazine*, 21 August 2002, 3.

3. See Kristopher Kaliebe and Adrian Sondheimer, "The Media: Relationships to Psychiatry and Children," *Academic Psychiatry* 26, no. 3 (September 2002): 210.

4. *For the Strength of Youth* (Salt Lake City: The Church of Jesus Christ of Latter-day Saints, 2001), 20.

5. Ibid.; emphasis added.

6. Boyd K. Packer, "The Instrument of Your Mind and the Foundation of Your Character," 2 February 2003, 6, http://speeches.byu.edu/reader/reader.php?id=478.

7. Snoop Dogg, http://thinkexist.com/quotation/it-s-so-easy-for-a-kid-to-join-a-gang-to-do-drugs/541418.html.

8. Marilyn Manson and Neil Strauss, *The Long Hard Road Out of Hell* (New York: HarperCollins, 1998), 265.

9. "First Presidency Preface," in *Hymns of The Church of Jesus Christ of Latter-day Saints* (Salt Lake City: The Church of Jesus Christ of Latter-day Saints, 1985), x.

10. Jessica Simpson, http://www.brainyquote.com/quotes/authors/j/jessica_simpson.html.

11. See Gene. R. Cook, "Ways to Avoid Discouragement," BYU–Idaho Devotional, 29 November 1988.

12. Tara Parker-Pope, "For Clues on Teenage Sex, Experts Look to Hip-Hop," *The New York Times*, 6 November 2007, http://query.nytimes.com/gst/fullpage.html?res=9E05E5D7103AF935A35752C1A9619C8B63&sec=&spon=&pagewanted=1.

13. Trent Reznor, "Hurt," in *The Downward Spiral.* Audio CD. TVT/Interscope Records, 1994.

14. See Randal Wright, *25 Mistakes LDS Parents Make and How to Avoid Them* (Salt Lake City: Deseret Book Distributors, 2007). 80.

15. Madonna, in J. Randy Taraborrelli, *Madonna: An Intimate Biography* (New York: Simon & Schuster, 2001), 8.

16. For one study, see Sophia Turczynewycz, Eric McGary, Ashlae Shepler, Laura Fink, and John Drain, "Rock On! The Cognitive Effects of Music," 19 April 2002, http://jrscience.wcp.muohio.edu/nsfall01/FinalArticles/Draft1.RockOnThe Cognitive.html.

17. Gary Toms, "Hip-Hop's Negative Impact on Kids," 1 August 2006, http://www.associatedcontent.com/article/47127/ hiphops_negative_impact_on_kids.html?page=2.

18. 50 Cent, http://thinkexist.com/quotes/50_cent/.

19. See Frances Rauscher and Gordon Shaw, *Neurological Research* 19, no. 1 (February 1997).

20. *For the Strength of Youth*, 23.

21. Sharon G. Larsen, "Your Celestial Guide," *Ensign,* May 2001, 87.

CHAPTER 15: WHY ARE THERE GUIDELINES FOR DANCING?

1. *For the Strength of Youth* (Salt Lake City: The Church of Jesus Christ of Latter-day Saints, 2001), 21.

2. See ibid., 20.

3. See Catherine Donaldson-Evans, "Players Break a Sweat with Video Games," 9 July 2004, http://www.foxnews.com/ story/0,2933,125114,00.html; "Dance Dance Revolution," http://en.wikipedia.org/wiki/Dance_dance_revolution.

4. Marie K. Hafen, "For Your Journeys in the Land," Ricks College Devotional, 3 October 2000, http://www.byui.edu/ Presentations/Transcripts/Devotionals/2000_10_03_Hafen.htm.

5. *For the Strength of Youth*, 21.

6. See "Most Marriages Due to Dancing," *The New York Times,* 9 May 1907, http://query.nytimes.com/gst/abstract.html? res=9C06E2DC133EE033A2575AC1A9639C946697D6CF.

7. *For the Strength of Youth*, 20.

8. Valerie Ninemire, "Is Cheerleading Getting too Sexy? No More Bumpin' and Grindin'," 20 March 2005, http://cheerlead ing.about.com/od/coachingcheerleading/a/cheerlaws.htm.

9. *For the Strength of Youth*, 21.

10. Ibid.

11. Ezra Taft Benson, in Conference Report, October 1970, 24.

12. Ezra Taft Benson, in Conference Report, April 1959, 79–80.

13. Brigham Young, in *Teaching of Presidents of the Church: Brigham Young* (Salt Lake City: The Church of Jesus Christ of Latter-day Saints, 1997), 188.

14. Joseph F. Smith, in *Teaching of Presidents of the Church: Joseph F. Smith* (Salt Lake City: The Church of Jesus Christ of Latter-day Saints, 1998), 377.

15. David O. McKay, quoted by Ezra Taft Benson, in Conference Report, April 1969, 14.

16. *For the Strength of Youth*, 21.

17. Ibid.

CHAPTER 16: WHY SHOULD I USE CLEAN LANGUAGE?

1. Gordon B. Hinckley, "'I Am Clean,'" *Ensign,* May 2007, 62.

2. Leland Gregory, *Idiots at Work* (New York: Andrews McMeel, 2004), 120, 193, 195.

3. See Lenore Sandel, *The Relationship between Language and Intelligence,* Review of Historical Research: Summary #5, April 1998.

4. *For the Strength of Youth* (Salt Lake City: The Church of Jesus Christ of Latter-day Saints, 2001), 22.

5. Henry B. Eyring, "God Helps the Faithful Priesthood Holder," *Ensign,* November 2007, 58.

6. See David Whitmer, in B. H. Roberts, *A Comprehensive History of The Church of Jesus Christ of Latter-day Saints,* 6 vols. (Salt Lake City: The Church of Jesus Christ of Latter-day Saints, 1930), 1:131.

7. *For the Strength of Youth*, 22.

8. Spencer W. Kimball, "President Kimball Speaks Out on Profanity," *New Era,* January 1981, 4.

9. *For the Strength of Youth*, 20.

10. Bruce C. Hafen, *A Disciple's Life* (Salt Lake City: Deseret Book, 2002), 148.

11. Neal A. Maxwell, "The Pathway of Discipleship," *Ensign,* September 1998, 10.

12. Author unknown. Quoted in Vaughn J. Featherstone, "The Last Drop in the Chalice," 24 September 1985, http://speeches.byu.edu/reader/reader.php?id=6988.

13. *For the Strength of Youth*, 22.

CHAPTER 17: WHY SHOULD I BE HONEST?

1. *For the Strength of Youth* (Salt Lake City: The Church of Jesus Christ of Latter-day Saints, 2001), 31.

2. See ibid.

3. "Academic dishonesty," http://en.wikipedia.org/wiki/Academic_dishonesty.

4. *For the Strength of Youth*, 31.

5. "Enron Employees Ride Stock to Bottom," 14 January 2002, http://archives.cnn.com/2002/LAW/01/14/enron.employees/; see also "Arthur Andersen," http://en.wikipedia.org/wiki/Arthur_Andersen.

6. Richard C. Hollinger and Jason L. Davis, *2002 National Retail Security Survey Final Report; University of Florida* (Gainsville, Flo.: University of Florida, 2003), 4.

7. "Cabbie Returns Bag of Diamonds," 18 November 2005, http://www.cbsnews.com/stories/2005/11/18/national/main1059255.shtml.

8. Gordon B. Hinckley, "'An Honest Man—God's Noblest Work,'" *Ensign,* May 1976, 61.

9. See http://www.wallettest.com.

CHAPTER 18: WHY SHOULD I KEEP THE SABBATH DAY HOLY?

1. James E. Faust, "The Lord's Day," *Ensign,* November 1991, 34.

2. Brigham Young, *Discourses of Brigham Young,* compiled by John A. Widtsoe (Salt Lake City: The Church of Jesus Christ of Latter-day Saints, 1954), 165.

3. *For the Strength of Youth* (Salt Lake City: The Church of Jesus Christ of Latter-day Saints, 2001), 32.

4. Spencer W. Kimball, *The Miracle of Forgiveness* (Salt Lake City: Bookcraft, 1969), 96–97.

5. Boyd K. Packer, "Washed Clean," *Ensign,* May 1997, 10.

6. Dallin H. Oaks, "The Gospel in Our Lives," *Ensign,* May 2002, 34.

7. Jeffrey R. Holland, Doctrine and Covenants CES Video, "Upon My Holy Day."

8. Spencer W. Kimball, *The Teachings of Spencer W. Kimball,* ed. Edward L. Kimball (Salt Lake City: Bookcraft, 1982), 220.

9. Mark E. Petersen, in Conference Report, April 1975, 72. See also D&C 59:9–10.

10. Dallin H. Oaks, "Sacrament Meeting and the Sacrament," *Ensign,* November 2008, 19.

11. Jeffrey R. Holland, "To Young Women," *Ensign,* November 2005, 29; emphasis in original.

12. D. Todd Christofferson, "A Sense of the Sacred," 7 November 2004, 6, http://speeches.byu.edu/reader/reader/php?id=8555.

CHAPTER 19: WHY SHOULD I FAST?

1. Plato, *Laws,* Book I, section 626E.

2. *For the Strength of Youth* (Salt Lake City: The Church of Jesus Christ of Latter-day Saints, 2001), 34.

3. *Gospel Principles* (Salt Lake City: The Church of Jesus Christ of Latter-day Saints, 1997), 165.

4. See Richard G. Scott, "We Love You—Please Come Back," *Ensign,* May 1986, 10–12.

5. David O. McKay, *Pathways to Happiness: Inspirational Discourses of David O. McKay* (Salt Lake City: Bookcraft, 1957), 120.

6. Joseph B. Wirthlin, "The Law of the Fast," *Ensign,* May 2001, 73.

7. See Spencer J. Condie, "Becoming a Great Benefit to Our Fellow Beings," *Ensign,* May 2002, 44–46.

8. See World Resource Institute, http://www.wri.org.

9. "Frequently Asked Questions," http://www.freerice.com/faq.html.

10. Wirthlin, "The Law of the Fast," 74.

11. See *For the Strength of Youth,* 35.

12. Joseph Smith, *The History of the Church,* edited by B. H. Roberts, 2d ed. 7 vols. (Salt Lake City: The Church of Jesus Christ of Latter-day Saints, 1932–51), 7:413; spelling standardized.

13. Gordon B. Hinckley, "The State of the Church," *Ensign,* May 1991, 52–53.

14. See http://www.squidoo.com/world-hunger.

15. *For the Strength of Youth*, 35.

CHAPTER 20: WHY SHOULD I PRAY ALWAYS?

1. See "Do Teens Pray? How Often?" http://www.youthandreligion.org/news/5-2-2002.html.

2. Brigham Young, in *Journal of Discourses,* 26 vols. (Liverpool: Latter-day Saints' Book Depot, 1854–86), 12:103.

3. "Mind and Spirit," from the Health Library section of CentraState Healthcare System, http://www.centrastate.com.

4. LDS Bible Dictionary, s.v. "Prayer"; emphasis added.

5. "SMS History, Facts and Data," http://www.mobilesmsmarketing.com/sms_history_facts_data.php; Tom Charity, "Korean Teenagers to Develop Carpal Tunnel Syndrome Due to Text Messaging," 4 May 2007, http://www.htlounge .net/articles/3171/1/Korean-Teenagers-To-Develop-Carpal-Tunnel-Syndrome-Due-To-Text-Messaging.

6. *For the Strength of Youth* (Salt Lake City: The Church of Jesus Christ of Latter-day Saints, 2001), 40.

7. See "Do Teens Pray? How Often?" http://www.youthandreligion.org/news/5-2-2002.html.

8. Joseph Smith, *The History of the Church,* edited by B. H. Roberts, 2d ed. 7 vols. (Salt Lake City: The Church of Jesus Christ of Latter-day Saints, 1932–51), 6:305.

9. Ibid.

10. H. Burke Peterson, "Prayer—Try Again," *Ensign,* June 1981, 75.

11. Gene R. Cook, *Receiving Answers to Our Prayers* (Salt Lake City: Deseret Book, 1996), 11.

12. Richard G. Scott, "Using the Supernal Gift of Prayer," *Ensign,* May 2007, 8–11.

CHAPTER 21: WHY SHOULD I STUDY MY SCRIPTURES DAILY?

1. See Boyd K. Packer, "The Play and the Plan," Address at Church Educational System fireside, Kirkland Washington Stake center, 7 May 1995, 1–9.

2. See Susan Easton Black, *Finding Christ through the Book of Mormon* (Salt Lake City: Deseret Book, 1987), 16.

3. David A. Bednar, "Understanding the Importance of Scripture Study," Ricks College, 6 January 1998.

4. Boyd K. Packer, in Conference Report, October 1986, 20.

5. Neleh Dennis, in David Randall, "Neleh Dennis of Layton, UT to Star on 'Survivor,'" *BYU Daily Universe,* 12 February 2002, http://newsnet.byu.edu/story/36615.

6. Sheri Dew, "We Are Not Alone," *Ensign,* November 1998, 96.

7. Boyd K. Packer, "Teach the Scriptures," Address to CES Religious Educators, Temple Square Assembly Hall, 14 October 1977, 21; emphasis added.

8. Anthony Sweat, "Reading Motivation: Factors Influencing Daily Scripture Study," study and paper for Utah State University, Logan, Utah, 2004, 12.

9. See Ville Heiskanen and Marcel van de Hoef, "Garmin, TomTom navigate turf war while cellphone firms eye the spoils," *Business Report,* 18 November 2007, http://www.busrep.co.za/index.php?fSectionId=2515&fArticleId=4131993.

10. Brent L. Top and Bruce A. Chadwick, "Helping Teens Stay Strong," *Ensign,* March 1999, 27; emphasis added.

11. James E. Faust, "The Power of Self-Mastery," *Ensign,* May 2000, 44.

12. Howard W. Hunter, "Reading the Scriptures," *Ensign,* November 1979, 64; emphasis added.

CHAPTER 22: WHY SHOULD I PAY TITHING?

1. U2, "God Part II," *Rattle & Hum,* Island Records, 1987.

2. Joseph F. Smith, *Gospel Doctrine* (Salt Lake City: Deseret Book, 1971), 229.

3. Arthur C. Brooks, "The Privilege of Giving," *Marriott Alumni Magazine,* Winter 2008, 18.

4. Gordon B. Hinckley, quoted by Lynn G. Robbins, "Tithing—A Commandment Even for the Destitute," *Ensign,* May 2005, 36.

5. Spencer W. Kimball, *The Teachings of Spencer W. Kimball,* ed. Edward L. Kimball (Salt Lake City: Bookcraft, 1982), 212.

6. Gordon B. Hinckley, "The Sacred Law of Tithing," *Ensign,* December 1989, 4; emphasis added.

7. Robert D. Hales, "Tithing: A Test of Faith with Eternal Blessings," *Ensign,* November 2002, 27; emphasis added.

8. Gordon B. Hinckley, "Inspirational Thoughts," *Ensign,* July 1998, 4.

9. The Freeman Institute, "Stupid-Criminals Hall of Shame," http://www.freemaninstitute.com/hall_of_shame.htm.

10. Smith, *Gospel Doctrine*, 225.

11. The Urban Institute, "Profiles of Individual Charitable Contributions by State, 2002," National Center for Charitable Statistics. Full report available at http://nccsdataweb.urban.org/kbfiles/421/stgive_02.pdf.

12. Brigham Young, *Discourses of Brigham Young,* compiled by John A. Widtsoe (Salt Lake City: Deseret Book, 1954), 174.

13. Thomas S. Monson, "Life's Greatest Decisions," CES Fireside for Young Adults, 7 September 2003.

14. Gordon B. Hinckley, General Authority Training, October 2001, quoted in D. Allen Anderson, "Faith in and a Testimony of . . . ," July 2005, http://www.lds.org.sg/sg_messages_July2005.htm.

15. "Live the Law of Tithing," http://mormon.org/mormonorg/eng/basic-beliefs/the-commandments/live-the-law-of-tithing.

16. See Gordon B. Hinckley, "We Walk by Faith," *Ensign,* May 2002, 73–74.

17. Brooks, "The Privilege of Giving," 19.

18. Hales, "Tithing: A Test of Faith with Eternal Blessings," 26–27; emphasis added.

CHAPTER 23: WHY SHOULD I WRITE IN A JOURNAL?

1. Personal family records of John Hilton III.

2. Henry B. Eyring, "Remembrance and Gratitude," *Ensign,* November 1989, 12–13.

3. Spencer W. Kimball, *The Teachings of Spencer W. Kimball,* ed. Edward L. Kimball (Salt Lake City: Bookcraft, 1982), 349.

4. Richard G. Scott, *Finding Peace, Happiness, and Joy* (Salt Lake City: Deseret Book, 2007), 45.

5. See Chad M. Burton and Laura A. King, "The health benefits of writing about intensely positive experiences," *Journal of Research in Personality* 38, no. 2 (2004): 150–63.

6. Spencer W. Kimball, "President Kimball Speaks Out on Personal Journals," *New Era,* December 1980, 26.

7. Henry B. Eyring, "O Remember, Remember," *Ensign,* November 2007, 66–67.

8. David A. Bednar, "Understanding the Importance of Scripture Study," Ricks College Devotional, 6 January 1998, http://www.byui.edu/Presentations/Transcripts/Devotionals/1998_01_06_Bednar.htm.

CHAPTER 24: WHY SHOULD I BE GRATEFUL?

1. Joseph Smith, quoted in Ezra Taft Benson, *God, Family, Country* (Salt Lake City: Deseret Book, 1974), 199.

2. See Chad M. Burton and Laura A. King, "The health benefits of writing about intensely positive experiences," *Journal of Research in Personality* 38, no. 2 (2004): 150–63.

3. Joseph B. Wirthlin, *Press On* (Salt Lake City: Deseret Book, 2007), 218.

4. *For the Strength of Youth* (Salt Lake City: The Church of Jesus Christ of Latter-day Saints, 2001), 6.

5. Wirthlin, *Press On*, 218.

6. Marvin J. Ashton, "And in Everything Give Thanks," 1 September 1991, 4, http://speeches.byu.edu/reader/reader .php?id=7074.

7. Henry B. Eyring, "Remembrance and Gratitude," *Ensign,* November 1989, 12.

8. Wirthlin, 224.

9. Ibid.

10. International Literacy Day, 7 September 2001, "Facts about Illiteracy," http://www.sil.org/literacy/LitFacts.htm.

11. Wirthlin, *Press On,* 218.

12. Ashton, "And in Everything Give Thanks," 5.

13. Gordon B. Hinckley, in Conference Report, October 1964, 117.

14. Gordon B. Hinckley, "A Prophet's Counsel and Prayer for Youth," *Ensign,* January 2001, 4.

15. Ibid.

CHAPTER 25: WHY SHOULD I HONOR MY PARENTS?

1. *Expenditures on Children by Families, 2007,* United States Department of Agriculture, March 2008, 20.

2. Russell M. Nelson, "Listen to Learn," *Ensign,* May 1991, 22–23.

3. Gordon B. Hinckley, "Some Lessons I Learned as a Boy," *Ensign,* May 1993, 59.

4. Thomas S. Monson, "Be Thou an Example," *Ensign,* May 2005, 112.

5. M. Russell Ballard, *When Thou Art Converted* (Salt Lake City: Deseret Book, 2001), 203.

6. Ezra Taft Benson, "To the Young Women of the Church," *Ensign,* November 1986, 81.

7. Ezra Taft Benson, "To the Elderly in the Church," *Ensign,* November 1989, 6.

CHAPTER 26: WHY IS IT SO IMPORTANT I GAIN AN EDUCATION?

1. "Relationship between Reading Literacy and Education Outcomes," *The Daily,* 7 June 2006, http://www.statcan.ca/ Daily/English/060607/d060607a.htm.

2. Camilla Eyring Kimball, as quoted in *A Heritage of Faith: Talks Selected from the BYU Women's Conferences,* eds. Mary E. Stovall and Carol Cornwall Madsen (Salt Lake City: Deseret Book, 1988), 7–8.

3. U.S. Census Bureau, 2000.

4. National Center for Higher Education Management Systems, 2002.

5. Gordon B. Hinckley, "A Prophet's Council and Prayer for Youth," *New Era,* January 2001, 8, 10–11.

6. Ibid., 8.

7. See Spencer J. Condie, *Russell M. Nelson: Father, Surgeon, Apostle* (Salt Lake City: Deseret Book, 2003), 147, 153–56, 215–18.

8. "Education," http://newsroom.lds.org/ldsnewsroom/eng/background-information/education.

9. Spencer W. Kimball, "Men of Example," Address to Religious Educators, 12 September 1975, 9–10.

10. Ibid.

11. Gordon B. Hinckley, "The Perpetual Education Fund, *Ensign,* May 2001, 53.

12. See Gordon B. Hinckley, "Seek Learning," *New Era,* September 2007, 2, 4–5.

13. Richard L. Evans, quoted in David A. Bednar, "Your Whole Soul as an Offering unto Him," 5 January 1999; emphasis added, http://www.byui.edu/Presentations/Transcripts/Devotionals/1999_01_05_Bednar.htm.

14. Digest of Educational Statistics, http://nces.ed.gov/programs/digest/d07/tables/dt07_255.asp.

15. Hinckley, "Seek Learning," 4.

CHAPTER 27: WHY SHOULD I ATTEND SEMINARY AND INSTITUTE?

1. James E. Faust, "The Enemy Within," *Ensign,* November 2000, 44.

2. "Interceptor Body Armor Components," http://www.globalsecurity.org/military/systems/ground/interceptor.htm.

3. Henry B. Eyring, "Remarks at An Evening with President Gordon B. Hinckley," Address to CES Religious Educators, 7 February 2003, 1; emphasis added.

4. Boyd K. Packer, "Teach the Scriptures," Address to CES Religious Educators, 14 October 1977, 4.

5. "Statistical Information," http://newsroom.lds.org/ldsnewsroom/eng/statistical-information.

6. L. Tom Perry, "Receive Truth," *Ensign,* November 1997, 61–62.

7. John Bartkowski, quoted in Elaine Jarvik, "LDS Teens tops in living faith," *Deseret News,* 15 March 2005, A01. See also Christian Smith and Melinda Lundquist Denton, *Soul Searching: The Religious and Spiritual Lives of American Teenagers* (New York: Oxford University Press, 2005).

8. Spencer W. Kimball, "Circles of Exaltation," Address to Religious Educators, 28 June 1968, 4; emphasis added.

9. Perry, "Receive Truth," 61.

10. Gordon B. Hinckley, *Faith: The Essence of True Religion* (Salt Lake City: Deseret Book, 1989), 122.

11. Gordon B. Hinckley, "The Miracle Made Possible by Faith," *Ensign,* May 1984, 47.

12. John A. Widstoe, *Evidences and Reconciliations* (Salt Lake City: Bookcraft, 1960), 16–17.

CHAPTER 28: WHY SHOULD I SERVE A MISSION?

1. Spencer W. Kimball, "Circles of Exaltation," Address to Religious Educators, 28 June 1968, 2.

2. Gordon B. Hinckley, "Some Thoughts on Temples, Retention of Converts, and Missionary Service," *Ensign,* November 1997, 52.

3. Gordon B. Hinckley, "To the Bishops of the Church," *Worldwide Leadership Training Meeting,* 19 June 2004, 27.

4. "Statistical Report, 2007," *Ensign,* May 2008, 25.

5. Gordon B. Hinckley, "Of Missions, Temples, and Stewardship," *Ensign,* November 1995, 52; emphasis added.

6. Gordon B. Hinckley, "News of the Church," *Ensign,* May 1985, 97.

7. Richard G. Scott, "Now Is the Time to Serve a Mission!" *Ensign,* May 2006, 89–90.

8. David A. Bednar, "Becoming a Missionary," *Ensign,* November 2005, 47.

9. Ibid.

10. Ibid.; emphasis added.

11. Spencer W. Kimball, "'It Becometh Every Man,'" *Ensign,* October 1977, 3.

12. Scott, "Now Is the Time to Serve a Mission!" 90.

13. Paraphrased from Gordon B. Hinckley, *Teachings of Gordon B. Hinckley* (Salt Lake City: Deseret Book, 1997), 360–61.

14. Hinckley, "Of Missions, Temples, and Stewardship," 51–52.

15. Brigham Young, in *Journal of Discourses,* 26 vols. (Liverpool: Latter-day Saints' Book Depot, 1854–86), 8:53.

16. Orson F. Whitney, in Conference Report, April 1918, 73.

17. Ezra Taft Benson, *The Teachings of Ezra Taft Benson* (Salt Lake City: Bookcraft, 1988), 213.

18. Heber C. Kimball, quoted in Gordon B. Hinckley, "An Ensign to the Nations," *Ensign,* November 1989, 53; emphasis added.

19. Hinckley, "Some Thoughts on Temples, Retention of Converts, and Missionary Service," *Ensign,* November 1997, 52.

CHAPTER 29: WHY SHOULD I REPENT NOW AND NOT LATER?

1. Spencer W. Kimball, *The Teachings of Spencer W. Kimball,* ed. Edward L. Kimball (Salt Lake City: Bookcraft, 1982), 48; emphasis in original.

2. See "Study: Americans Procrastinating More and More," 11 January 2007, http://www.foxnews.com/story/0,2933,243102,00.html.

3. M. Russell Ballard, "Purity Precedes Power," *Ensign,* November 1990, 36.

4. *For the Strength of Youth* (Salt Lake City: The Church of Jesus Christ of Latter-day Saints, 2001), 2; emphasis added.

5. Robert D. Hales, "Fulfilling Our Duty to God," *Ensign,* November 2001, 40.

6. Spencer W. Kimball, *The Miracle of Forgiveness* (Salt Lake City: Bookcraft, 1969), 117; emphasis added.

7. Henry B. Eyring, "Do Not Delay," *Ensign,* November 1999, 34.

8. Jeffrey R. Holland, "For Times of Trouble," 18 March 1980, 5; emphasis in original, http://speeches.byu.edu/reader/reader.php?id=6763.

CONCLUSION: SOMETIMES WE DO NOT NEED TO KNOW *WHY*

1. Richard G. Scott, "Trust in the Lord," *Ensign,* November 1995, 17.

2. Lance B. Wickman, "But If Not," *Ensign,* November 2002, 30.

3. Robert D. Hales, "Healing Soul and Body," *Ensign,* November 1998, 14–15; emphasis in original.

4. David A. Bednar, "For Such a Time As This," 16 March 2001; emphasis in original, http://www.byui.edu/Presentations/Transcripts/WomensWeek/2001_03_16_Bednar.htm.

5. Paraphrased from Thomas S. Monson, *Inspiring Experiences That Build Faith: From the Life and Ministry of Thomas S. Monson* (Salt Lake City: Deseret Book, 1994), 23.

6. Joseph Smith, *Lectures on Faith* (Salt Lake City: Deseret Book, 1985), 1; emphasis added.

7. Boyd K. Packer, "What Is Faith?" in *Faith* (Salt Lake City: Deseret Book, 1983), 42.

SHOULD I KEEP THE COMMANDMENTS? • WHY ARE THERE SO MANY COMMANDMENTS AND RULES? • WHY DO SOME PEOPL
BREAK THE COMMANDMENTS APPEAR HAPPY? • WHY ARE SOME COMMANDMENTS MORE IMPORTANT THAN OTHERS—OR AR
• WHY SHOULD I LISTEN TO AND FOLLOW THE PROPHET? • WHY IS IT SO IMPORTANT TO LISTEN TO GENERAL CONFERENCE
Y DO MODERN PROPHETS SOMETIMES TEACH THINGS THAT ARE DIFFERENT FROM WHAT PAST PROPHETS TAUGHT? • WH
LD I LISTEN TO PROPHETS WHO ARE SO MUCH OLDER THAN I AM? • WHY DOES IT MATTER WHO MY FRIENDS ARE? • WHY I
TO STILL BE FRIENDS WITH PEOPLE IF THEY AREN'T LDS? • WHY CAN A FRIEND STILL BE BAD IF THEY AREN'T PRESSURIN
O BREAK THE COMMANDMENTS? • WHY IS IT WRONG FOR ME TO "COVER" FOR MY FRIENDS AND NOT TELL ON THEM? ISN'
WHAT GOOD FRIENDS DO? • WHY SHOULD I KEEP THE WORD OF WISDOM? • WHY SHOULDN'T I "TRY" ALCOHOL JUST TO SE
T IT TASTES LIKE? • WHY SHOULDN'T I TAKE SOMETHING INTO MY BODY IF SCIENCE SAYS IT'S GOOD FOR ME? • WHY SHOUL
ID DRINKING HIGHLY CAFFEINATED SOFT DRINKS OR "ENERGY" DRINKS? • WHY SHOULDN'T I PIERCE OR TATTOO MY BODY
Y IS HAVING TWO PAIRS OF EARRINGS SUCH A BIG DEAL? OR IS IT? • WHY IS IT WRONG TO GET A RELIGIOUS TATTOO, SUC
SCRIPTURE REFERENCE OR "CTR"? • WHY SHOULDN'T I GET A TATTOO OR PIERCING IF IT IS ACCEPTABLE IN MY CULTURE?
SHOULD I DRESS MODESTLY? • WHY CAN'T I WEAR A STRAPLESS PROM DRESS ONE NIGHT OF THE YEAR? • WHY SHOULDN
SKIN SHOW BETWEEN MY SHIRT AND MY PANTS? • WHY IS IT A BIG DEAL IF BOYS "SAG" THEIR PANTS OR HAVE LONG HAIR
Y SHOULD I BE SEXUALLY PURE? • WHY IS IT GOING TOO FAR TO PASSIONATELY KISS SOMEONE? • WHY ARE NCMOS BAD?
IS IT WRONG TO BE PHYSICALLY INTIMATE WITH SOMEONE IF I LOVE THEM? • WHY SHOULDN'T I DATE UNTIL I'M 16? • WH
THE MAGICAL AGE? IS IT ALL THAT DIFFERENT THAN 15? • WHY ISN'T IT A GOOD IDEA TO HANG OUT AT THE HOUSE OF SOMI
OF THE OPPOSITE GENDER WHO I REALLY "LIKE"? • WHY IS IT STILL CONSIDERED A DATE IF A GROUP OF MY FRIENDS GOE
HE PARK TO MEET A GROUP OF THE OPPOSITE GENDER WHOM SOME OF US LIKE? • WHY SHOULDN'T I STEADY DATE IN HIG
OOL? • WHY DATE OTHER PEOPLE IF I ONLY LIKE ONE PERSON? • WHY IS IT WRONG TO STEADY DATE SOMEONE IN HIG
OOL IF WE BOTH HAVE HIGH STANDARDS? • WHY IS IT OK TO STEADY DATE AFTER MY MISSION, BUT NOT BEFORE? • WH
ULD I GET MARRIED IN THE TEMPLE? • WHY IS IT WRONG TO MARRY SOMEONE OUTSIDE THE CHURCH AND TEMPLE IF I AM I
E WITH THAT PERSON? • WHY SHOULDN'T I MARRY SOMEONE AND THEN HOPE HE OR SHE WILL LATER CONVERT TO TH
RCH? • WHY IS THE LORD OPPOSED TO HOMOSEXUAL MARRIAGE? • WHY SHOULD I WANT TO HAVE CHILDREN WHEN I'M MAI
? • WHY SHOULD I WANT TO BRING INNOCENT CHILDREN INTO SUCH A WICKED WORLD? • WHY IS IT MORE INFLUENTIAL T
E CHILDREN THAN A HIGH-POWERED CAREER? • WHY DO MEMBERS OF THE CHURCH TEND TO HAVE BIGGER FAMILIES THA
ER PEOPLE? • WHY CAN'T I WATCH WHATEVER I WANT? • WHY CAN'T I WATCH A MOVIE IF IT ONLY HAS ONE OR TWO "BAI
TS? • WHY IS IT WRONG TO WATCH A MOVIE THAT GLORIFIES VIOLENCE OR IMMORALITY IF IT IS HISTORICALLY ACCURATE
Y SHOULDN'T I PLAY VIDEO GAMES WHERE I FIGHT AND KILL PEOPLE IF I KNOW IT'S JUST PRETEND? • WHY SHOULDN'T I VIEV
RNOGRAPHY? • WHY ARE ROMANCE NOVELS SOMETIMES CONSIDERED PORNOGRAPHY? • WHY IS PORNOGRAPHY A BIG DEA
DOESN'T HURT ANYBODY? • WHY SHOULD I SEE MY BISHOP IF I NEED TO REPENT FOR PORNOGRAPHY USE? • WHY DOES TH
IC I LISTEN TO MATTER? • WHY CAN'T I LISTEN TO A SONG THAT ONLY HAS A COUPLE OF SWEAR WORDS IF I HEAR WORS
N THAT EVERY DAY AT SCHOOL? • WHY DOES IT MATTER HOW LOUD MY MUSIC IS? • WHY SHOULD I LISTEN TO OR SING TH
RCH HYMNS? • WHY ARE THERE GUIDELINES FOR DANCING? • WHY IS FREAK DANCING BAD? • WHY SHOULD I GO TO CHURC
CES? • WHY SHOULD I STILL GO TO DANCES IF I DON'T LIKE DANCING? • WHY SHOULD I USE CLEAN LANGUAGE? • WH
ULDN'T I GOSSIP OR TALK BEHIND PEOPLE'S BACKS? • WHY SHOULDN'T I MAKE FUN OF PEOPLE, EVEN IF I'M JOKING? • WH
ULD I WATCH MY TONGUE, EVEN WHEN PLAYING SPORTS? • WHY SHOULD I BE HONEST? • WHY SHOULDN'T I ILLEGALL
WNLOAD MUSIC, MOVIES, OR SOFTWARE? WHY SHOULDN'T I COPY MY FRIEND'S HOMEWORK ASSIGNMENT IF I ALREAD
W THE MATERIAL? • WHY IS IT WRONG IF I PURPOSELY LEAVE OUT PART OF THE TRUTH, EVEN THOUGH I'M NOT "LYING"?
Y SHOULD I KEEP THE SABBATH DAY HOLY? • WHY SHOULDN'T I TEXT MESSAGE IN SACRAMENT MEETING? • WHY SHOULDN
EAR FLIP-FLOPS TO CHURCH? • WHY SHOULDN'T I SKIP SUNDAY SCHOOL? • WHY SHOULD I FAST? • WHY DOES WHAT TIM
URCH STARTS HAVE LITTLE TO DO WITH HOW LONG I FAST? • WHY SHOULD I STILL PAY FAST OFFERINGS IF MY PARENT
EADY PAY? • WHY SHOULD I HAVE SOMETHING I'M FASTING FOR? • WHY SHOULD I PRAY ALWAYS? • WHY DOES IT SEEM LIP
ETIMES I DON'T GET AN ANSWER TO MY PRAYERS? • WHY SHOULD I TAKE OFF MY HAT AND USE WORDS LIKE "THEE" AN
Y" WHEN I PRAY? • WHY SHOULD I PRAY BY MYSELF IF I PRAY WITH MY FAMILY EVERY DAY? • WHY SHOULD I STUDY MY SCRI
ES DAILY? • WHY IS IT SO IMPORTANT THAT I STUDY MY SCRIPTURES EVERY DAY? • WHY ARE THE SCRIPTURES SO HARD T
ERSTAND SOMETIMES? • WHY IS IT MORE IMPORTANT TO STUDY THE SCRIPTURES FOR A SET AMOUNT OF TIME INSTEAD OF
AMOUNT OF PAGES? • WHY SHOULD I PAY TITHING? • WHY DOES GOD NEED ME TO PAY TITHING IF HE CAN JUST CREATE GOL
MONEY? • WHY DO SOME PEOPLE WHO PAY TITHING STILL NOT HAVE A LOT OF MONEY? • WHY CAN'T I ENTER THE TEMPLE
N'T PAY TITHING? • WHY SHOULD I WRITE IN A JOURNAL? • WHY SHOULDN'T I JUST WRITE DOWN THE "GOOD" STUFF IN M
RNAL? • WHY SHOULD I TAKE NOTES DURING CHURCH MEETINGS AND SCRIPTURE STUDY? • WHY CAN'T I HAVE MY BLO
APBOOK, OR VIDEO RECORDINGS COUNT AS MY JOURNAL? • WHY SHOULD I BE GRATEFUL? • WHY SHOULD WE THANK GO
BLESSINGS BEFORE ASKING FOR MORE BLESSINGS? • WHY SHOULD I BE GRATEFUL IF THERE IS SO MUCH I DON'T HAVE? • WI
AYING "THANK YOU" A SIGN OF AN EDUCATED PERSON? • WHY SHOULD I HONOR MY PARENTS? • WHY SHOULDN'T I TALK BA
MY PARENTS? • WHY IS HONORING MY PARENTS MORE THAN SIMPLY OBEYING THEM? • WHY SHOULD I LISTEN TO MY PARENT
EN IF I THINK THEY ARE WRONG? • WHY IS IT SO IMPORTANT I GAIN AN EDUCATION? • WHY SHOULD I GO TO COLLEGE IF I CA
KE A LOT OF MONEY WITHOUT IT? • WHY SHOULD I STILL GET A DEGREE IF I'LL NEVER WORK IN THAT FIELD? • WHY SHOULD
THER MY EDUCATION IF I AM GOING TO BE A STAY-AT-HOME MOTHER? • WHY SHOULD I ATTEND SEMINARY AND INSTITUTE?
Y IS SEMINARY MORE IMPORTANT THAN ANY OTHER SCHOOL CLASS? • WHY IS IT SO IMPORTANT THAT I ENROLL IN ALL FOU
RS OF SEMINARY? • WHY IS INSTITUTE JUST AS IMPORTANT AS SEMINARY? • WHY SHOULD I SERVE A MISSION? • WHY D
NEED A RAISED BAR FOR MISSIONARY STANDARDS? • WHY CAN'T I JUST SERVE A MISSION WHEN I AM OLDER WITH MY SPOU
TEAD OF WHEN I AM 19? • WHY DO BOYS HAVE TO SERVE A MISSION AND GIRLS DON'T? • WHY SHOULD I REPENT NOW A
LATER? • WHY SHOULD I TALK TO MY BISHOP ABOUT CERTAIN SINS? • WHY DO I NEED THE SAVIOR'S ATONEMENT TO

WHY SHOULD I KEEP THE COMMANDMENTS? • WHY ARE THERE SO MANY COMMANDMENTS AND RULES? • WHY DO SOME PE
HO BREAK THE COMMANDMENTS APPEAR HAPPY? • WHY ARE SOME COMMANDMENTS MORE IMPORTANT THAN OTHERS—OR
HEY? • WHY SHOULD I LISTEN TO AND FOLLOW THE PROPHET? • WHY IS IT SO IMPORTANT TO LISTEN TO GENERAL CONFERE
WHY DO MODERN PROPHETS SOMETIMES TEACH THINGS THAT ARE DIFFERENT FROM WHAT PAST PROPHETS TAUGHT?
HOULD I LISTEN TO PROPHETS WHO ARE SO MUCH OLDER THAN I AM? • WHY DOES IT MATTER WHO MY FRIENDS ARE? • W
OK TO STILL BE FRIENDS WITH PEOPLE IF THEY AREN'T LDS? • WHY CAN A FRIEND STILL BE BAD IF THEY AREN'T PRESSU
E TO BREAK THE COMMANDMENTS? • WHY IS IT WRONG FOR ME TO "COVER" FOR MY FRIENDS AND NOT TELL ON THEM?
HAT WHAT GOOD FRIENDS DO? • WHY SHOULD I KEEP THE WORD OF WISDOM? • WHY SHOULDN'T I "TRY" ALCOHOL JUST TO
HAT IT TASTES LIKE? • WHY SHOULDN'T I TAKE SOMETHING INTO MY BODY IF SCIENCE SAYS IT'S GOOD FOR ME? • WHY SHO
AVOID DRINKING HIGHLY CAFFEINATED SOFT DRINKS OR "ENERGY" DRINKS? • WHY SHOULDN'T I PIERCE OR TATTOO MY B
WHY IS HAVING TWO PAIRS OF EARRINGS SUCH A BIG DEAL? OR IS IT? • WHY IS IT WRONG TO GET A RELIGIOUS TATTOO,
S A SCRIPTURE REFERENCE OR "CTR"? • WHY SHOULDN'T I GET A TATTOO OR PIERCING IF IT IS ACCEPTABLE IN MY CULTUR
HY SHOULD I DRESS MODESTLY? • WHY CAN'T I WEAR A STRAPLESS PROM DRESS ONE NIGHT OF THE YEAR? • WHY SHOUL
LET SKIN SHOW BETWEEN MY SHIRT AND MY PANTS? • WHY IS IT A BIG DEAL IF BOYS "SAG" THEIR PANTS OR HAVE LONG H
WHY SHOULD I BE SEXUALLY PURE? • WHY IS IT GOING TOO FAR TO PASSIONATELY KISS SOMEONE? • WHY ARE NCMOS BA
HY IS IT WRONG TO BE PHYSICALLY INTIMATE WITH SOMEONE IF I LOVE THEM? • WHY SHOULDN'T I DATE UNTIL I'M 16?
IS THE MAGICAL AGE? IS IT ALL THAT DIFFERENT THAN 15? • WHY ISN'T IT A GOOD IDEA TO HANG OUT AT THE HOUSE OF SO
NE OF THE OPPOSITE GENDER WHO I REALLY "LIKE"? • WHY IS IT STILL CONSIDERED A DATE IF A GROUP OF MY FRIENDS G
O THE PARK TO MEET A GROUP OF THE OPPOSITE GENDER WHOM SOME OF US LIKE? • WHY SHOULDN'T I STEADY DATE IN
CHOOL? • WHY DATE OTHER PEOPLE IF I ONLY LIKE ONE PERSON? • WHY IS IT WRONG TO STEADY DATE SOMEONE IN
CHOOL IF WE BOTH HAVE HIGH STANDARDS? • WHY IS IT OK TO STEADY DATE AFTER MY MISSION, BUT NOT BEFORE?
HOULD I GET MARRIED IN THE TEMPLE? • WHY IS IT WRONG TO MARRY SOMEONE OUTSIDE THE CHURCH AND TEMPLE IF I A
OVE WITH THAT PERSON? • WHY SHOULDN'T I MARRY SOMEONE AND THEN HOPE HE OR SHE WILL LATER CONVERT TO
HURCH? • WHY IS THE LORD OPPOSED TO HOMOSEXUAL MARRIAGE? • WHY SHOULD I WANT TO HAVE CHILDREN WHEN I'M M
IED? • WHY SHOULD I WANT TO BRING INNOCENT CHILDREN INTO SUCH A WICKED WORLD? • WHY IS IT MORE INFLUENTIA
AVE CHILDREN THAN A HIGH-POWERED CAREER? • WHY DO MEMBERS OF THE CHURCH TEND TO HAVE BIGGER FAMILIES T
THER PEOPLE? • WHY CAN'T I WATCH WHATEVER I WANT? • WHY CAN'T I WATCH A MOVIE IF IT ONLY HAS ONE OR TWO "B
ARTS? • WHY IS IT WRONG TO WATCH A MOVIE THAT GLORIFIES VIOLENCE OR IMMORALITY IF IT IS HISTORICALLY ACCURAT
HY SHOULDN'T I PLAY VIDEO GAMES WHERE I FIGHT AND KILL PEOPLE IF I KNOW IT'S JUST PRETEND? • WHY SHOULDN'T I V
ORNOGRAPHY? • WHY ARE ROMANCE NOVELS SOMETIMES CONSIDERED PORNOGRAPHY? • WHY IS PORNOGRAPHY A BIG D
IT DOESN'T HURT ANYBODY? • WHY SHOULD I SEE MY BISHOP IF I NEED TO REPENT FOR PORNOGRAPHY USE? • WHY DOES
USIC I LISTEN TO MATTER? • WHY CAN'T I LISTEN TO A SONG THAT ONLY HAS A COUPLE OF SWEAR WORDS IF I HEAR WO
HAN THAT EVERY DAY AT SCHOOL? • WHY DOES IT MATTER HOW LOUD MY MUSIC IS? • WHY SHOULD I LISTEN TO OR SING
HURCH HYMNS? • WHY ARE THERE GUIDELINES FOR DANCING? • WHY IS FREAK DANCING BAD? • WHY SHOULD I GO TO CHU
ANCES? • WHY SHOULD I STILL GO TO DANCES IF I DON'T LIKE DANCING? • WHY SHOULD I USE CLEAN LANGUAGE? • W
HOULDN'T I GOSSIP OR TALK BEHIND PEOPLE'S BACKS? • WHY SHOULDN'T I MAKE FUN OF PEOPLE, EVEN IF I'M JOKING? • W
HOULD I WATCH MY TONGUE, EVEN WHEN PLAYING SPORTS? • WHY SHOULD I BE HONEST? • WHY SHOULDN'T I ILLEGA
OWNLOAD MUSIC, MOVIES, OR SOFTWARE? • WHY SHOULDN'T I COPY MY FRIEND'S HOMEWORK ASSIGNMENT IF I ALRE
NOW THE MATERIAL? • WHY IS IT WRONG IF I PURPOSELY LEAVE OUT PART OF THE TRUTH, EVEN THOUGH I'M NOT "LYING
HY SHOULD I KEEP THE SABBATH DAY HOLY? • WHY SHOULDN'T I TEXT MESSAGE IN SACRAMENT MEETING? • WHY SHOULD
WEAR FLIP-FLOPS TO CHURCH? • WHY SHOULDN'T I SKIP SUNDAY SCHOOL? • WHY SHOULD I FAST? • WHY DOES WHAT T
HURCH STARTS HAVE LITTLE TO DO WITH HOW LONG I FAST? • WHY SHOULD I STILL PAY FAST OFFERINGS IF MY PARE
LREADY PAY? • WHY SHOULD I HAVE SOMETHING I'M FASTING FOR? • WHY SHOULD I PRAY ALWAYS? • WHY DOES IT SEEM L
OMETIMES I DON'T GET AN ANSWER TO MY PRAYERS? • WHY SHOULD I TAKE OFF MY HAT AND USE WORDS LIKE "THEE"
THY" WHEN I PRAY? • WHY SHOULD I PRAY BY MYSELF IF I PRAY WITH MY FAMILY EVERY DAY? • WHY SHOULD I STUDY MY SC
URES DAILY? • WHY IS IT SO IMPORTANT THAT I STUDY MY SCRIPTURES EVERY DAY? • WHY ARE THE SCRIPTURES SO HARD
NDERSTAND SOMETIMES? • WHY IS IT MORE IMPORTANT TO STUDY THE SCRIPTURES FOR A SET AMOUNT OF TIME INSTEAD O
ET AMOUNT OF PAGES? • WHY SHOULD I PAY TITHING? • WHY DOES GOD NEED ME TO PAY TITHING IF HE CAN JUST CREATE
R MONEY? • WHY DO SOME PEOPLE WHO PAY TITHING STILL NOT HAVE A LOT OF MONEY? • WHY CAN'T I ENTER THE TEMPL
DON'T PAY TITHING? • WHY SHOULD I WRITE IN A JOURNAL? • WHY SHOULDN'T I JUST WRITE DOWN THE "GOOD" STUFF IN
OURNAL? • WHY SHOULD I TAKE NOTES DURING CHURCH MEETINGS AND SCRIPTURE STUDY? • WHY CAN'T I HAVE MY BL
CRAPBOOK, OR VIDEO RECORDINGS COUNT AS MY JOURNAL? • WHY SHOULD I BE GRATEFUL? • WHY SHOULD WE THANK G
OR BLESSINGS BEFORE ASKING FOR MORE BLESSINGS? • WHY SHOULD I BE GRATEFUL IF THERE IS SO MUCH I DON'T HAVE?
SAYING "THANK YOU" A SIGN OF AN EDUCATED PERSON? • WHY SHOULD I HONOR MY PARENTS? • WHY SHOULDN'T I TALK B
O MY PARENTS? • WHY IS HONORING MY PARENTS MORE THAN SIMPLY OBEYING THEM? • WHY SHOULD I LISTEN TO MY PARE
VEN IF I THINK THEY ARE WRONG? • WHY IS IT SO IMPORTANT I GAIN AN EDUCATION? • WHY SHOULD I GO TO COLLEGE IF I
AKE A LOT OF MONEY WITHOUT IT? • WHY SHOULD I STILL GET A DEGREE IF I'LL NEVER WORK IN THAT FIELD? • WHY SHOU
URTHER MY EDUCATION IF I AM GOING TO BE A STAY-AT-HOME MOTHER? • WHY SHOULD I ATTEND SEMINARY AND INSTITU
HY IS SEMINARY MORE IMPORTANT THAN ANY OTHER SCHOOL CLASS? • WHY IS IT SO IMPORTANT THAT I ENROLL IN ALL F
EARS OF SEMINARY? • WHY IS INSTITUTE JUST AS IMPORTANT AS SEMINARY? • WHY SHOULD I SERVE A MISSION? • W
E NEED A RAISED BAR FOR MISSIONARY STANDARDS? • WHY CAN'T I JUST SERVE A MISSION WHEN I AM OLDER WITH MY SPO
ISTEAD OF WHEN I AM 19? • WHY DO BOYS HAVE TO SERVE A MISSION AND GIRLS DON'T? • WHY SHOULD I REPENT NO
OT LATER? • WHY SHOULD I TALK TO MY BISHOP ABOUT CERTAIN SINS? • WHY DO I NEED THE SAVIOR'S ATONEMENT TO